The First Blitz

Bombing London in the First World War

OSPREY
PUBLISHING

Dedication

To the memory of all those who died in London's first Blitz, whether on the ground or in the air.

THE FIRST BLITZ

Bombing London in the First World War

IAN CASTLE

First published in Great Britain in 2015 by Osprey Publishing,
PO Box 883, Oxford, OX1 9PL, UK
PO Box 3985, New York, NY 10185-3985, USA
E-mail: info@ospreypublishing.com
Osprey Publishing, part of Bloomsbury Publishing Plc

ISBN: 978 1 4728 1529 3
ePub ISBN: 978 1 4728 1 531 6
PDF ISBN: 978 1 4728 1 530 9
Index by Zoe Ross
Cartography by The Map Studio (Zeppelin raids) and bounford.com
(Bomber raids)
Artwork by Christa Hook
Typeset in Adobe Garamond Pro and Alternative Gothic
Originated by PDQ Media, Bungay, UK
Printed in China through World Print Ltd

15 16 17 18 19 10 9 8 7 6 5 4 3 2 1

Front cover: A Zeppelin airship over London, illuminated by
searchlights, 1916. (Topfoto)

Contents page: Part of a poster fron 1915, depicting a raid on
London (National Army Museum).

Osprey Publishing supports the Woodland Trust, the UK's leading
woodland conservation charity. Between 2014 and 2018 our
donations will be spent on their Centenary Woods project in the UK.
www.ospreypublishing.com

ACKNOWLEDGEMENTS
My fascination with the first air war over London was ignited many
years ago by a plaque on a building in Farringdon Road, Clerkenwell.
It referred to a Zeppelin raid on the night of 8/9 September 1915 and
it set me on a course which eventually resulted in the publication of
two books by Osprey, London 1914–17: The Zeppelin Menace and
London 1917–18: The Bomber Blitz. Now, as we reach the centenaries
of those ground-breaking air raids on London, Osprey has decided to
republish updated versions of these books in this single volume.

This book was only possible because of the diligent and methodical
work of numerous anonymous clerks of the Royal Flying Corps,
Royal Naval Air Service, Metropolitan Police and London Fire Brigade
who meticulously filed away every letter, report and document they
received until eventually, years later, they found their way to the
National Archives in Kew, London. Without their efforts this book
would have been very different and the maps a shadow of what they
are. It never ceases to amaze me that the mere click of a button on a
computer keypad at Kew can put those 100-year-old documents
directly in one's hands just 20 minutes later.

Throughout the time working on these books I received open and
generous help from a number of individuals. I must therefore
particularly thank Colin Ablett for access to his library and permission
to use photos from his collection. In Austria my friend Martin Worel
meticulously produced German translations for me and I am indebted
to Marton Szigeti in Germany who has been generous with his vast
knowledge of the German 'Giants'. And back in England I must
mention David Marks. He shares my fascination with all things
dirigible and has granted me open access to items in his unparalleled
collection.

Finally I would like to thank Christa Hook, the artist who produced
the artwork that features so prominently in this book. I sent Christa
childish scribbles and notes and she returned them as works of art.

RANK ABBREVIATIONS

British:

General	Gen
Lieutenant-General	Lt Gen
Major-General	Maj Gen
Lieutenant Colonel	Lt Col
Major	Maj
Captain	Capt
Lieutenant	Lt
Flight Lieutenant	Flt Lt
Second-Lieutenant	2nd Lt
Sub-Lieutenant	Sub-Lt
Flight Sub-Lieutenant	Flt Sub-Lt

German:

Generalleutnant	GenLt
Korvettenkäpitan	Kvtkpt
Hauptmann	Hptmn
Kapitanleutnänt	Kptlt
Oberleutnant	Oblt
Oberleutnant-zur-See	Oblt-z-S
Leutnant	Lt
Vizefeldwebel	Vfw
Unteroffizier	Uffz

CONTENTS

Introduction 7

The Growing Aerial Threat to London 9

The Zeppelin Raids – The Men That Mattered 12

Preparing for the Zeppelin War 17

The 1915 Zeppelin Raids 25

The 1916 Zeppelin Raids 56

The 1917 Zeppelin Raids 93

The End of the Zeppelin War 100

The Coming of the Bombers 102

The Bomber Raids – The Men That Mattered 103

Preparing for the Bomber Blitz 109

The 1917 Bomber Raids 117

The 1918 Bomber Raids 169

The Aftermath of the First Blitz 190

Select Bibliography 193

Appendix 1: In Touch With London's First Blitz 194

Appendix 2: Chronology 196

Appendix 3: The Forces Engaged in London's First Blitz 198

Index 205

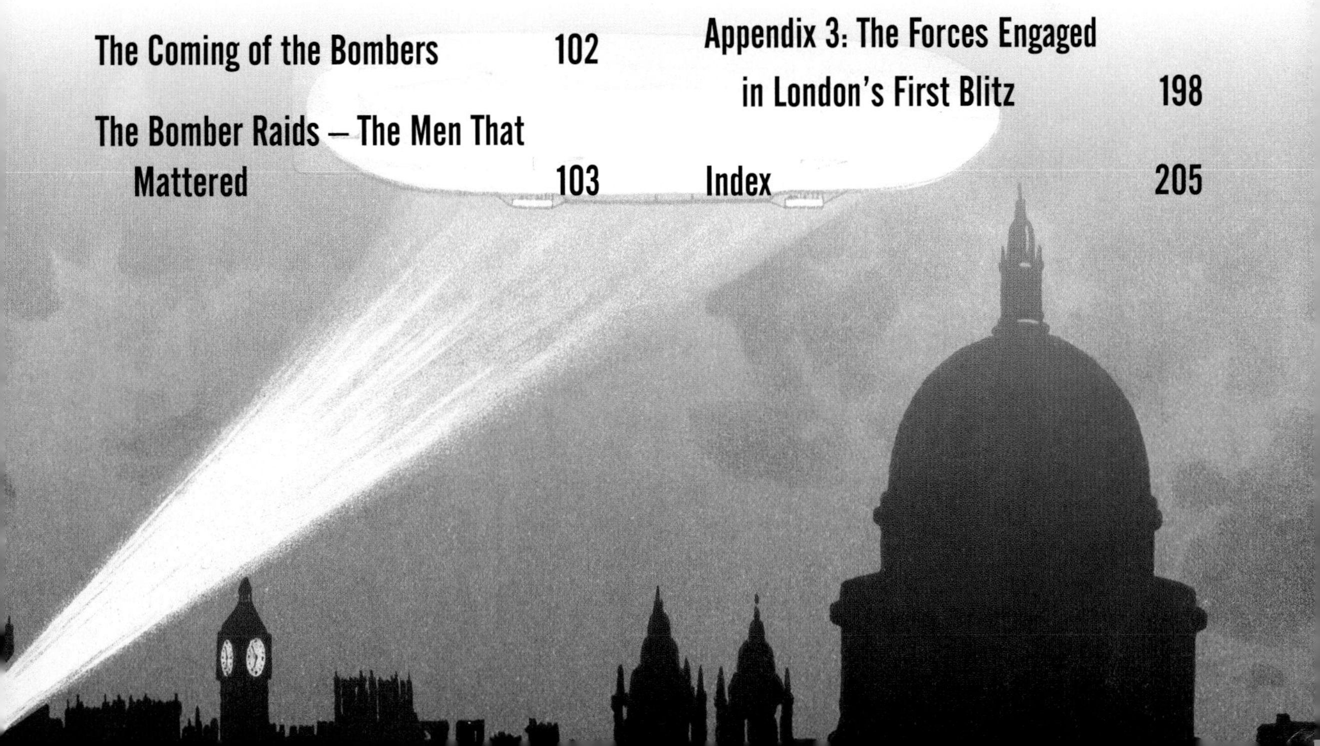

INTRODUCTION

The rapid descent to war experienced in the hot summer of 1914 alerted scaremongers in Britain to the possibility of immediate aerial bombardment of London and other major industrial cities. The publicity and propaganda surrounding the development of Germany's fleet of airships had spread far and wide, and the spectre of these great leviathans of the air sowing their seeds of death and destruction in the streets of London suddenly became very real.

Two days after Britain declared war on Germany, the editor of *The Times* newspaper informed his readers that the enemy boasted a force of 11 airships serving with their armed forces – but he claimed, reassuringly, that only two were capable of reaching Britain. The following day, 7 August, preparations for the air defence of London began when a single, unarmed aircraft took up station at Hendon, a north-western suburb of the city. Then, the next day, the Admiralty added to the defence by assigning three 1-pdr 'pom-pom' guns to anti-aircraft duties in Whitehall, close to the seat of government. But no attack materialized. In fact almost ten months would pass before German airships finally appeared menacingly over the streets of London. Yet even then Britain had little answer to the threat, and not until the late summer of 1916 could the armed forces offer a serious and deadly response.

Even before Germany launched her Zeppelin offensive against London, however, the German army held high hopes of sending bomber aircraft against the city. In the early weeks of the war, as the German army pushed the Allies back and the 'race to the sea' was underway, Wilhelm Siegert, commander of

At the beginning of the war many in Britain feared immediate aerial attack by Germany's much-vaunted fleet of airships. Despite this German propaganda picture highlighting these fears, it would not be until January 1915 that the first Zeppelin bombs fell on Britain.

the army's Flieger-Battalion Nr. 4 proposed the creation of a force to open a strategic bombing campaign against the hub of the British Empire and seat of its government. The limited range of the aircraft available at that time, however, meant that any bombing unit required a base close to the French port of Calais, which offered the shortest route to London. Confident of reaching that goal the Oberste Heeresleitung (OHL) – Army High Command – approved the creation of a force for the task, allowing Siegert to select the best pilots and observers, and within a few weeks they were formed at an airfield about 6 miles south of Ostend, at Ghistelles (Gistel) in occupied Belgium. Formed as Fliegerkorps der Obersten Heeresleitung, this highly secret unit adopted the unlikely codename Brieftauben-Abteilung Ostende – the Ostend Carrier Pigeon Detachment – to disguise its identity. But when, in November 1914, the German advance ground to a halt with Calais out of reach, the OHL shelved Siegert's plan, though it was not forgotten. The aeroplane's time would come, but for now, Germany waited for its airship fleets to strike the first blow against London from the air.

THE GROWING AERIAL THREAT TO LONDON

GERMANY TAKES TO THE AIR

The father of rigid airship development was Count Ferdinand von Zeppelin. Others had experimented with the principles of lighter-than-air flight, but it was Zeppelin's creation, *Luftschiff* (airship) *Zeppelin 1,* which first took to the air in July 1900, that offered the greatest promise. His first flight preceded that of the Wright brothers by three years when in 1903 they coaxed their flimsy Wright Flyer into the air for the first manned, controlled and powered flight by a heavier-than-air machine – an aeroplane. Although both tentative and primitive, these skyward leaps marked the first steps on a journey that would bring airship and aeroplane to battle over the darkened streets of London just 12 years later.

Count Zeppelin continued to develop his airships and, despite a number of potentially crushing setbacks, he persevered and engendered massive support from the German people. After fire destroyed his fourth airship in 1908, a public fund raised 6 million Marks to enable him to continue his work. This influx of money financed the creation of the Luftschiffbau Zeppelin GmbH (Zeppelin Airship Company) and also the Deutsch Luftschiffahrts-Aktien-Gesellschaft (DELAG), the world's first commercial airline. DELAG airships soon became a common sight over Germany. The population stared skywards in admiration and wonder; Count Zeppelin's airships became a source of national pride and, for many onlookers, they provided a highly visible demonstration of German technical superiority.

Ferdinand von Zeppelin (1838–1917). Zeppelin retired from the army in 1891 and concentrated on airship development. In 1900 he launched his first steerable rigid airship, based on original designs of aviation pioneer David Schwarz, who had died three years earlier.

The German military had already shown an interest in the count's work and in 1909 the army purchased two of his airships, numbering them Z.I and Z.II. After a period of evaluation, the army ordered two more. Not to be outdone, the navy placed its first order in April 1912, with a second following in 1913. Zeppelin, however, was not the only builder of rigid airships. In 1909 a rival company set up business. Fronted by Johann Schütte, Professor of Naval Architecture at Danzig University, and funded principally by an industrialist, Karl Lanz, Luftschiffbau Schütte-Lanz GmbH built its first airship in 1911 before selling its second model, SL.2, to the army in 1914.

Although more streamlined, Schütte-Lanz airships were not greatly dissimilar in appearance to the Zeppelin, although there was one significant structural difference. While the Zeppelin Company based construction on a latticed aluminium framework – later replaced by duralumin, an aluminium alloy – those of Schütte-Lanz utilized laminated plywood. However, this wooden construction did not meet favour with senior naval officers who felt it liable to suffer catastrophic failure under continual exposure to moisture in operations over the North Sea. As such, Schütte-Lanz airships generally received more favour from the army than the navy. But in Britain when the raids began, to those on the ground looking up in awe and horror as these vast dirigibles (steerable airships) passed overhead, all airships were simply 'Zeppelins'. At the start of the war Germany possessed 11 airships, as the editor of *The Times* had correctly informed his readers; ten commanded by the army – of which three were former DELAG commercial airships now used mainly for training new crews – and one by the navy.

'NO LONGER AN INACCESSIBLE ISLAND'

In Britain, concern over Germany's airship programme grew until in 1908 the government authorized an examination of the threat posed by airships and what advantage Britain might gain from their use. As a result, the Admiralty began a programme to build its own rigid airship, hoping to evaluate the threat in practical ways. The resultant airship, *His Majesty's Airship 1r*, also known as *Naval Airship No. 1* – or popularly as *'The Mayfly'* – was, like its namesake in nature, short-lived, wrecked by a squall in September 1911 before she even flew. At the same time, aeroplane development, a late starter in Britain, was gradually advancing. The first recognized aeroplane flight in Britain had only taken place in October 1908, and lasted just 27 seconds. In comparison, the following year, the French aviator Louis Blériot made his dramatic flight across the English Channel, prompting the visionary author H.G. Wells to echo the earlier warning of the newspaper baron, Lord Northcliffe, when he wrote, 'in spite of our fleet, this is no longer, from the military point of view, an inaccessible island.'

Gradually the British military turned its attention towards aviation. In April 1911 the Balloon Section of the Royal Engineers disbanded to reform as the Air Battalion, while their headquarters at Farnborough was renamed the Army Aircraft Factory. The Royal Navy also began experimenting with aircraft and a year later the efforts by both organizations were concentrated in a single Royal Flying Corps, with a military wing, a naval wing, a flying school at Upavon in Wiltshire and the base at Farnborough, renamed again as the Royal Aircraft Factory. It soon became clear, however, that this imposed relationship between the army and navy flyers was an uneasy one. Despite the army upholding its traditional responsibility to protect the homeland, the military wing revealed in June 1914, on the eve of war, that there was still no aerial home defence organization and, furthermore, all existing squadrons were committed to providing aerial reconnaissance for any British Expeditionary Force (BEF) destined for Europe. After an uneasy relationship lasting just two years the naval wing left the Royal Flying Corps (RFC) in July 1914 to set up its own independent organization, governed directly by the Admiralty, and named the Royal Naval Air Service (RNAS). Shortly after the commencement of the war, the Admiralty formally accepted responsibility for the home defence tasks it had already been performing.

As the clouds of war gathered, both the RFC and RNAS gradually increased their strength, acquiring a diverse range of aircraft with which to fight this very first war in the air. The next four years witnessed remarkable advancements in aviation and in the methods available to defend against aerial attack.

THE AIR WAR TAKES OFF

Although the perceived menace presented by Germany's airship fleet at the beginning of the war was great, by the autumn of 1916 its threat to London was virtually over. Zeppelins had failed to deliver the anticipated killer blow. But Germany did not let matters rest there; the effect on morale of bombing London remained a great prize. Despite its losses, their navy remained committed to the development of airships to counter Britain's improved defences, but the army, disillusioned, turned its attention to the potential offered by aeroplanes to carry an effective bomb load to London. By the spring of 1917 aeroplanes were finally available with the required range. From airfields in Belgium the air assault on London stepped up a notch, signalling the advent of the capital's first Blitz.

But that lay in the future. For now, London awaited the attack of the Zeppelin raiders.

THE ZEPPELIN RAIDS – THE MEN THAT MATTERED

First Lord of the Admiralty, Winston S. Churchill

While serving in government as Home Secretary, Churchill displayed a keen interest in naval development, leading to his appointment as First Lord of the Admiralty in October 1911. Fascinated by the developing science of aviation he enrolled for flying lessons in 1913. Although senior army figures saw the future of aircraft in a purely passive reconnaissance role, Churchill quickly recognized its offensive potential.

He was also a prime mover in the separation of the naval wing from the Royal Flying Corps and the formation of the RNAS. On 29 July 1914 he decreed that naval aircraft should regard defence against aerial attack their prime responsibility and expressed his opinion that London, the Woolwich Arsenal and the naval dockyards at Chatham and Portsmouth were all prime targets for attack. Then, in September 1914, with the RFC in Belgium with the BEF, Churchill officially accepted responsibility for home defence on behalf of the Admiralty. At a time when many

Winston Churchill (1874–1965). Churchill took up the post of First Lord of the Admiralty in 1911 and continued until May 1915. He was an enthusiastic supporter of aviation development and was the prime mover in establishing London's earliest aerial defence.

were still coming to terms with this new danger from the skies, Churchill created the initial defence of Britain against aerial attack, with his first line of defence centred on the RNAS squadron based at Dunkirk in France.

In January 1915, Churchill outlined the latest plans for London's defence, asserting that within the London-Sheerness-Dover triangle about 60 rifle-armed aeroplanes stood permanently on standby to repel air invaders – and added, bullishly, that some pilots were even prepared to ram Zeppelins in the air!

Churchill, for one, did not see a future for the Zeppelin; 'this enormous bladder of combustible and explosive gas … these gaseous monsters' as he once described them. For a time though it looked as if he had misjudged their potential, but by the end of the war the military career of the airship was over. However, Churchill was not to oversee their final demise. As the prime architect of the disastrous Gallipoli campaign he was removed from office in May 1915.

Major-General David Henderson, RFC

After army service in the Sudan in 1898, Henderson served in the Anglo-Boer War as an intelligence officer under Sir George White, enduring the siege of Ladysmith. From October 1900 to September 1902 he served under Lord Kitchener as director of military intelligence, and on his return from the war Henderson published highly respected books on intelligence and reconnaissance.

Confirming his reputation as an adventurous spirit, Henderson gained his pilot's licence in 1911 at the age of 49. He immediately developed a strong belief in the future of air power. In September 1913, having been selected to represent the army in discussions on the development of aviation, he was appointed Director-General of Military Aeronautics at the War Office, exerting control over all aspects of the military wing of the RFC – recruitment, training and equipment.

On the outbreak of war in 1914, Henderson went to France as head of the RFC. However, the rapid expansion of the organization combined with the workload generated as director of military aviation affected his health, and in August 1915 he handed over control at the front to Brigadier-General Hugh Trenchard and returned to the War Office. He faced much criticism for the failure of the RFC to stop the Zeppelin raids on London in 1915, but he persevered, developing the RFC until it was a match for both airship and aeroplane raiders. Towards the end of the war he also played a hugely important role in the amalgamation of the RFC and RNAS into a single Royal Air Force in April 1918.

Maj Gen David Henderson, RFC (1862–1921). A former army intelligence officer, in 1911 (aged 49) he learned to fly, making him the world's oldest pilot at that time. Appointed to the RFC in September 1912, he became Director of Military Aeronautics a year later.

Admiral Sir Percy Scott, RN

Sir Percy Moreton Scott joined the Royal Navy as a cadet in September 1866 and progressed to the rank of Admiral in 1913. Throughout his career he devoted much of his time to the improvement of naval gunnery. In October 1899, Scott, as captain of HMS *Terrible*, arrived in South Africa shortly after the commencement of the Second Anglo-Boer War and came to public attention when he designed and built land mountings for 4.7in guns from his ship, enabling them to serve at the Siege of Ladysmith. Scott repeated this feat the following year when *Terrible* arrived in China during the Boxer uprising. He continued his involvement in naval gunnery until he retired in 1913. In November 1914 the Admiralty recalled Scott as a gunnery advisor, and he also became involved in anti-submarine work. Then, following the poor anti-aircraft gun response to the London Zeppelin raid of 8/9 September 1915, he was tasked with creating an effective gun defence for the capital.

Konteradmiral Paul Behncke

As the Deputy Chief of the German Naval Staff, Behncke became one of the most vociferous supporters for a bombing campaign against London. As early as August 1914, following the advance of the German army into Belgium, Behncke proposed

the construction of airship bases on the Belgium coast to facilitate raids against Britain. He highlighted the importance of London as a target and expected these raids 'to cause panic in the population which may possibly render it doubtful that the war can be continued'.

Yet Behncke's proposals met opposition at the highest level – from Kaiser Wilhelm II. With his close ties to the British royal family and the genuine belief, like so many others, that the war would soon be over, the Kaiser forbade the bombing of Britain. Despite, this Behncke continued to press for an air campaign, yet it was not only the opposition of the Kaiser which prevented

ABOVE: Admiral Sir Percy Moreton Scott, Royal Navy (1853–1924). Scott, a gunnery expert, was called upon to take command of London's anti-aircraft guns after their poor showing during Heinrich Mathy's raid in L.13 on the night of 8/9 September 1915.

LEFT: Konteradmiral Paul Behncke, Reichskriegsmarine (1866–1937). As Deputy Chief of the Naval Staff he was one of the most persistent campaigners in persuading the Kaiser to approve aerial bombing raids on London. He highlighted the importance of London as a target and in particular the Admiralty buildings in Whitehall, as well as the docks. (Colin Ablett)

them taking place. Even by October 1914, neither the army nor the navy were yet in a position to begin raiding as they lacked suitable bases and had few airships.

Behncke continued lobbying, along with others, for permission to bomb London and, under increasing pressure, the Kaiser finally accepted the reality of a limited bombing campaign on England in January 1915. However, on the Kaiser's insistence, London remained excluded. Undeterred, Behncke kept up his campaign and produced a list of recommended targets that included the Admiralty buildings, Woolwich Arsenal, the Bank of England and the Stock Exchange. In February, the Kaiser accepted the London docks as a legitimate target, but still clung naively to the notion that he could specifically forbid attacks on residential areas, royal palaces and important monuments. Yet the combination of unsophisticated bombing methods and the proximity of countless tightly packed streets around the docks meant these restrictions were impossible to observe. Then, in May 1915, the Kaiser approved bombing east of the Tower of London, followed in July by the inclusion of the whole of London. Behncke finally had his wish.

Fregattenkapitän Peter Strasser

Strasser joined the German navy as a 15 year old, before entering the naval academy at Kiel. He made good progress through the ranks, serving on a number of ships between 1897 and 1902, during which time he became expert in naval gunnery. After this period at sea, Strasser joined the Navy Office as a gunnery specialist, but in 1911 he volunteered for aviation training. Two years later, in September 1913, Kvtkpt Strasser was offered command of the Naval Airship Division.

Strasser, displaying his inspirational leadership qualities to the full, quickly galvanized the moribund division and instilled fresh confidence and pride into his men. He then made his mark on the naval hierarchy, pushing his ideas for the development of the Airship Division all the way to the top at a time when some were considering disbanding the division altogether, eventually earning promotion to Fregattenkapitän. Although a harsh disciplinarian, Strasser also took great care of his men, and those that passed through his rigorous training schedule developed a fine *esprit de corps* and hero-worship for their commander. Despite numerous setbacks during the war, Strasser never lost his unswerving faith in the Zeppelin, although Vizeadmiral Reinhard Scheer reined in his aggressive independence a little following his appointment as Commander-in-Chief of the High Seas Fleet in January 1916. However, Strasser's devotion to the Airship Division received recognition in November 1916 with his appointment as Führer der Luftschiffe, carrying the equivalent rank of Admiral second class.

Fregattenkapitän Peter Strasser, Reichskriegsmarine (1876–1918). Strasser took command of the Naval Airship Division in September 1913 following the death of its commander, Kvtkpt Friedrich Metzing, in the crash of Zeppelin L.1. An inspirational and charismatic leader, he regularly flew on missions to understand first hand the difficulties his crews experienced, although many considered him a 'Jonah' as those airships often returned early with mechanical problems. In spite of mounting Zeppelin losses, he maintained an unshaken belief in the value of airships right to the end.

POLICE WARNING.

WHAT TO DO
WHEN THE
ZEPPELINS COME.

Sir Edward Henry, the Commissioner of the Metropolitan Police, has issued a series of valuable instructions and suggestions as to the action that should be taken by the ordinary householder or resident in the event of an air raid over London.

New Scotland Yard, S.W.
June 26, 1915.

In all probability if an air raid is made it will take place at a time when most people are in bed. The only intimation the public are likely to get will be the reports of the anti-aircraft guns or the noise of falling bombs.

The public are advised not to go into the street, where they might be struck by falling missiles; moreover, the streets being required for the passage of fire engines, etc., should not be obstructed by pedestrians.

In many houses there are no facilities for procuring water on the upper floors. It is suggested, therefore, that a supply of water and sand might be kept there, so that any fire breaking out on a small scale can at once be dealt with. Everyone should know the position of the fire alarm post nearest to his house.

All windows and doors on the lower floor should be closed to prevent the admission of noxious gases. An indication that poison gas is being used will be that a peculiar and irritating smell may be noticed following on the dropping of the bomb.

Gas should not be turned off at the meter at night, as this practice involves a risk of subsequent fire and of explosion from burners left on when the meter was shut off. This risk outweighs any advantage that might accrue from the gas being shut off at the time of a night raid by aircraft.

Persons purchasing portable chemical fire extinguishers should require a written guarantee that they comply with the specifications of the Board of Trade, Office of Works, Metropolitan Police, or some approved Fire Prevention Committee.

No bomb of any description should be handled unless it has shown itself to be of incendiary type. In this case it may be possible to remove it without undue risk. In all other cases a bomb should be left alone, and the police informed.

E. R. HENRY.

PREPARING FOR THE ZEPPELIN WAR

The development of airships opened the path for a new branch of warfare: strategic bombing. With aviation still a new science, there were no established rules or tactics for aerial conflict. As such, the role of aviators on both sides constantly evolved, each devising and implementing strategies and counter-strategies in response to changing circumstances.

BRITISH STRATEGY AND TACTICS

At the outbreak of war, the Royal Flying Corps mustered five squadrons, of which four were active and had departed for France with the BEF. No. 1 Squadron, formerly assigned to airships, remained behind at Brooklands in Surrey, to be re-equipped with aeroplanes. On paper, the RFC claimed about 190 aircraft, but many of these were unfit for service. The four squadrons that went to France took 63 aircraft of various types; of those left in Britain, perhaps as few as 20 were fit for service.

The RNAS established a number of air stations along the coast, mainly between the Humber and the Thames, where it based its 39 aeroplanes, 52 seaplanes and a flying boat – but perhaps only half of these were operational. Amongst its eclectic collection the RNAS included one Vickers F.B.4 'Gunbus', the only fighter aircraft in Britain at that time, mounting a single machine gun in the observer's cockpit. In August 1914, as part of its commitment to the defence of London, the RNAS took over Hendon airfield in north-west London.

This folded leaflet, distributed with the *Daily News*, offers simple advice for householders to employ during an air raid. Inside the leaflet, the *Daily News* offers readers free 'Zeppelin Bombardment Insurance' – for those who subscribe to the newspaper.

On 5 September 1914 Churchill outlined his home defence plan. He announced that the front line – formed by the RNAS in France – would engage enemy airships close to their own bases, attack those bases and establish aerial control over a wide area extending from Dunkirk. An aerial strike force formed the second line, located 'at some convenient point within a range of a line drawn from Dover to London, with local defence flights at Eastchurch (Isle of Sheppey) and Calshot (Southampton Water)'. Other aircraft with an interceptor role occupied stations along the east coast. The RNAS pilots based at Hendon formed the final line in the airborne defence plan.

Other defensive moves saw additional anti-aircraft guns assigned to key military installations, while instructions for the implementation of a blackout came into effect on 1 October. The Commissioner of Police issued an order that all powerful outside lights be extinguished, while street lights be either extinguished or the tops of lamps shaded with black paint. Railway lighting was to be reduced to a minimum, lights inside shops and other premises were to be shaded and lights on buses and trams should just be sufficient for the collection of fares. Notices also instructed the public to ensure they had well-fitting curtains. The war, as a journalist observed, had ushered in a new dark age.

> For the first time Londoners knew what it was to be hampered a little by the darkness. They took it in the Londoners' way, good-humouredly, which is almost more than might have been expected, because the idea that his city might be in danger has scarcely yet penetrated the Londoner's easy going mind … taking the whole thing as a not very good, but tolerable joke.

In October 1914, the RNAS requested RFC assistance in defending London. In response, four aircraft from No. 1 Squadron were dispatched, two to Hounslow and two to Joyce Green (near Dartford). By the end of the year the Admiralty defence plan had formalized and about 40 RNAS aircraft based at 12 stations covering the approaches to Britain's east coast between Killingholme (near Grimsby) in the north and Dover in the south. In addition, over 20 seaplanes remained on stand-by.

This system provided a two-tier defence. It took a long time for an aircraft to climb to a height where it could engage an enemy airship. This plan anticipated that those aircraft based inland would receive enough warning of a raid on London to ascend to meet it, while in the meantime those on the coast would attain the altitude needed to intercept the raiders on their return journey.

Aircraft production increased rapidly to meet the demand from both the RFC and RNAS, and by the end of 1914 they had together ordered almost a thousand new aircraft. The Royal Aircraft Factory at Farnborough had been working on producing a stable and easy-to-fly machine for reconnaissance and scouting duties. This resulted in the B.E. (Blériot Experimental) series, of which

the government approved the production of the BE2c variant in great quantities. However, when fast and nimble German fighters began to appear on the Western Front, the slow and steady BE2c became an easy victim. Back in England, and relegated to home defence duties, these very same qualities, combined with new developments in armaments, eventually saw the BE2c develop into an excellent night-flying anti-Zeppelin platform.

Although London could now, on paper at least, boast an aerial defence force, in reality it offered little opposition to raiding airships. The British understood that the use of highly inflammable hydrogen as a lifting gas, contained in a number of separate gas cells within the rigid framework, presented a great weakness in airship design, but struggled for a means to exploit this. Ordinary bullets carried little threat, merely puncturing individual gas cells with only a limited immediate effect on overall performance. Therefore, at the beginning of the war, many pilots flew into action armed with single-shot, breech-loading Martini-Henry cavalry carbines, of Zulu War vintage, firing a new 'flaming bullet'. This .45-calibre bullet contained an incendiary compound, but pilots struggled to hold their aircraft steady while using both hands to fire the carbine.

A number of bombs were available for use against airships. The main problem with these being that the pilot needed to coax his aircraft up above the hostile

The Imperial War Museum's BE2c (Blériot Experimental 2c) The Royal Aircraft Factory-designed BE2c had a 90 hp engine, a wing span of 36ft 10in and was 27ft 3in long. Outclassed on the front line in France, it proved an ideal anti-Zeppelin night-fighter at home.

airship to drop them, and yet the available aircraft did not have the ability to out-climb the airships. The aerial armoury included the 20lb explosive Hales bomb and 10lb and 20lb incendiary bombs. Another weapon in this early arsenal was the fearsome-sounding 'Fiery Grapnel'. This device comprised a four-pointed hook, loaded with explosives, that was trailed on a cable below the aircraft until, hopefully, it caught on the outer skin of an airship and could be detonated. Never a favourite with the pilots, it was never tested in combat.

To boost the initial provision of guns in Whitehall, London received a further ten weapons detailed to serve in an anti-aircraft role, but all generally lacked the elevation or range to hit airships. Special constables, enrolled in the Royal Naval Volunteer Reserve, manned these three 6-pdr Hotchkiss guns and five 1-pdr 'pom-poms', but both had an effective anti-aircraft range below a Zeppelin's operational height. In addition, the Royal Marines manned two 3in naval guns in the capital, one at Tower Bridge, and the other in Green Park. Behind this flimsy defensive façade, London lay open and exposed to attack.

GERMAN PLANS

At the outbreak of war the German army had ten operational airships (nine Zeppelins and one Schütte-Lanz), although this figure included the three commercial DELAG Zeppelins acquired for training purposes. The army assigned four airships to the Western Front and three to the east. The navy had just one airship, L.3, which came into service at the end of May 1914. The army, tactically naive when it came to the deployment of their airships, had lost three of those in the west within three weeks of the start of the war. All were claimed by enemy fire while flying at relatively low level. Before the month was out they had also lost one at the Battle of Tannenberg in the east. Just two Zeppelins and one Schütte-Lanz remained operational, along with the navy's single airship, and with that detailed for naval patrol work, any threat to Britain from the air had temporarily evaporated.

New airships, ordered before the war, gradually began to arrive and by the end of August 1914 the navy doubled its strength with the acquisition of L.4. This was the first of ten M-class airships, evenly distributed between the army and navy, based on the same design as the pre-war L.3. The order reached completion in February 1915.

With more airships on the production line, the requirement now was for sheds in which to house them. Early in 1913 the navy selected a remote spot at Nordholz, near Cuxhaven, to build an airship base, complete with four revolving sheds; this provision would enable take-off whatever the wind direction. While Nordholz was prepared, the navy rented a hangar at Fuhlsbüttel, near Hamburg. The army initially based their airships in Belgium for service in the west but later relocated to Germany.

With increasing demands from the armed services, the Zeppelin Company proposed to produce a bigger airship by adapting a commercial design they had been working on. This design introduced duralumin (an aluminium alloy) to replace aluminium, which made the framework even lighter without a reduction in strength. This model, the P-class, with a hull of 536ft would be 18ft longer than the L.3 design and, with a 61ft diameter, would be 13ft wider. This additional size increased the gas capacity from 880,000 to 1,126,000 cubic feet. The effect of the greater capacity was to increase the ceiling of the new Zeppelins from about 6,500 to 10,500ft. Adding a fourth engine increased speed from 52 to 63mph. The new design also increased crew safety and comfort by providing fully enclosed gondolas (the cars suspended from the hull) for the first time. The armed services readily accepted the new design and ordered 22, while plans to build new sheds went ahead too, the navy expecting those at Tondern and Hage to be ready by the end of the year. Both services also placed new orders with Schütte-Lanz.

The army took delivery of LZ.38, the first of the eagerly awaited P-class Zeppelins, on 3 April 1915. The navy waited another five weeks for their first vessel, the L.10, and the order was complete by the end of 1915. The first of the navy's new sheds at Nordholz opened in late January 1915, at Tondern in late March and at Hage in April.

The revolving shed at Nordholz was originally 597ft long and designed to hold two airships. As larger airships were ordered, the angular extensions were added to increase the length to 656ft. One officer described Nordholz as 'the most God-forsaken hole on earth.'

German army and navy airship bases

No.	Home base	London raid	Service
LZ.38	Evere	31 May/1 June 1915	Army
L.10	Nordholz	17/18 August 1915	Navy
SL.2	Berchem Ste. Agathe	7/8 September 1915	Army
LZ.74	Namur*	7/8 September 1915	Army
L.13	Hage	8/9 September 1915	Navy
L.15	Nordholz	13/14 October 1915	Navy
L.31	Ahlhorn	24/25 August 1916	Navy
SL.11	Spich	2/3 September 1916	Army
L.31	Ahlhorn	23/24 September 1916	Navy
L.33	Nordholz	23/24 September 1916	Navy
L.45	Tondern	19/20 October 1917	Navy

* Namur was a navy airship base used by the army at times.

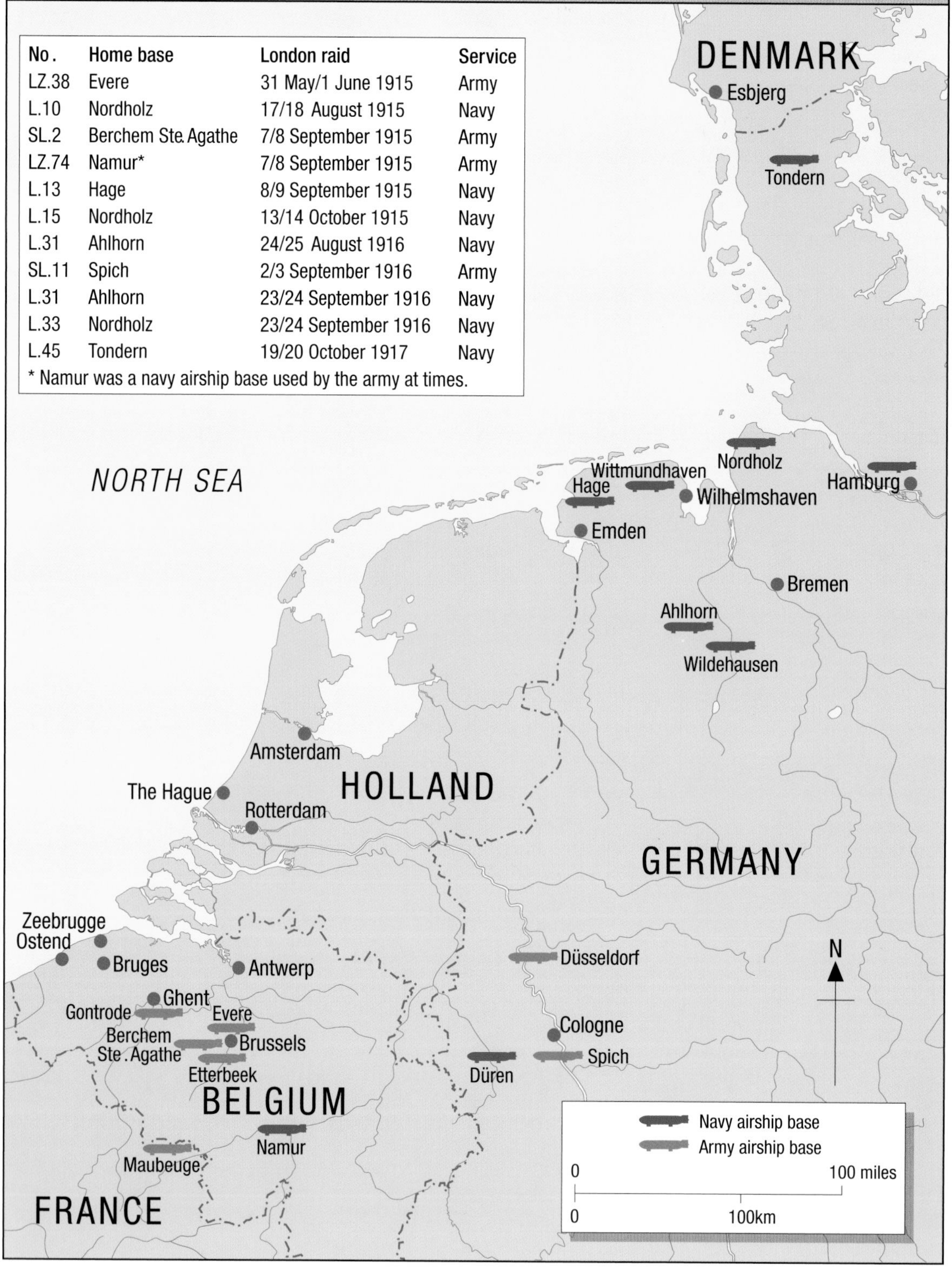

DENMARK

Esbjerg

Tondern

NORTH SEA

Wittmundhaven
Hage
Nordholz
Hamburg
Wilhelmshaven
Emden

Bremen

Ahlhorn
Wildehausen

Amsterdam

HOLLAND

The Hague
Rotterdam

GERMANY

Zeebrugge
Ostend
Bruges
Antwerp
Düsseldorf

Gontrode
Ghent
Evere
Berchem
Ste. Agathe
Brussels
Etterbeek

Cologne
Spich

Düren

BELGIUM

Namur

Maubeuge

FRANCE

N

| | Navy airship base |
| | Army airship base |

0 _____ 100 miles

0 _____ 100km

Yet while the army and navy awaited delivery of their new airships, Kaiser Wilhelm firmly blocked any attempt to bomb England, despite the determined efforts of men like the Deputy Chief of the Naval Staff, Konteradmiral Paul Behncke, backed by Kvtkpt Peter Strasser.

While the German airship commanders strained at the leash to bomb England, but were prevented from doing so by Kaiser Wilhelm, British airmen experienced no such restrictions. Heeding Churchill's directive that the defence of Britain started at the airship bases in Europe, the RNAS launched a successful raid on the army airship shed at Düsseldorf on 8 October 1914, incinerating Zeppelin Z.IX. Another raid, on 21 November, daringly targeted Friedrichshafen, the home of the Zeppelin Company, causing some damage although it narrowly missed destroying the navy's new L.7 as it approached completion. Then, on Christmas Day 1914, the British attempted an ambitious combined air and sea operation, with seaplanes attacking the nearly completed Nordholz sheds. The raid failed and was to be the last of its kind, but the Germans were not aware of this. The German navy, concerned that these raids would destroy their airships before they had even begun to attack England, increased the pressure on Kaiser Wilhelm to sanction air attacks. Finally, on 9 January 1915, he gave his qualified approval. There were to be no attacks on London, but the Thames estuary and east coast of Britain were now legitimate targets.

THE 1915 ZEPPELIN RAIDS

THE CAMPAIGN BEGINS

The Kaiser's approval immediately spurred the German Naval Airship Division into action, with Strasser ordering four of his airships to attack England on 13 January 1915. However, bad weather forced the abandonment of the raid. The weather was probably Britain's greatest ally in restricting German determination to bomb the nation into submission. Heavy rain absorbed by the outer envelope of an airship added tons of extra weight, as did snow and ice, forcing them dangerously low. When ice froze on the propellers, sharp fragments flung backwards with terrific force could puncture the outer envelope and internal gas cells. Thunder, lightning and fog each offered their own dangers. Strong headwinds could bring progress to a halt, while crosswinds could blow an airship miles off course. Navigation itself was basic, with each airship carrying a magnetic compass and steering by dead reckoning over the sea. This process used a combination of speed and compass direction to calculate a position, but the direction and speed of the wind greatly affected accuracy. Over land, crews used maps to identify ground features and towns, often illuminating them with magnesium-burning parachute flares. However, if the wind pushed the ship off course then landfall over England was easy to misjudge, adding confusion to later aerial identification of targets. From April 1915 airship commanders benefited from the use of radio bearings to pinpoint their position, but the accuracy often left much to be desired. At the same time British stations were able to intercept and plot these transmissions too,

Bomb damage in Bartholomew Close caused during the raid of 8/9 September 1915. Kptlt Heinrich Mathy dropped a single 300kg high-explosive bomb from Zeppelin L.13, the largest yet dropped on London. The bomb killed two men, gouged a great hole in the ground and shattered surrounding business premises. (IWM, LC 30)

forcing airship commanders to keep communications to a minimum. There was also the constant threat of mechanical breakdown. After surmounting all these dangers, there remained one more obstacle to overcome, namely the aircraft and anti-aircraft guns of Britain's Home Defence organization. Initially, though, this opposition was limited.

After the first aborted mission, Strasser ordered a second six days later, on the night of 19/20 January 1915. This time two navy M-class Zeppelins, L.3 and L.4, successfully crossed the North Sea, but were blown off course from their intended target of the Humber. Instead, unopposed by the RNAS and RFC, they released their bombs over Great Yarmouth, King's Lynn and a number of small Norfolk villages. Konteradmiral Paul Behncke received the news of this first successful Zeppelin raid with great delight, enthusiastically shared by the German population. Back in England, shocked families mourned the deaths of four innocent civilians while 16 others received treatment for their injuries.

On 12 February, in the face of constant pressure, the Kaiser relented further and declared the London docks a permitted target. Two weeks later navy Zeppelin L.8 flew from Düsseldorf to attack London but strong headwinds made the attack impossible. She sought refuge at Gontrode army airship base near Ghent in Belgium, but then, on her return journey, a combination of small-arms fire and engine failure forced her down and strong winds destroyed her on the ground.

The Army Airship Service launched its four available airships against England on 17 March, but heavy fog over the English Channel forced them back. Returning to base, one airship suffered damage on landing and three days later, while attacking Paris, enemy fire forced down another. Then, on 13 April, anti-aircraft fire brought down a third vessel, LZ.35, near Ypres. Fortunately for the army they took delivery of the last of their M-class airships – LZ.37 – in March and their interim O-class LZ.39 and the first of their P-class airships – LZ.38 – in April 1915.

With the army licking its wounds, the onus returned to Strasser and the Naval Airship Division. On 14 April Kptlt Heinrich Mathy in L.9 bombed around Blyth and Wallsend in the north-east of England, but the damage was negligible. One British aircraft took off from RNAS Whitley Bay and patrolled over Newcastle but, with no searchlights in operation, L.9 escaped undetected.

The following day three airships – L.5, L.6 and L.7 – set out to raid the Humber, but strong winds again blew them off course. L.5 and L.6 released bombs over Suffolk and Essex before returning to base.

Strasser came to the conclusion that his older M-class Zeppelins, with their limited endurance and lifting capabilities, were not up to the task of attacking England, and put further plans on hold until his new P-class airships were ready. Now the pendulum swung back to the Army Airship Service, and in particular to Hptmn Erich Linnarz.

Army Zeppelin LZ.38, the first P-class to enter service. LZ.38 was 536ft long and powered by three 210 hp Maybach engines (later P-class vessels had four engines). Commanded by Hptmn Erich Linnarz, she was the first airship to bomb London.

Linnarz, appointed to command the first of the new Zeppelins, began very careful planning, for the general feeling amongst airship crews was that the Kaiser would soon have to declare London open to airship attack. On 29/30 April Linnarz bombed Ipswich and Bury St Edmunds from LZ.38; thick coastal mist prevented RNAS Yarmouth from opposing the raid. Linnarz returned on the night of 9/10 May. This time he made two successful bombing runs over Southend on the south coast of Essex. LZ.38 continued its probing raids and on the night of 16/17 May, dropped bombs on Ramsgate and Oxney, near Dover in Kent. For the first time a searchlight illuminated a Zeppelin raid and a defence pilot – Flt Sub-Lt Redford Mulock, RNAS – actually saw a Zeppelin, although LZ.38 easily out-climbed him. Linnarz bombed Southend again on the night of 26/27 May, but with little advance warning, the five RNAS aircraft that took off were unable to climb high enough before LZ.38 turned for home. The sum total of material damage accumulated on these four raids only amounted to about £17,000 (1915 value), but they claimed the lives of six civilians and caused injuries to a similar number. Although not destruction on a grand scale, it proved valuable experience for Linnarz and the crew of LZ.38, experience they were about to put to devastating effect.

THE FIRST LONDON RAID –
THE ARMY CLAIMS THE PRIZE

In May 1915 the Kaiser, under constant pressure, gave his reluctant approval for the bombing of the British capital east of the Tower of London. Overlooking a number of stipulations imposed by the Kaiser, the Army Airship Service prepared to lead the way.

At about dusk on the evening of Monday 31 May, Linnarz ascended in LZ.38 from the base at Evère, just north of Brussels, while LZ.37 took off from Namur. Damage to its outer envelope forced LZ.37 to return early, but, unhindered, Linnarz flew over Margate at 9.42pm headed for the now-familiar landmark of Southend. From there he steered a westerly course for the capital.

It was now almost ten months since Britain had declared war on Germany. The feared Zeppelin onslaught on London had not materialized and the tentative probes at East Anglia, Essex and Kent had little effect on Londoners. Although the streets remained darkened, most people went about their lives as normal. The Metropolitan Police received notification of an impending raid at about 10.55pm. While they were still absorbing this unexpected news, a shocked sub-inspector of the Special Constabulary observed a Zeppelin approaching Stoke Newington Station. Moments later bombs began to fall.

The first bomb on London, an incendiary, fell just south of the railway station on a house at 16 Alkham Road, the home of a clerk, Albert Lovell. It smashed through the roof, setting fire to the bedroom and back room on the top floor. The bewildered Mr Lovell, his wife, children and two guests tumbled from the house without injury and the fire brigade arrived promptly to extinguish the blaze. Linnarz passed on over Stoke Newington High Street before turning onto a course heading south, directly on a line leading towards the Tower of London and parallel with Stoke Newington Road/Kingsland Road in the direction of Hoxton. In Cowper Road, a Mr C. Smith was in bed when he heard 'a terrible rushing of wind and a shout of "Fire" and "The Germans are here."' He rushed his children down to the basement, then went outside to find the neighbouring house on fire. An incendiary bomb had crashed through the roof; passing through the top floor it set fire to a first-floor bedroom where Samuel Leggatt's five children were sleeping. Leggatt fought his way into

The first house in London to be bombed from the air: 16 Alkham Road, in Stoke Newington.

the room, suffering burns to his face and hands, but, helped by neighbours, pulled four of his children to safety and led them away to hospital. Tragically, in the confusion, the family believed neighbours had taken in the youngest child, three-year-old Elsie, but a policeman later discovered her blackened body under debris in the room. Another of the Leggatt's daughters, Elizabeth May, died in hospital a few days later.

Linnarz, in LZ.38, continued flying south, deploying a heavy concentration of bombs as he went. Two incendiaries fell on 187 Balls Pond Road, a three-storey house owned by a builder, Thomas Sharpling. A police constable who saw the bombs fall said that he 'heard the sound of machinery in the air, and suddenly the house burst into flames.' Sharpling and his family scrambled clear while a lodger leapt from a window into a blanket, but later searchers discovered the charred bodies of two other lodgers kneeling by their bed as if in prayer: Henry Good, a 49-year-old labourer, and his wife Caroline.

Other incendiary bombs fell relatively harmlessly in Southgate Road, yet they provided a rude awakening for the residents. One of them, Mr A.B. Cook, later recalled that people were unaware what was happening at first: 'People flung up their windows and saw an astonishing sight, the roadway a mass of flames … Flames reached a height of 20ft … The sky was red with the light of flames.' In Southgate Grove the sound of the bombs affected a fragile 67-year-old spinster, Eleanor Willis, so badly that she died from shock three days later.

LZ.38 continued wreaking destruction through the streets of Hoxton and continued over Shoreditch High Street. Here, at 11.08pm, three incendiaries fell on the roof of the Shoreditch Empire music hall, where a late performance was in progress. The manager calmly addressed the audience who then left in an orderly manner as the band 'played lively airs'. Further along the High Street bombs fell on Bishopsgate Goods Station, then, within a mile of the Tower of London, Linnarz turned away to the south-east and bombed Spitalfields. Crossing the Whitechapel Road and then heading east over Commercial Road, bombs hit a bonded warehouse full of whisky and a synagogue, before two explosive bombs fell in the roadway in Christian Street; 12 passers-by received injuries and one, an eight-year-old boy called Samuel Reuben, who was on his way home from the cinema, died. One of the badly injured, Leah Lehrman, died two days later. These bombs fell only 600 yards from the London Western Dock.

A Zeppelin incendiary bomb. The interior was packed with a mixture of Benzol, tar and Thermite, which burned at an extremely high temperature, easily setting wood and combustible materials alight. The outside of the bomb was covered with tarred rope which helped keep the liquid contents inside and the fire burning. The bomb in the photo is that which struck 16 Alkham Road and was retained by the occupier for many years.

London's first Zeppelin raid – Nevill Road, Stoke Newington

Shortly after 11pm on Monday 31 May 1915, Zeppelin LZ.38 appeared unannounced over Stoke Newington in north London. The commander, Erich Linnarz, later described the tense moment as he prepared to release the first bombs on the capital:

'My finger hovered on the button that electrically operated the bombing apparatus. Then I pressed it. We waited. Minutes seemed to pass before, above the humming song of the engines, there rose a shattering roar … A cascade of orange sparks shot upwards, and a billow of incandescent smoke drifted slowly away to reveal a red gash of raging fire on the face of the wounded city.'

The first bomb fell on Alkham Road, the next in Chesholm Road, then Dynevor Road before LZ.38 steered over Nevill Road. An incendiary bomb crashed through the roof of an outbuilding at the back of the Nevill Arms, but failed to ignite. Two houses further on, at No. 27, another incendiary smashed through the roof causing a tremendous conflagration. Five rooms were gutted and two badly damaged. Alfred West, the 26-year-old son of the owner, suffered burns to his face. The fire was eventually extinguished by the police and neighbours as LZ.38 continued on its path of destruction.

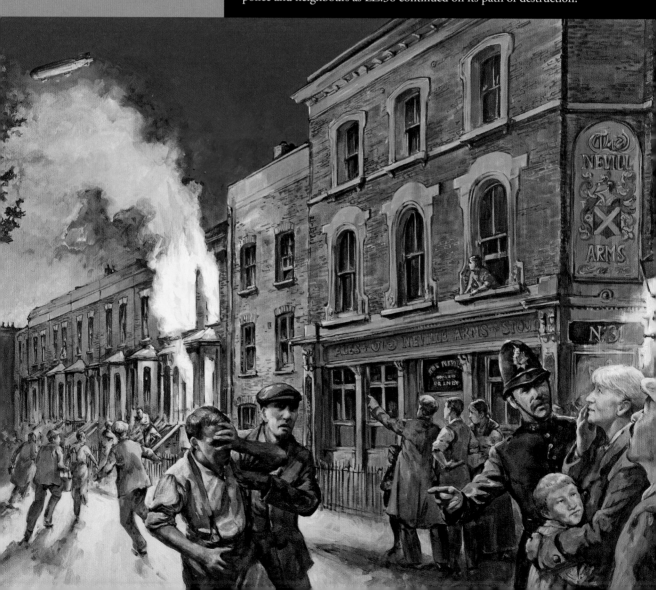

The 31 May/1 June 1915 raid on London: LZ.38 (Hptmn Erich Linnarz)

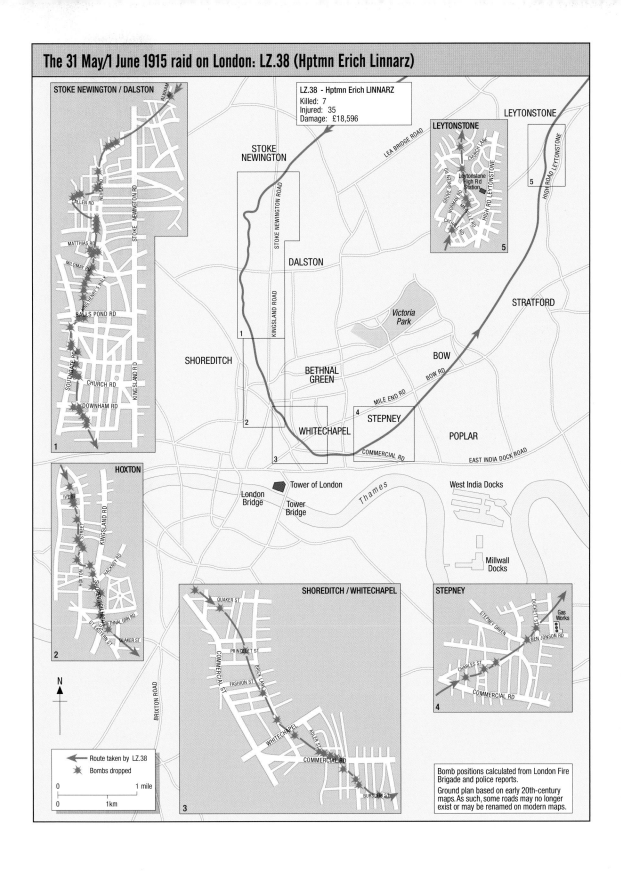

LZ.38 - Hptmn Erich LINNARZ
Killed: 7
Injured: 35
Damage: £18,596

STOKE NEWINGTON / DALSTON

LEYTONSTONE

STOKE NEWINGTON

LEYTONSTONE

DALSTON

STRATFORD

SHOREDITCH

BETHNAL GREEN

BOW

STEPNEY

WHITECHAPEL

POPLAR

HOXTON

Tower of London

London Bridge

Tower Bridge

Thames

West India Docks

Millwall Docks

SHOREDITCH / WHITECHAPEL

STEPNEY

N

Route taken by LZ.38

Bombs dropped

0   1 mile
0   1km

Bomb positions calculated from London Fire Brigade and police reports.

Ground plan based on early 20th-century maps. As such, some roads may no longer exist or may be renamed on modern maps.

Large crowds gathered in the streets throughout the bombed area but the police reported that the behaviour was generally good and no panic ensued. However, there was an incident where a mob attacked a Russian nightwatchman as he left the burning premises of a bamboo furniture manufacturer in Hoxton Street, believing him to be German and the cause of the fire. Tension simmered the following day (1 June), and anti-German feeling ran high in Hoxton and Shoreditch where mobs attacked and damaged a number of shops owned by persons believed to be of German nationality.

Linnarz turned north-east and, passing over Stepney, dropping four explosive and two incendiary bombs, which caused only minor damage. Almost 3 miles further on he dropped an incendiary over Stratford at about 11.30pm, that smashed through the roof of 26 Colegrave Road, passing through the bedroom of Peter Gillies and his wife, within 5ft of where they lay asleep. A neighbour who saw the bomb fall said, 'I heard the droning of an aeroplane but I could not see anything. According to the noise it came lower and then I saw the bomb drop. It was simply a dark object and I saw it drop through the roof of number 26.' Then, half a mile further on, LZ.38 dropped five bombs over Leytonstone, causing minor damage before heading back towards Southend and out over the coast near Foulness.

The main bombing run, from Stoke Newington to Stepney, lasted 20 minutes. The Fire Brigade attended 41 fires; members of the public extinguished others. Seven premises were completely burnt out, but the largest fire occurred at 31 Ivy Street, Hoxton, gutting a cabinetmaker's and timber yard. The Fire Brigade calculated material damage for the night at £18,596, with seven killed. Some 3,000lb of bombs were dropped (the police recorded 91 incendiary and 28 explosive bombs and two grenades).

The night of 31 May was dark, with no moon, and, although the atmosphere remained fairly clear, no searchlights located LZ.38 and no guns opened fire, and hardly anyone actually saw her as she passed over the capital. The RNAS managed to get 15 aircraft airborne, but only one pilot, flying from Rochford near Southend, saw LZ.38. Engine trouble forced him down before he could climb high enough to engage.

There could be no hiding the fact: a Zeppelin had passed freely over London and, facing no opposition, had bombed civilian targets at will, before departing without a shot fired in return. The German government in Berlin enthusiastically but falsely claimed that the raid 'threw numerous bombs on the wharves and docks of London.' In Britain, the government slapped an immediate press restriction on reporting airship raids, limiting coverage to official communications.

FIRST BLOOD

The German Army Airship Service took the laurels for the first successful raid on London, a fact not well received by the Navy Airship Division. The navy now prepared to send its first P-class Zeppelin, L.10, into action against Britain. On the afternoon of 4 June, L.10 and the Schütte-Lanz airship SL.3 set off, but only L.10 headed for London. The commander of L.10, Kptlt Klaus Hirsch, misjudged his position and, believing he could not reach the city, instead bombed what he thought was the naval base at Harwich. Hirsch in fact had been carried south-west by strong winds and his bombs actually fell on Gravesend, within easy reach of the city. Fog hampered British defensive sorties that night and neither L.10 nor SL.3, which sought targets in the north of England, encountered any opposition.

Two days later, on the night of 6/7 June, another raid took place, and for the first time both the navy and army sent airships out on the same night. The navy sent Kptlt Mathy in L.9 to 'attack London if possible, otherwise a coastal town according to choice'. Weather conditions forced Mathy to switch his target to Hull, where his bombs caused widespread devastation and claimed 26 lives.

The army raid that night comprised three Zeppelins – LZ.37, LZ.38 and LZ.39 – and resulted in a fresh disaster for the Army Airship Service. Hauptmann Linnarz knew the route to London well now, but LZ.38 developed engine trouble early in the flight, forcing him to return to his base at Evère. Meanwhile, LZ.37 and LZ.39 ran into thick fog over the North Sea and abandoned the raid too. Advised by the Admiralty of their return, four aircraft of No. 1 (RNAS) Squadron, based at airfields near Dunkirk in France, set out to intercept them or bomb their Belgium sheds. Linnarz had already docked LZ.38 when two Henri Farman aircraft arrived over Evère. Their bombs destroyed the shed and with it LZ.38, only six days after it had successfully bombed London. Meanwhile, one of the other pilots, Flt Sub-Lt R.A.J. Warneford, flying a Morane-Saulnier Parasol, caught sight of the returning LZ.37 and turned in pursuit. Her commander, Oblt van der Haegen, made a dash for his base, attempting to keep his assailant at bay with machine-gun fire. As LZ.37 descended, Warneford climbed above her and released six bombs over the doomed airship. LZ.37 exploded into a mass of burning flame and crashed down to earth, onto the Convent of St. Elisabeth in Ghent, killing two nuns and a civilian. Miraculously, one of her crew survived. After an eventful return journey Warneford became an instant hero, an antidote to the growing anger in Britain caused by the inability of the home defences to engage the Zeppelin raiders. He immediately received the award of the Victoria Cross, but did not live long to enjoy his success; ten days after his exploits he was killed when his plane crashed near Paris.

The vulnerability of the Belgian hangars now became apparent and outweighed the benefit they offered of a shorter route to England. Both the army and navy abandoned any further plans for their regular use.

The navy returned to the offensive on the night of 15/16 June. Two P-class Zeppelins, L.10 and L.11, left Nordholz and headed for Tyneside, but only L.10 reached the target. On his return the commander of L.10, Kptlt. Klaus Hirsch, reported to Strasser that the evening had never really become dark, pointing out that the June and July nights were too short to provide effective cover for air attacks. Strasser agreed with Hirsch and the initial flurry of raiding by the naval airships ended. The army, meanwhile, with its last two operational airships (Z.XII and LZ.39) dispatched to the eastern front, temporarily had no offensive capability.

The success of Warneford in bringing down LZ.37 with bombs confirmed for many in authority that this remained the most likely method of destroying airships. A theory much in evidence suggested that a layer of inert gas surrounded the hydrogen cells contained within the outer envelope, preventing their ignition by incendiary bullets. As such, the belief became prevalent that an airship could only be destroyed by a major trauma caused by an explosive bomb – a theory seemingly confirmed by Warneford's singular success. In fact, ten days before the destruction of LZ.37, the War Office informed the RFC that it believed the 'flaming bullets' were 'useless against Zeppelins'. However, incendiary bullets used in combination with explosive bullets were the answer, but it was not until 1916 that the authorities finally recognized this.

In Britain the uneasy relationship between the War Office and Admiralty as to the responsibility for Home Defence continued. When Arthur Balfour replaced Churchill as First Lord of the Admiralty in May 1915, just before the first London raid, he felt the defence of London was not a naval responsibility. In June, the Admiralty requested that the War Office take on the role and, after some posturing, the War Office finally stated that they hoped to be able to fulfil the obligations for home defence by January 1916.

In June 1915 the RFC had 20 aircraft detailed to support the RNAS in the defence of London. These flew from Brooklands, Farnborough, Dover, Hounslow, Joyce Green, Northolt, Shoreham and Gosport. All 20 carried an armament of bombs, except two Vickers Gunbuses based at Joyce Green that mounted machine guns and two BE2c aircraft at Dover fitted with the Fiery Grapnel. Unfortunately, nine of these aircraft were the unsuitable Martinsyde S1 Scout, unsteady in the air, with a low ceiling and sluggish climbing ability.

Despite this necessary co-operation, relations between the War Office and the Admiralty were not always harmonious, and, against this lack of a unified defence, the Zeppelins returned in August 1915 after a two-month absence. By this time the Kaiser had relented under pressure and approved unrestricted bombing of London.

THE SECOND LONDON RAID – THE NAVY STRIKES

Fresh from operations with the fleet, the Naval Airship Division resumed its air campaign against Britain on the night of 9/10 August and, despite launching four P-class Zeppelins – L.10, L.11, L.12 and L.13 – against London, none reached the target. Oberleutnant-zur-See Werner Peterson in L.12 caused minor

damage in Dover, but, illuminated by a searchlight, he came under anti-aircraft fire. With two gas cells punctured, L.12 began to lose height. Limping homewards, Peterson ordered all excess weight overboard to lighten his ship, but she came down in the sea off Zeebrugge. A torpedo boat towed her into Ostend where British pilots made a number of unsuccessful attempts to bomb her. While she was being lifted on to the dock by crane, the front portion of L.12 burst into flames. Peterson was left to salvage what he could from the rear portion which remained in the water.

Undeterred and making the most of the dark skies of the new moon, Strasser authorized another raid on London three days later, on the night of 12/13 August. Zeppelin L.9 joined the three survivors of the previous raid, but a combination of strong headwinds and engine problems prevented any of them reaching the city. Only L.10 reached England, where it bombed Harwich, but four aircraft that ascended from RNAS Yarmouth failed to intercept her.

Eleven weeks had now passed since the Army Airship Service had successfully bombed London, and Strasser was unceasing in his determination to strike an equal blow for the navy. He launched his next raid on the dark and moonless night of 17/18 August, sending L.10, L.11, L.13 and L.14 against the capital. The frustrated Kptlt Mathy in L.13 turned for home early again with engine trouble, the third time in three raids for the new airship. Kptlt Alois Böcker, commanding L.14, also returned with engine problems. Further south L.11, commanded by Oblt-z-S Horst von Buttlar, flew across Kent, dropping bombs at Ashford and on villages near Faversham before setting course for home, although his report falsely claimed great success in bombing Woolwich, some 40 miles from Ashford. Elsewhere, however, Strasser could take comfort, for finally a navy Zeppelin had reached London.

This photograph was taken from the command gondola of L.11 at the start of the raid of 9/10 August 1915 against London. The other Zeppelins are, from left to right, L.10, L.12 and L.13. None reached the capital and L.12 was damaged by anti-aircraft fire.

The stricken L.12 being towed back to Ostend. The RNAS flew nine sorties in an attempt to bomb the wreck, but, encountering heavy anti-aircraft fire, all were unsuccessful and one pilot, Flt Lt D.K. Johnston, was killed.

Oberleutnant-zur-See Friedrich Wenke brought L.10 in over the coast about 6 miles north of Felixstowe at around 9.00pm. Steering southwards, he skirted Felixstowe, avoided Harwich, and followed the River Stour to Manningtree in Essex. From there he steered by the railway line to Colchester and passed over Witham at about 9.50pm, before skirting the north of Chelmsford at Broomfield. From there L.10 headed west towards Waltham Abbey. The two RNAS aircraft at Chelmsford did not get airborne until 45 minutes after L.10 had passed, but over Waltham Abbey a searchlight caught the airship and the anti-aircraft gun stationed there managed to fire off two rounds before L.10 moved out of range and headed for London. Wenke later reported that the London searchlights found it very difficult to hold him in their beams at his height of 10,200ft (almost two miles). However, he then appears to have become disorientated, possibly confusing the great six-mile line of reservoirs running down the Lea Valley from Waltham to Walthamstow with the line of the River Thames. For in his report he stated that he was flying a little to the north of the Thames and began his bombing run between Blackfriars and London Bridges. Perhaps the roads running between the reservoirs added to his confusion, appearing like the Thames bridges from altitude in the dark. The anti-aircraft gun at Edmonton opened fire with no result, then his first bomb, an incendiary, fell at 10.32pm as he flew over Lloyd Park in Walthamstow.

Flying south over Hoe Street he dropped two incendiaries south of Hoe Street Station, followed by a string at the junction with the Lea Bridge Road. Here bombs destroyed four flats on Bakers Avenue, and damaged 20 tenements at Bakers Almshouses; three incendiary bombs that landed on the Leyton Tram Depot at 10.37pm caused serious fires. An explosive bomb also landed in the road between the almshouses and the depot, ripping up tramlines and causing

The 17/18 August 1915 raid on London: L.10 (Oblt-z-S Friedrich Wenke)

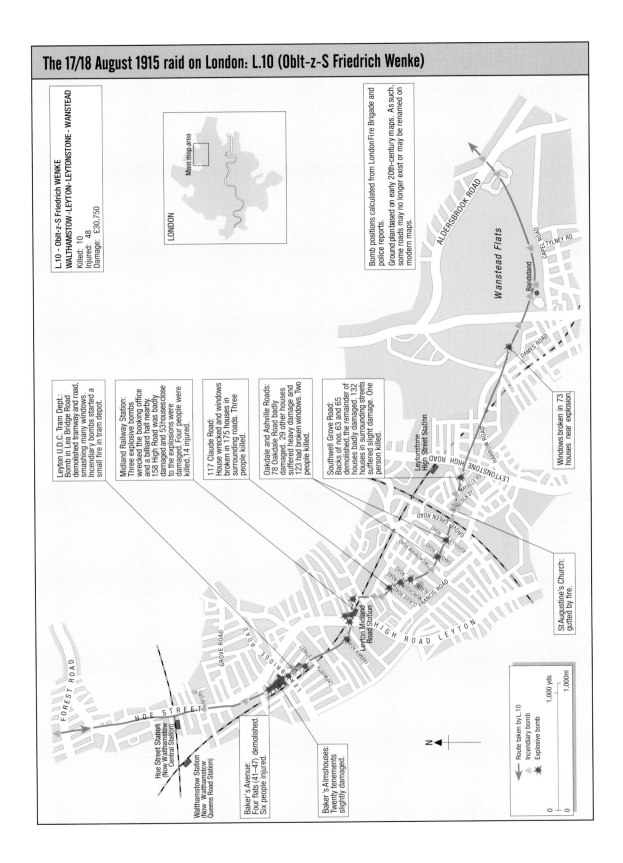

L.10 - Oblt-z-S Friedrich WENKE
WALTHAMSTOW - LEYTON - LEYTONSTONE - WANSTEAD
Killed: 10
Injured: 48
Damage: £30,750

LONDON

Main map area

Bomb positions calculated from London Fire Brigade and police reports.
Ground plan based on early 20th-century maps. As such, some roads may no longer exist or may be renamed on modern maps.

Leyton U.D.C. Tram Dept.: Bomb in Lea Bridge Road demolished tramway and road, smashing many windows. Incendiary bombs started a small fire in tram depot.

Midland Railway Station: Three explosive bombs wrecked the booking office and a billiard hall nearby. 158 High Road was badly damaged and 53 houses close to the explosions were damaged. Four people were killed, 14 injured.

117 Claude Road: House wrecked and windows broken in 175 houses in surrounding roads. Three people killed.

Oakdale and Ashville Roads: 78 Oakdale Road badly damaged. 29 other houses suffered heavy damage and 123 had broken windows. Two people killed.

Southwell Grove Road: Backs of nos. 63 and 65 demolished, the remainder of houses badly damaged. 132 houses in surrounding streets suffered slight damage. One person killed.

Windows broken in 73 houses near explosion.

St Augustine's Church: gutted by fire.

Baker's Avenue: Four flats (41–47) demolished. Six people injured.

Baker's Almshouses: Twenty tenements slightly damaged.

Hoe Street Station (Now Walthamstow Central Station)

Walthamstow Station (Now Walthamstow Queens Road Station)

Leytonstone High Street Station

Leyton Midland Road Station

FOREST ROAD
HOE STREET
GROVE ROAD
LEA BRIDGE ROAD
CAPWORTH STREET
FRANCIS ROAD
HIGH ROAD LEYTON
CLAUDE ROAD
NICHOLSON ROAD
ABBOTS ROAD
TWICKENHAM ROAD
OAKDALE ROAD
ASHVILLE ROAD
GROVE GREEN ROAD
LONDON ST
MAYVILLE RD
LEYTONSTONE HIGH ROAD
HARROW ROAD
DAMES ROAD
ALDERSBROOK ROAD
Wanstead Flats
Bandstand
CAPE ROAD
TYLNEY RD

N

Route taken by L.10
Incendiary bomb
Explosive bomb

0   1,000 yds
0   1,000m

Friedrich Wenke reported that L.10's initial bombs fell between Blackfriars and London Bridge, as recorded in this illustration that appeared in a German newspaper. Wenke was wrong: his bombs fell near the great reservoirs in the Lea Valley.

damage to the depot. Another explosive bomb landed on the Midland Road Station at Leyton causing significant local damage, and others fell close by as L.10 continued on a south-east line across the streets of Leyton. One, which exploded in Claude Road, killed three members of the same family, while two explosive bombs that dropped in Oakdale Road and Ashville Road killed two people and injured 20, as well as badly damaging 30 houses and smashing the windows of another 123 properties. Wenke then steered over Leytonstone, where three incendiaries in Lincoln Street gutted St Augustine's Church, just a few yards from where Linnarz's final bombs had fallen during the first London raid. Wenke's final bombs landed at about 10.43pm on the open space of Wanstead Flats. As L.10 steered away in the direction of Brentwood those left in her wake evaluated the damage. Seven men, two women and a child were dead, with another 48 people sustaining injuries. The London Fire Brigade estimated material damage to property at £30,750.

Approaching Chelmsford, Wenke released two final bombs, but one failed to explode. The two aircraft that took off from Chelmsford after L.10 passed on the way to London were still in the air when she returned. These aircraft, Caudron G.3s, were tricky to handle at the best of times and not ideal for night flying. Flight Sub-Lieutenant H.H. Square, flew in pursuit of L.10, but was unable to claw his way up high enough and abandoned the chase. Both Square and the pilot of the other Caudron, Flt Sub-Lt C.D. Morrison, suffered bad accidents on landing and their aircraft were destroyed. L.10 escaped that night, but, as with

Zeppelin L.10, the first of the Naval Airship Division airships to bomb London. L.10 entered service in May 1915, based at Nordholz. She participated in five raids on England before lightning destroyed her on 3 September 1915.

LZ.38, success was short lived. Returning from a North Sea patrol 16 days later, commanded by Kptlt Hirsch, she flew into a tremendous thunderstorm. It seems that lightning ignited leaking hydrogen, causing L.10 to explode and crash into an area of tidal flats off Cuxhaven; the entire crew perished.

This German propaganda postcard published in 1915 may illustrate SL.2 attacking the Isle of Dogs on 7 September 1915. Most of the 11 bombs fell along West Ferry Road, while one demolished three houses in Gaverick Street and another hit a sailing barge.

THE THIRD RAID – SOUTH-EAST LONDON TARGETED

Avoiding the period of the full moon, raids on Britain commenced again on the night of 7/8 September. This time the army returned to the fray, with three airships heading for London. A heavy ground mist blanketed the coastal airfields, thwarting any attempts to oppose the raid.

LZ.77, commanded by Hptmn Alfred Horn, came in over the Essex coast at about 10.55pm just south of Clacton, but quickly became lost. Having flown erratically over Essex and Suffolk for a few hours, Horn eventually unloaded six bombs over villages around Framlingham and departed over Lowestoft at about 2.25am.

The other two airships were more successful, though there is evidently much confusion in the reports of the routes they took over London, mainly because they both passed through the same area. It seems likely that Hptmn Richard von Wobeser steered the recently rebuilt SL.2 in over the coast at Foulness at about 10.35pm, and took a westerly course over Billericay and Chigwell before turning south over Tottenham

and heading for the Thames. Flying over the Millwall Docks at about 11.35pm, von Wobeser dropped 11 bombs, all of which landed on the western side of the Isle of Dogs, along the line of West Ferry Road. One explosive bomb landing in Gaverick Street demolished three houses and injured 11 people. Only one bomb caused slight damage to the dock itself and an incendiary landed on a sailing barge moored off the dock entrance; both men on board later died of their injuries. SL.2 then crossed the Thames, turned eastwards, and dropped an incendiary on the Foreign Cattle Market, Deptford, which the Army Service Corps used as a depot, destroying some boxes of tea and bags of salt. However, a short distance further on a bomb dropped on the home of 56-year-old William Beechey, at 34 Hughes Fields, killing him, his wife Elizabeth and three of their children aged between 11 and three. Continuing eastwards, von Wobeser steered SL.2 over Greenwich, where eight incendiaries fell, four of them harmlessly in Greenwich Park. He continued over Charlton where he dropped more incendiaries, and finally to Woolwich where a last explosive bomb landed close to the Dockyard Station. The Woolwich anti-aircraft guns only received notice of the approach of SL.2 at 11.50pm and opened fire two minutes later, loosing off four rounds, but had no time to switch on the searchlight. The gunners estimated her to be flying at about 8,000ft and travelling at between 50 and 60mph. By 11.54pm, SL.2 was out of range, crossing back over the Thames and passing close to the Royal Albert Dock. She headed out on a north-east course, passing over Bradwell-on-Sea at 1.38am on the morning of 8 September.

Shortly before midnight, as von Wobeser's raid ended, Hptmn Friedrich George, commanding LZ.74, approached the northern outskirts of London. Having made landfall over Clacton at about 10.40pm, George took a westerly course, flying over Mersea Island and Chipping Ongar to Broxbourne. There he turned south and, on approaching London, he released 45 bombs to lighten his ship. George believed he was over Leyton, but his bombs fell on Cheshunt, some 15 miles north of central London, causing significant damage among the horticultural nurseries and large houses that proliferated in the area. The anti-aircraft gun at Waltham Abbey opened fire at 11.55pm; its crew estimated LZ.74 to be flying at a height of 9,000ft and travelling at about 40mph, but the searchlight was unable to get a fix on the target. LZ.74 continued south and passed out of range of the gun at 11.59pm. Later accounts suggest George had dropped all but one of his bombs on Cheshunt, but official reports indicate that he must have retained almost half his load.

Following a course due south, Hptmn George brought LZ.74 directly over the City of London. Shortly after midnight he dropped one sighting incendiary in the Fenchurch Street area, causing a small fire in a bonded warehouse. Then, passing directly over the Tower of London, the Zeppelin followed a course towards the south-east, dropping two explosive bombs on Keetons Road,

The 7/8 September 1915 raid on London: SL.2 (Hptmn Richard von Wobeser) and LZ.74 (Hptmn Friedrich George)

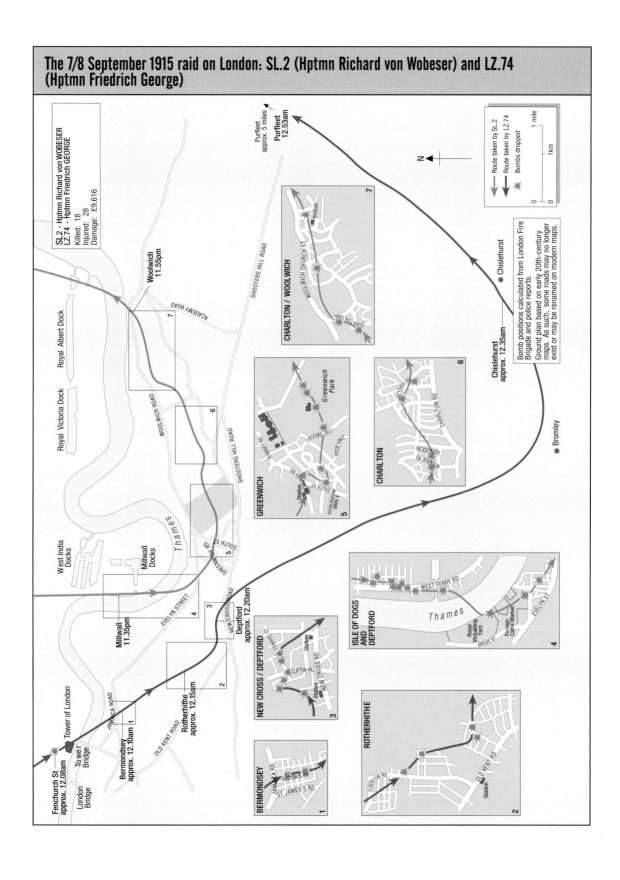

Bermondsey, within half a mile of the Surrey Commercial Docks and, in Ilderton Road, Rotherhithe, another fell on a house let out in tenements, killing six and injuring five people. LZ.74 then turned towards New Cross, dropping another nine bombs and causing more death and destruction, before departing London on a south-easterly course, reaching the Bromley/Chislehurst area at about 12.35am. There, LZ.74 turned north-east and passed close to the Purfleet anti-aircraft guns, which opened fire at 12.53am. The searchlight only caught her momentarily, her speed estimated at 40mph and height at 10,000ft. The gun ceased firing two minutes later. LZ.74 was still flying at between 40 and 50mph when she attracted more anti-aircraft fire, from Harwich at 2.11am, before she passed out to sea four minutes later.

In total 18 people were killed in the raid and at least 28 injured. However, official estimates put material damage at only £9,616.

Kptlt Heinrich Mathy. Mathy transferred to the Airship Division in January 1915 and became the best-known of all the airship commanders. He took part in 15 raids against England, four of these on London.

THE FOURTH RAID – CENTRAL LONDON BLASTED

The success of the Army Airship Service raid immediately stung Strasser into action. The following night he launched L.11, L.13 and L.14 against London, while the older L.9 headed north and bombed the chemical plant and ironworks at Skinningrove, between Redcar and Whitby.

Weather conditions were favourable for once, and there were high hopes of success as the London-bound airships set out. However, only an hour into the flight L.11 developed engine trouble and returned to base at Nordholz. Kptlt Böcker in L.14 had reached Norfolk when he too encountered problems with his engines. Realizing he could not reach London, he eventually off-loaded his bombs around East Dereham, 14 miles west of Norwich, then set course for home.

This left the spotlight on Kptlt Heinrich Mathy, the 32-year-old commander of L.13 – and he did not disappoint Strasser. On his three previous flights Mathy had returned early with engine problems, but this time there would be no recurrence. L.13 made landfall over King's Lynn at about 8.45pm. He followed the line of the River Ouse and Bedford Level Canal to Cambridge, from where the glow on the southern horizon illuminated the route to London. From Cambridge, Mathy appears to have followed the road running through Buntingford to Ware in Hertfordshire, before he circled to the north-west of London and set his course for the city.

Coming in over the suburb of Golders Green, Mathy dropped two explosive and ten incendiary bombs at about 10.40pm, damaging three houses as he checked his bombsight. Following the Finchley Road for a while, L.13 then veered off over Primrose Hill and Regent's Park. By-passing Euston Station at a height of about 8,500ft, he slowed his speed to 37mph and dropped his first bomb on central London, an incendiary, which fell on Woburn Square in Bloomsbury at about 10.45pm. Continuing over Russell Square, he dropped more incendiaries before releasing his first explosive bomb; it landed in the central gardens of Queen's Square, just missing the surrounding hospital buildings, but shattering hundreds of windows. Approaching Holborn, L.13 released a number of bombs close to Theobalds Road. One damaged the offices of the National Penny Bank and blew out the front of The Dolphin Public House on the corner of Lamb's Conduit Passage. The blast killed 23-year-old Henry Coombs who was standing by the entrance to the pub and injured 16 others.

Having bombed Gray's Inn, Mathy then steered a little to the north over Gray's Inn Road, dropping one explosive and two incendiary bombs on Portpool Lane, severely damaging a number of tenements, killing three children and injuring about 25 other people. Twisting to the south-east over Clerkenwell Road, the Zeppelin meted out more damage in Leather Lane and Hatton Garden, and badly damaged buildings in Farringdon Road between Cross Street and Charles Street (now Greville Street). From there L.13 passed over Smithfield Market and entered the City of London, the financial heart of Britain. Amongst his bombload Mathy carried onboard a single massive 300kg bomb, the first unleashed on Britain. He called it the 'Love Gift' and dropped it in the middle of his bombing run; it fell on Bartholomew Close, just a short distance from St Bartholomew's Hospital (St Bart's) and blasted a hole in the ground eight feet deep. All around was destruction. Fire gutted a printing works while the concussion of the blast shattered shopfronts, scattering battered remnants of stock across the road. Two men emerging from a public house started to run for cover as they saw L.13 overhead but they 'were blown to pieces' by the blast. The clock hanging in the close offered silent witness to the destruction – it stopped at 10.59pm. From the control gondola of L.13 Mathy watched the bomb fall and observed: 'The explosive effect … must be very great, since a whole cluster of lights vanished in its crater.'

Now, having passed just to the north of St Paul's Cathedral, at least ten more incendiary bombs rained down on the narrow streets surrounding the Guildhall: Wood Street, Addle Street, Basinghall Street and Aldermanbury. However, despite fierce fires breaking out, which gutted at least two warehouses, the historic Guildhall escaped harm. Most of London's anti-aircraft guns had been firing away at L.13 from about 10.50pm with no effect, and an urgent message issued from central control three minutes later exasperatedly stated: 'All firing too low. All shells bursting underneath. All bursting short.' An official

The 8/9 September 1915 raid on London: L.13 (Kptlt Heinrich Mathy)

L.13 - Kptlt Heinrich MATHY
Killed: 22
Injured: 87
Damage: £530,787

Bomb positions calculated from London Fire Brigade and police reports.

Ground plan based on early 20th-century maps. As such, some roads may no longer exist or may be renamed on modern maps.

LONDON

Main map area

N

Route taken by L.13
Bombs dropped by L.13

0   500 yds
0   500m

GOLDERS GREEN

1. HIGHFIELD RD
2. ALBA GDNS
3. RUSSELL GDNS

To Golders Green
5 miles
(See below)

memorandum later stated: 'Ideas both as to the height and size of the airship appear to have been somewhat wild.' However, the guns, and 20 searchlights that Mathy counted, may have proved distracting because he passed within 300 yards of the Bank of England without taking any action. An American reporter, William Shepherd, who witnessed the scene wrote:

> Among the autumn stars floats a long, gaunt Zeppelin. It is dull yellow – the colour of the harvest moon. The long fingers of searchlights, reaching up from the roofs of the city are touching all sides of the death messenger with their white tips. Great booming sounds shake the city. They are Zeppelin bombs – falling – killing – burning. Lesser noises – of shooting – are nearer at hand, the noise of aerial guns sending shrapnel into the sky.

Shepherd watched as one shell burst quite close, and someone next to him shouted, 'Good God! It's staggering!', but the airship moved steadily on. Next, L.13 crossed London Wall, where Alfred Grosch was working at the telephone exchange. He recalls what he saw as he looked out of the window:

The burnt-out premises of Messrs Glen and Co., Woollen Merchants, at 4–5 Addle Street. A single incendiary bomb dropped by L.13 caused this damage.

> A streak of fire was shooting down straight at me, it seemed, and I stared at it hardly comprehending. The bomb struck the coping of a restaurant a few yards ahead, then fell into London Wall and lay burning in the roadway. I looked up, and at the last moment the searchlight caught the Zepp, full and clear. It was a beautiful but terrifying sight.

Mathy now approached Liverpool Street Station preparing a horrific finale. Just outside Broad Street Station, only 50 yards from the entrance to Liverpool Street Station, an explosive bomb smashed into a No. 35A bus, passing over the driver's head, down through the floor to explode under the conductor's platform at the rear. The driver was wandering in the road in shock, staring at his hand from which a number of fingers were missing, the conductor was dead and the passengers, all thrown to the front of the bus were 'shockingly injured and killed.' Other bombs fell around the station, causing great destruction around Norton Folgate and the southern end of Shoreditch High Street.

Two buses were hit by bombs dropped from L.13. This No. 8 bus was in Norton Folgate, north of Liverpool Street Station, when a bomb exploded in the road, killing the driver, F. Kreppel, and eight passengers.

One bomb landed in the street and blasted a passing No. 8 bus. It killed the driver and eight passengers. Another bomb blew a hole in the roadway over a railway tunnel, severing the water main and damaging the electricity and gas mains. The last anti-aircraft gun in central London ceased firing at 11.00pm, but as Mathy steered away northwards, the gun on Parliament Hill put a shell uncomfortably close to him as he passed over Edmonton, persuading him to climb to a little over 11,000ft as he turned for home.

Only three BE2cs, from RNAS Yarmouth, took to the air but they did not see L.13 and one pilot, Flt Sub-Lt G.W. Hilliard, died in a landing accident. The damage inflicted was the highest recorded for any single airship raid of the war, London suffering to the extent of £530,787. Amongst the rubble, the bodies of 22 Londoners awaited recovery and 87 more bore injuries that would remind them of this terrible night for the rest of their lives.

CONCERNS FOR LONDON'S DEFENCE

Concerns over London's vulnerability to aerial attacks increased with each incursion over the capital. Four raids had hit the city, and, during the last, thousands observed L.13 sailing relatively unmolested over the heart of London. No aeroplanes appeared in opposition, while falling shrapnel from anti-aircraft shells fired at the airship caused more damage on the ground than in the air. Politicians demanded answers, the newspapers posed questions, dubbing the night 'Murder by Zeppelin', and the public felt alone and unprotected in the face of the previously unimagined horrors of aerial bombardment. However, although the Germans predicted that the bombing would cause panic on the streets of the city, they were wrong. It did nevertheless engender a universal anger amongst the population, shocked that Germany could indiscriminately target women and children in this way. From all quarters there arose a demand for a significant counter to the Zeppelin menace.

In response, the Secretary of State for War, Lord Kitchener, ordered Maj Gen David Henderson, Director-General of Military Aeronautics and commander of the RFC, to his office. Kitchener, under great pressure himself, demanded of Henderson, 'What are you going to do about these airship raids?' Even though Henderson pointed out that the defence of London was in the hands of the RNAS, Kitchener threatened to hold Henderson personally responsible if the RFC did not oppose the next raid. Accordingly, on 9 September, Henderson ordered BE2cs to both Writtle (near Chelmsford) and Joyce Green and began to overhaul his resources.

Matters were stirring in the corridors of the Admiralty too. In September, in an effort to improve the situation, they appointed the gunnery expert Admiral Sir Percy Scott, recently recalled from retirement, as sole commander of London's artillery defence. Scott wasted no time in attending to his task. A quick inventory

A Vickers 3-pdr quick-firing gun mounted on a Lancia chassis. The mobile anti-aircraft battery set up headquarters at Kenwood House in Hampstead under Lt Col Alfred Rawlinson, an army officer recently appointed to the Royal Naval Volunteer Reserve as deputy to Sir Percy Scott.

told him that his command amounted to 12 guns manned by part-time crews; he ignored the ineffective and outdated 'pom-poms'. He immediately sent to France for a 75mm auto-cannon, a gun far in advance of anything available at that time in Britain. With this weapon, an anti-aircraft gun mounted on an automobile chassis, he formed the nucleus of a mobile anti-aircraft battery. From all available sources, he pressed guns into service and at the same time established fixed gun positions with linked searchlight stations, while recruiting and training the personnel to operate them. Fortunately for London, three more attempted raids on consecutive nights in September all failed and it was a month before a Zeppelin reached London again.

Major-General Henderson meanwhile sent out reconnaissance parties to find suitable sites for new forward airfields positioned astride the north-eastern approaches to London. He secured farmland at Suttons Farm near Hornchurch and at Hainault Farm near Romford, adding them to the RFC roster. In addition, an observer cordon was organized to operate beyond the forward airfields, in telephone communication with the War Office. In a very short time portable canvas hangars arrived at the new airfields, landing grounds were marked out and a group of newly qualified pilots, awaiting overseas postings, reported for duty on London's new front line. Initial plans only required this hastily arranged response to provide cover from 4–12 October 1915, but an extension was authorized. The day after it had originally been due to expire, the Zeppelins returned to the capital.

THE FIFTH RAID – 'THEATRELAND' AND THE ARTILLERY RESPONSE

It had been Strasser's intention to commence raids on Liverpool in October, but the weather forecast for the night of 13/14 October precluded that. Instead, he launched five Zeppelins against London. Alongside L.11, L.13 and L.14, Strasser now had two new airships, L.15 and L.16, both fitted with four new 240hp engines, an improvement on the 210hp versions carried by the others. The airship fleet planned to rendezvous over the North Sea prior to launching the attack, but with no sign of Oblt-z-S von Buttlar's L.11, Heinrich Mathy, leading the raid from L.13, ordered the other ships to move off. They reached the coast of north-east Norfolk near Bacton between 6.20pm and 6.45pm; then at North Walsham, about 5 miles inland, the fleet encountered mobile machine-gun fire, the new first line of defence. As the four airships continued towards London, the leading trio gradually drew away from Oblt-z-S Werner Peterson in L.16 and lost contact.

The Admiralty received early advice of the impending raid via reports from the North Sea lightships and increased radio traffic. At 5.30pm the six RFC airfields around London received a warning order of Zeppelin activity. This was followed at 6.55pm by an order for Northolt, Joyce Green, Suttons Farm and Hainault Farm to have an aircraft on stand-by; an hour later each airfield received instructions to get an aircraft into the air if weather permitted. Thick ground fog prevented any take-off from Northolt or Suttons Farm, but 2nd Lt F.H. Jenkins ascended from Hainault Farm at 8.00pm in a BE2c, followed 20 minutes later by Lt R.S. Tipton from Joyce Green. As these two aircraft laboured up into the sky – the BE2c taking some 50 minutes to climb to 10,000ft – the Zeppelins continued on their way.

It appears that L.13 and L.15 kept more or less together, flying over Thetford and Saffron Walden before diverging near Bishop's Stortford. Kptlt Böcker in L.14 had already separated from this pair, heading towards the Thames estuary where he intended to pass to the east of London before swinging around and approaching from the south. Mathy planned to circle around the west of the capital and come in from the south-west, while Kptlt Joachim Breithaupt in L.15, in his first raid on London, followed the shortest route in from the north.

At about 8.45pm, Breithaupt approached Broxbourne, Hertfordshire. A 13-pdr anti-aircraft gun opened fire on the looming airship, to which she replied with extraordinary accuracy, dropping three bombs and knocking over the guncrew, damaging a Royal Engineer lorry and destroying the officer's car. L.15 passed over Potters Bar, High Barnet, Elstree and then Wembley, before finally turning eastwards. Releasing ballast, she rose to 8,500ft and headed for the centre of London. As he progressed, Breithaupt kept Hyde Park on his port side until he approached the Thames close to the Houses of Parliament. As the anti-aircraft gun in Green Park opened on L.15 and two searchlights found her, a journalist watching her progress noted that 'she looked a thing of silvery beauty sailing serenely through the night'. The famous landmarks of London were clear even from a mile and half up in the sky and Breithaupt ordered bombing to commence at Charing Cross Station at 9.35pm. Just at that moment, an army officer on leave from Flanders was driving along the Strand in a taxi when the driver suddenly came to halt, got out and ran off. The officer looked up at the sky and later recalled:

Kptlt Joachim Breithaupt. Breithaupt took command of L.15 on 12 September 1915, having commanded L.6 for the previous four months. The 'Theatreland' raid of 13 October 1915 was the first time he had flown over Britain.

> Right overhead was an enormous Zeppelin. It was lighted up by searchlights, and cruised along slowly and majestically, a marvellous sight. I stood gaping in the middle of the Strand, too fascinated to move. Then there was a terrific explosion, followed by another and another.

The first bomb fell in Exeter Street, just off the Strand, in the heart of London's 'Theatreland'. The bomb hit a corner of the Lyceum Theatre, causing limited damage inside but killing one person and injuring two others in the street. Another bomb fell seconds later close to the corner of Exeter and Wellington streets. An interval was in progress at the Lyceum and many of the audience were buying refreshments from street traders and at The Old Bell public house. The bomb gouged a large crater in the road and fractured a gas main. As the dust settled, amid the debris, rubble and flames lay 17 bodies while another 21 people sustained terrible injuries. A third bomb fell in Catherine Street near the Strand Theatre. Scenes of devastation and horror confronted the theatregoers as they emerged into the bomb-scarred streets, but high above them Breithaupt continued on his path, disconnected from the trail of destruction below. He later recalled: 'The picture we saw was indescribably beautiful – shrapnel bursting all around (though rather uncomfortably near us), our own bombs bursting, and the flashes from the anti-aircraft batteries below.' Indeed, for the first time a Zeppelin commander was aware of a significant barrage of anti-aircraft fire.

The scene of devastation at the junction of Wellington and Exeter Streets in Covent Garden after Breithaupt's raid. The building on the right is the Old Bell public house. The bomb here killed 17 and injured 21.

The 13/14 October 1915 raid on London: L.15 (Kptlt Joachim Breithaupt), L.13 and L.14

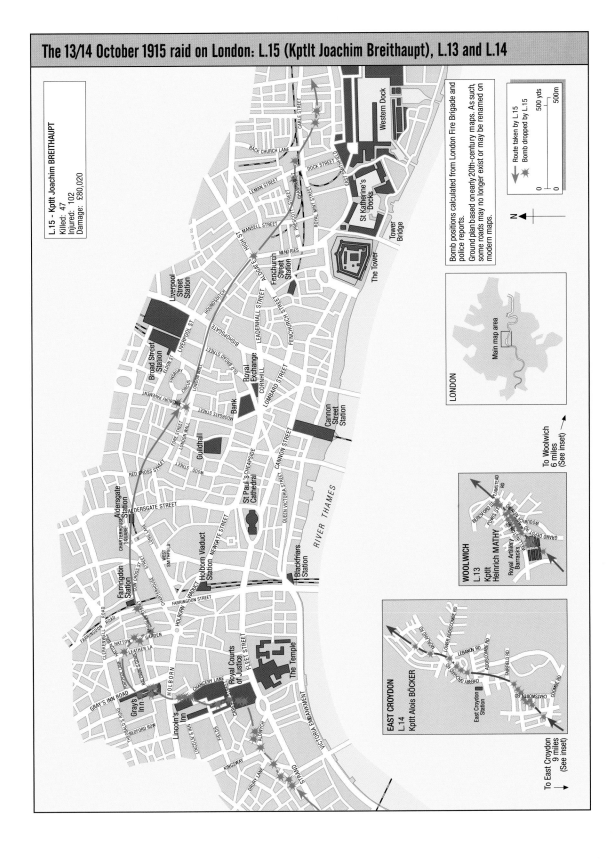

L.15 – Kptlt Joachim BREITHAUPT
Killed: 47
Injured: 102
Damage: £80,020

Bomb positions calculated from London Fire Brigade and police reports.
Ground plan based on early 20th-century maps. As such, some roads may no longer exist or may be renamed on modern maps.

Route taken by L.15
Bomb dropped by L.15

0   500 yds
0   500m

N

LONDON

Main map area

WOOLWICH
L.13
Kptlt
Heinrich MATHY

To Woolwich
6 miles
(See inset)

EAST CROYDON
L.14
Kptlt Alois BÖCKER

To East Croydon
9 miles
(See inset)

From Catherine Street, L.15 continued to Aldwych, where two bombs killed three people and injured 15. Incendiary bombs then fell on the Royal Courts of Justice as L.15 turned onto a northerly course before more explosive bombs fell on Carey Street and Lincoln's Inn, an explosive bomb in Old Square badly damaging the 17th-century stained-glass window of Lincoln's Inn Chapel. Chancery Lane suffered next, then L.15 crossed over Holborn, dropping more incendiaries and an explosive bomb on Gray's Inn before turning east again and releasing incendiaries over Hatton Garden and one in Farringdon Road, close to where bombs had fallen in the raid of 8/9 September.

Breithaupt now steered L.15 towards the City of London. Unknown to him, at the very same time Cdr Rawlinson (Sir Percy Scott's deputy) had been involved in a hair-raising dash across London from Wormwood Scrubs to the Honorable Artillery Company grounds near Moorgate with the new French 75mm auto-cannon. He swung the gun into action just as Breithaupt approached. With no time to lose, Rawlinson quickly estimated range and height and gave the order to fire. The high-explosive shell burst short of the target, but it was immediately clear

Damage caused on 13 October by an explosive bomb at Gray's Inn, one of London's four Inns of Court and home to many top barristers' chambers. (IWM, HO.5)

to Breithaupt that this was something new. He swiftly released two bombs, which fell in Finsbury Pavement, and started to climb. By the time the gun fired a second shot L.15 was over Aldgate, where she dropped an explosive bomb that landed on Minories, partly demolishing a hotel, bank and restaurant as well as causing damage to numerous other buildings in Houndsditch and Aldgate High Street. Rawlinson's second round burst above L.15, forcing Breithaupt to release water ballast to enable him to climb rapidly. Before turning away to the north, Breithaupt dropped two more explosive bombs, narrowly missing the Royal Mint. The raid had lasted only ten minutes.

In addition to Rawlinson's gun, Woolwich had fired 137 rounds, and guns at Clapton Orient football ground, Nine Elms, West Ham, Finsbury Park, Parliament Hill, Green Park, Tower Bridge, King's Cross, Foreign Office, Blackheath, Honor Oak, Barnes and Waterloo had added their firepower. Percy Scott's new defences had made their presence felt. However, the aerial response was less successful. A combination of ground mist and engine problems contrived to restrict the RFC response, while no RNAS aircraft flew defence sorties that night.

The corner of Minories and Aldgate High Street. The bomb partly demolished the London and South Western Bank and the hotel above, also severely damaging a restaurant next door. A woman injured in the explosion subsequently died.

Breithaupt's raid was by far the most successful of the night. Heinrich Mathy in L.13 had passed to the west of London, but lost his way, dropping 12 bombs around Guildford and Shalford in Surrey, while attempting to locate the Hampton waterworks. Then, flying eastwards, he unexpectedly found himself in close proximity to Böcker near Oxted.

Having crossed the Thames estuary, Böcker, in L.14, also lost his way, flying south until he reached the English Channel at Hythe. Circling over the nearby Otterpool Camp at about 9.05pm, he released eight bombs, killing 14 soldiers, wounding 12 and also killing 16 army horses. Böcker then turned back inland and, after dropping bombs on Frant and Tunbridge Wells, he encountered Mathy and L.13 at about 10.40pm. The two airships exchanged signals then diverged; Böcker headed north-west towards Croydon while Mathy flew north. At 11.19pm Böcker dropped 13 explosive bombs near the busy railway junction at East Croydon, but only one caused minor damage to the track; the rest demolished or damaged nearby houses, killing and injuring a number of civilians. From there Böcker turned eastwards intending to head home, but near

Bromley, he almost collided with L.13. Some accounts claim that the two commanders later exchanged words over the incident.

After this encounter Mathy flew on to attack Woolwich, although he thought he was attacking the Royal Victoria Dock on the other side of the Thames. L.13 flew in slowly, coming under intense anti-aircraft fire from the Woolwich guns. The first bomb dropped at 11.50pm and two or three minutes later it was all

Bomb damage at the rear of 92 Chamber Street, close to the Royal Mint. Four people (Frederick Coster, John Wilshan, Reuben Pizer and Mary Hearn) were injured in the explosion.

over. Although three explosive bombs and over 20 incendiaries hit the artillery barracks and arsenal, they recorded little significant damage. Casualties amounted to four men wounded in the barracks and nine in the arsenal, one of whom later died from his injuries.

The remaining two Zeppelins, L.16 and L.11 never got close to London. Peterson in L.16 lost touch with the others on the journey across East Anglia and at 9.35pm, as L.15 was bombing London, he came under anti-aircraft fire from the gun at Kelvedon Hatch, south of Chipping Ongar. Perhaps with memories of the raid of 9/10 August still fresh in his mind, when in command of L.12 he was forced down into the sea by anti-aircraft fire, Peterson turned away from London and dropped nearly 50 bombs on Hertford, 20 miles north of the city. In his report he incorrectly claimed hits on extensive factories or railway premises in East London. Von Buttlar in L.11 missed the rendezvous over the North Sea and came in over the coast about an hour after the others. He dropped a few bombs over the countryside of north-eastern Norfolk and returned home.

In all, total casualties for the raid amounted to 71 killed and 128 injured (in London and Croydon the total was 47 killed and 102 injured). Despite the improvement in London's defences, the Naval Airship Division suffered no casualties, although ground fire may have caused some engine damage to L.15, contributing to an eventful homeward voyage.

The Zeppelins did not come again in 1915. The arrival of the new moon in November brought the return of darkened skies, but with them came strong gales. Then, in both December 1915 and January 1916, the new moon heralded an extended period of fog, rain, sleet and snow.

Three explosive bombs dropped on Oval Road, East Croydon, from Kptlt Böcker's L.14 killed three civilians, wrecked six houses in the street and damaged four others.

THE 1916 ZEPPELIN RAIDS

A PERIOD OF CONSOLIDATION

In the lull between the 1915 and 1916 raids, both the German army and navy took delivery of more P-class airships. However, the navy lost the new L.18 in November, just ten days after commissioning her, in an accident at her home base at Tondern. In December, the first of ten new Q-class Zeppelins were delivered, five to each service. These new Zeppelins were basically P-class airships with the addition of two extra gas cells, increasing the length from 536ft to 585ft and improving lifting capacity and ceiling. Of more interest to Strasser, though, was the order, placed in July 1915, for the next development in airship design, the R-class, better known in Britain as the Super Zeppelins. These six-engined monsters were 650ft long and increased the lifting capacity and operational ceiling even further.

In Britain, the RFC's temporary defence arrangements for London ended, and by 26 October those pilots recently drafted in to serve on the forward airfields departed to other duties. A number of conferences then took place between the War Office and the Admiralty about the future responsibility for the defence of London. Finally, on 10 February 1916, an agreement stipulated that enemy aircraft approaching Britain were the navy's responsibility. Then, once they crossed the coastline, the responsibility passed to the army – and the RFC. Plans to reinstate October's temporary defence plan for London on a permanent basis received approval and a proposal for the formation of ten home defence squadrons was accepted. The War Office, now responsible for the defence of London, also

adopted Sir Percy Scott's plan for two gun rings around the capital, with a third ring of searchlights, known as 'aeroplane lights' beyond them. Initially Lord French, Commander-in-Chief, Home Forces, exercised command of the London guns through seven area sub-commanders. In February 1916 the War Office recalled Lt Col M. St L. Simon, R.E., from France to supervise the construction of gun and searchlight positions in the London area. Later, in December 1916, he became Anti-Aircraft Defence Commander, London.

A weakness in the patrol pattern flown by the RFC during the October raid was recognized and solved. With the second aircraft from each airfield not taking off until the first had landed, a gap appeared in the protective cover. By extending the patrols from 90 minutes to two hours, with the second aircraft beginning its ascent 30 minutes before the first was due to land, this gap closed and ensured unbroken air cover during a raid. Also in February 1916, the RFC grouped all the aircraft assigned to the London defences in No. 19 Reserve Aeroplane Squadron (RAS), with headquarters at Hounslow.

L.32, one of the new R-class airships, known by the British as the Super Zeppelins. With six 240hp engines and a length of 649ft 7in, these vessels were 113ft longer than the P-class and 64ft longer than the interim Q-class.

THE RAIDS RECOMMENCE

On the night of 31 January/1 February 1916, before all the defensive changes were in place, the Naval Airship Division launched nine Zeppelins on their biggest raid so far. The primary target this time was Liverpool, but difficult weather conditions and engine failures resulted in the fleet ranging over a wide area of the Midlands and the North, dropping bombs on what seemed appropriate targets. Despite 22 RFC and RNAS aircraft taking to the air, they met with no success in the thick foggy weather, while the rudimentary take-off and landing provisions made the whole process riddled with danger. Only six landed again without incident, and two pilots suffered fatal injuries in crash-landings. The German forces suffered too; Zeppelin L.19, on her first raid over England, came down in the North Sea on the return journey and her crew were lost in controversial circumstances. However, as far as the Naval Airship Division was concerned, Britain lay as open and vulnerable to their attacks as ever.

As the RFC and RNAS prepared for the next Zeppelin onslaught, work continued on the development of weapons to counter the threat. The principal armament remained the 20lb Hales bomb and a 16lb incendiary device. In February 1916 a new missile joined this limited arsenal – the Ranken dart – but, again, this weapon required a height advantage before use. More importantly, work was progressing on the development of explosive and incendiary bullets. Until now the Lewis gun had generally offered little threat to enemy airships, but that would soon change. However, this highly significant leap forward in the war against the Zeppelins was still a few months away.

March 1916 brought another respite for London when the German navy withdrew five of their newest airships in an attempt to solve the recurring problems of engine failure. In the meantime, in appalling weather, three of the older vessels raided the north of England on the night of 5/6 March, causing significant damage, particularly on Hull. Snowstorms and strong winds prevented any aircraft opposition.

A SHIFT IN FORTUNE

At the end of March the Zeppelins came again. This time, on the night of 31 March/1 April 1916, both the army and navy launched attacks. The army airships raiding East Anglia achieved nothing; three Zeppelins set out, but only one, LZ.90, came inland as far as Ipswich. She returned home without unloading her bombs.

The navy dispatched seven Zeppelins, with London as their target. Despite four of the most experienced Zeppelin commanders – Mathy, Böcker, Peterson and Breithaupt – taking part, none reached London, although both Böcker in L.14 and Peterson in L.16 claimed they had. Böcker, with Strasser on board, dropped his bombs on towns in Essex but claimed Tower Bridge as his target. Peterson falsely claimed hits on Hornsey in north London, but in fact his bombs fell on Bury St Edmonds. Elsewhere, L.22 – one of the new Q-class Zeppelins – switched targets and attacked Cleethorpes in Lincolnshire, where a bomb falling on a church hall killed 32 soldiers of the Manchester Regiment billeted inside, and injured another 48. The ever-present problem of mechanical failure forced L.9 and L.11 to return early, but the journey proved particularly dramatic for the crews of L.13 and L.15.

AN AIRFIELD AT NIGHT – ZEPPELIN ALERT!

An RFC pilot is shown here preparing for a Zeppelin patrol in early 1916. The devastating Zeppelin raids of September 1915 led to an urgent demand for the RFC to do more to oppose future raids. Accordingly, land was sought for two new airfields on the north-eastern approaches to London. Suitable farmland was acquired in Essex near Hornchurch at Suttons Farm, designated Landing Ground No. II, and Hainault Farm, near Romford, designated Landing Ground III. Suttons Farm comprised 90 acres of corn stubble bounded by low hedges.

Two BE2c aircraft were dispatched to Suttons Farm, with one pilot to be on stand-by each night for anti-Zeppelin duty. Besides carrying bombs fixed in racks under the wings, the BE2c also carried an upward-firing Lewis gun. Two canvas hangars designated for Suttons Farm were erected on 3 October and a landing ground marked, outlined with flares. Initially these were just old petrol cans with the tops cut off, half filled with petrol and cotton waste then set alight. By arranging the lines of flares in a specific order, individual landing grounds could be identified by disorientated pilots from the air. Although originally intended only as a temporary airfield, Suttons Farm became a permanent base, eventually home to a flight of No. 39 (Home Defence) Squadron – the most successful Zeppelin-fighting squadron of the war.

Mathy, in L.13 en route for London, attacked an explosives factory near Stowmarket, but a hit from a 6-pdr anti-aircraft gun holed two of L.13's gas cells. He turned for home, losing gas as he went. The crew jettisoned equipment and the remaining bombs to lighten the ship, allowing L.13 to limp back to base at Hage.

Breithaupt, who had bombed London so successfully the previous October, was not so lucky this time. L.15 flew in over Dunwich in Suffolk at 7.45pm, following a course to the Thames via Ipswich and Chelmsford. His route took him directly into the area defended by No. 19 RAS. Notified of the Zeppelin's approach, 2nd Lt H.S. Powell took off from Suttons Farm at 9.15pm, quickly followed by 2nd Lt A. de Bathe Brandon from Hainault Farm and 2nd Lt C.A. Ridley from Joyce Green. As these pilots urged their BE2c planes up into the night sky, Breithaupt turned towards Woolwich. Six minutes after take-off, Ridley spotted L.15 caught in a searchlight ahead of him, but several thousand feet higher. He attempted to close and opened fire with his Lewis gun at extreme range, but then the searchlight lost contact, and so did Ridley. When the searchlights picked up Breithaupt again, the anti-aircraft guns on the stretch of the Thames between Purfleet and Plumstead exploded into action. At about 9.45pm the Purfleet gun scored a direct hit. 2nd Lt Brandon had also spotted her and, as she turned away from the guns and lights, he set an interception course. L.15 started to lose height and the crew quickly established that two gas cells were virtually empty and two others leaking; to lighten the ship over 40 bombs were dropped on open ground near Rainham. At about 9.55pm Brandon closed with L.15 over Ingatestone, about 15 miles north-west of Purfleet, and from a position about 300 or 400ft above, he released three Ranken darts as the machine guns on the upper platform of L.15 opened fire at him. The darts missed the target, so Brandon came around again and prepared an incendiary bomb, but, fumbling in the dark, he took his eyes off the target and almost overshot. Having failed to find the launching tube, he rested the incendiary bomb in his lap and dropped more

Zeppelin L.15 was brought down about 15 miles north of Margate, following damage inflicted by the Purfleet anti-aircraft gun. The crew made desperate attempts to keep her aloft but she had lost too much hydrogen.

The crew of L.15 were eventually rescued and taken to Chatham aboard the destroyer HMS *Vulture*. These pictures show two of the crew under guard; the original captions identify the men as a warrant officer (left) and leading mechanic (right).

darts without result. Turning to make a third attack, the inexperienced Brandon – with only 30 hours' flying time behind him – became confused by the speed of action, found himself flying away from L.15 and lost contact.

Breithaupt was now free of pursuit, but was in a bad way. Jettisoning all excess weight, L.15 continued to lose height, and as he approached the coast he began to doubt whether he could nurse the ailing ship to Belgium. At 10.25pm he sent a last radio message – 'Require immediate assistance between Thames and Ostend – L.15' – then threw the radio overboard and flew out over Foulness. Just after 11.00pm the stress to L.15's frame proved too much, and at 2,000ft, following 'an ominous crack', her back broke and she crashed into the sea about 15 miles north of Margate. One of the crew, Obersignalmaat Willy Albrecht drowned; the others clambered up onto the top of the outer covering and waited. After five hours floundering uncomfortably at sea, a British destroyer rescued Breithaupt and the surviving 16 members of the crew, taking them to Chatham as prisoners of war. Attempts to tow L.15 failed and the wreckage finally sank off Westgate, near Margate.

The attack of 31 March/1 April marked the start of a run of five consecutive nights of raiding. Three of these were targeted on London, but because of strong winds only one airship, army Zeppelin LZ.90 commanded by Oblt Ernst Lehmann, got close. On 2 April he dropped 65 incendiary and 25 explosive bombs as he approached Waltham Abbey, causing only minimal damage to a farm, breaking windows, roof tiles and killing three chickens. Then, just after midnight, as the Waltham Abbey anti-aircraft guns opened up with a heavy bombardment, Lehmann turned for home. Seven aircraft from No. 19 RAS took off to intercept LZ.90 but only one claimed a sighting.

Strasser realized his raids were not having the effect he had originally anticipated, but he retained absolute belief that his airships would eventually bring Britain to its knees. To ensure he retained the support he needed, Strasser allowed the issue of reports such as that released to the Kaiser after the raid of 31 March/1 April. It falsely claimed success against specific targets in London including an aeroplane hangar in Kensington, a ship near Tower Bridge, fires in West India Docks and explosions at Surrey Docks as well as the destruction of a munitions boat at Tilbury Docks with massive casualties.

REORGANIZATION AND RE-ARMAMENT

In March 1916 those aircraft defending London were placed under the new No. 18 Wing, commanded by Lt Col Fenton Vesey Holt. Three weeks later, on 15 April, No. 19 RAS became No. 39 (Home Defence) Squadron. Its various detachments, currently spread around the outskirts of London, were concentrated at Suttons Farm and Hainault Farm. The headquarters flight remained for the time being at Hounslow, where all training continued to take place until a new airfield could be located north-east of London. As the squadron quickly began to take shape, it received the welcome news in June that home defence squadrons were finally able to divorce themselves entirely from training responsibilities, which they had until now combined with their defensive duties. With this positive change they became part of No. 16 Wing, which in July was simply designated Home Defence Wing.

While these pilots honed their skills, elsewhere technical developments were finally about to provide them with a weapon to strike fear into the hearts of the Zeppelin crews. Unknown to those men, who flew into battle suspended beneath more than a million cubic feet of highly inflammable hydrogen gas, British aircraft would soon be hunting them armed with machine guns firing a deadly combination of explosive and incendiary bullets.

Initial trials of John Pomeroy's .303 explosive bullet in June 1915 failed to convince the RFC authorities of its practicality. Later, in October, another bullet with both explosive and incendiary effects, underwent trials with the RNAS, designed by Flt Lt F.A. Brock (of the famous fireworks family). After further trials in February 1916, the Admiralty placed an order. Pomeroy persevered with his own bullet, and in May the RFC requested an initial batch while also ordering 500,000 of the Brock bullet; a similar-sized order for Pomeroy's bullet followed in August 1916. At least one aircraft from No. 39 Squadron used part of the trial batch of Brock bullets in action on 25 April. That same month the RFC also tested a phosphorus incendiary bullet produced by an engineer, J.F. Buckingham. All these bullets needed further enhancement and none stood out as being superior to the others, but they showed great promise. Orders for the Buckingham bullet followed too, and in June 1916 a new tracer bullet, the Sparklet, was added to the arsenal, developed by the makers of the Sparklet soda siphon. And this was the answer. Hydrogen only becomes flammable when mixed with oxygen; a combination of these new bullets would, it was hoped, blow a hole in the gas bags, letting hydrogen escape and mix with air, then a following incendiary bullet would ignite the combustible mixture.

THE LAST RAIDS OF SPRING

Bad weather thwarted an attempt by naval Zeppelins to attack London on the night of 24/25 April 1916. The following day the army sent five Zeppelins on a course for the city. Despite good weather, only Hptmn Erich Linnarz, the man who had captained LZ.38 on the first successful bombing of London 11 months earlier, came close to reaching the target. Linnarz now commanded LZ.97, one of the new Q-class Zeppelins, and was determined to reach London again. Coming in over West Mersea at about 10.00pm on 25 April, he followed the course of the Blackwater river inland. Passing Chelmsford, he headed west until, at about 10.45pm, he dropped over 40 incendiary bombs on a line from Fyfield to Chipping Ongar in Essex. These caused virtually no damage. Then, 15 minutes later, having steered a south-west course and believing he was over London, Linnarz began to bomb again. His second-in-command, Oblt Lampel, recalled the feelings of the crew at that moment:

> [The Commander's] hand is on the buttons and levers. 'Let go!' he cries. The first bomb has fallen on London! We lean over the side. What a cursed long time it takes between release and impact while the bomb travels those thousands of feet! We fear that it has proved a 'dud' – until the explosion reassures us. Already we have frightened them; away goes the second, an incendiary bomb. It blazes up underneath and sets fire to something, thereby giving us a point by which to calculate our drift and ground speed.

But Linnarz's crew had miscalculated, and this second batch of bombs actually dropped over Barkingside, some 8 miles north-east of the city. LZ.97 followed a curving route southwards towards Newbury Park as searchlights flicked to and fro across the sky. Oberleutnant Lampel described them 'reaching after us like gigantic spiders' legs; right, left and all around.' Then the guns opened up. LZ.97 circled over Seven Kings then headed back towards the east, dropping a single bomb on Chadwell Heath.

However, Linnarz was not yet out of danger. Barkingside lay in the midst of the airfields of the newly organized No. 39 Squadron. With word of the Zeppelin's approach, two aircraft took off from both Suttons Farm and Hainault Farm. Captain A.T. Harris (later Air Marshal Arthur 'Bomber' Harris), commanding B Flight at Suttons Farm, was first up at 10.30pm and 15–20 minutes later he saw the searchlights reaching out to the north. At 7,000ft he observed LZ.97 turning and climbing over Seven Kings. Struggling up to 12,000ft, Harris made for the Zeppelin, which passed over him 2,000ft higher up. In spite of the long range, he opened fire with his Lewis gun, but almost immediately the new Brock explosive ammunition jammed. He turned, got behind Linnarz's ship, cleared his gun and fired again – but once more it jammed.

2nd Lt William Leefe Robinson. Robinson transferred from the Worcestershire Regiment to the RFC in March 1915. After initially serving as an observer in No. 4 Squadron in France, he qualified as a pilot at Upavon in September 1915. A year later he was awarded the V.C. and became a national celebrity.

Then, as he worked to clear it a second time, his BE2c slipped off course and the target disappeared into the blackness of the night.

The other pilot from Suttons Farm, 2nd Lt William Leefe Robinson, took off about 15 minutes after Harris. Then, having climbed to 7,000ft and attracted by the sweeping searchlights, he caught sight of LZ.97. Climbing towards her, he opened fire, but estimated the target to be 2,000ft or more above him. Three times he got into position below LZ.97, but each time his gun jammed; he fired off only 20 rounds before losing sight of her. Linnarz and LZ.97 escaped, but it was a sobering experience for Oblt Lampel who later wrote: 'It is difficult to understand how we managed to survive the storm of shell and shrapnel.'

After the departure of LZ.97, the skies over London were empty for many weeks. The navy Zeppelins' commitment to the German fleet in connection with the Battle of Jutland (31 May–1 June 1916) and then the advent of short summer nights prevented any more raids on Britain for almost three months.

LONDON'S AERIAL DEFENCE MAKES READY

With this lull in the German offensive, the RFC was able to continue its reorganization. However, in June 1916, with the approach of the Allied offensive on the Somme, the demands for more aircraft on the Western Front led to a reduction in the February home defence proposal from ten to eight squadrons, but even then less than half the aircraft required were available to bring these squadrons up to strength. Further pressure reduced this force again in July to six squadrons, with the promise of additional squadrons later in the year to compensate. No. 39 Squadron was in fact one of the few up to full strength, with 24 aircraft, including six of the new BE12. This single-seat version of the BE2c had an improved engine, giving it a better rate of climb and, for the first time on home defence, a Vickers machine gun fitted with interrupter gear. This allowed firing through the propeller arc – a major improvement on the upward-firing, bracket-mounted Lewis used on the BE2c. In August, No. 39 Squadron finally grouped all three flights on the north-eastern approaches to London as the Hounslow flight took up residence at a new airfield at North Weald Bassett.

At the end of June positive feedback on RFC trials of the new bullets paved the way for pilots to discard bombs from their armament. The recommended load for a BE2c pilot was now a Lewis gun firing a mixture of explosive, incendiary and tracer ammunition along with a box of Ranken darts. However, the RNAS steadfastly refused to abandon bombs entirely.

On the ground, although great improvements were apparent in the number of guns and searchlights available, at 271 guns and 258 searchlights, these figures remained far short of the planned national levels of 490 each.

RETURN OF THE RAIDERS

The navy airships returned to the offensive on the night of 28/29 July. This raid was remarkable only in the fact that it saw the arrival over England of the first R-class or Super Zeppelin, L.31, commanded by Heinrich Mathy. In the pipeline for over a year, the design had suffered a number of production delays, but finally it was ready. At some 650ft long and with a diameter of 78ft, its 19 gas cells contained almost 2 million cubic feet of hydrogen, a vast increase over the 1.2 million of the Q-class and the 1.1 million of the P-class. This increase in gas capacity allowed the Super Zeppelins to climb to 17,400ft. However, at an operational height of 13,000ft the six engines could reach 60mph when loaded with between three and four tons of bombs. While hopes were high for this long-awaited addition to the Zeppelin fleet, their arrival over Britain coincided with the introduction of explosive and incendiary bullets to home defence squadrons.

This ten-Zeppelin raid caused virtually no damage. Mechanical problems caused four to return early and fog severely restricted the impact of the others. However, it proved a useful exercise for Mathy and his new ship. Eight naval

Zeppelin L.31 was the first of the 'Super Zeppelins' to appear over Britain, on 28 July 1916. The photo shows L.31 flying over the German battleship *Ostfriesland*, one of those that bombarded Scarborough, Hartlepool and Whitby in December 1914.

Zeppelins followed up with a raid two days later. All headed for the east coast, except Mathy in L.31 who steered for London, but unpredicted high winds disrupted the attack leaving L.31 to wander briefly over Kent before returning to Nordholz. The naval airships set out again on the night of 2/3 August. Following a similar pattern, five headed for East Anglia as Mathy in L.31 made another strike for London. As in the previous raid, Mathy only reached Kent, where vigorous defensive fire from batteries on the south coast forced him away.

Mathy was joined by another of the Super Zeppelins – L.30, commanded by Horst von Buttlar, now promoted to Kapitänleutnant – on the night of 8/9 August, when nine naval airships raided the north-east coast, Hull in particular suffering badly. A short lull followed as the cycle of the full moon passed; then, on the night of 24/25 August the navy Zeppelins returned.

THE SIXTH LONDON RAID – THE SUPER ZEPPELINS REACH THE CAPITAL

Thirteen naval Zeppelins set out on the sixth London raid. L.16 and L.21 came in over Suffolk and Essex, where they caused minor damage before turning for home. L.32, another Super Zeppelin on its first raid over England and with Strasser on board, reached Kent. Greatly delayed by strong winds at altitude, the commander, Werner Peterson, decided it was too late to strike for London, so having flown along the coast from Folkestone to Deal he dumped his bombs at sea and returned. Nine others dropped out with mechanical difficulties or through delays caused by the strong winds. Only one airship made for London: L.31 commanded by Heinrich Mathy.

Mathy appeared off Margate at 11.30pm, and for once the bad weather worked in his favour. The night was wet with extensive low cloud, and, although the engines could be heard, L.31 became visible only momentarily between gaps in the cloud. Mathy followed the line of the Thames and, having passed between North Woolwich and Beckton, he turned south-west over Blackwall. This took him over the Millwall Docks on the Isle of Dogs, where he dropped his first bombs on or adjoining West Ferry Road. These destroyed a number of small houses and an engineering works, falling only a few yards from those dropped by SL.2 on 7 September 1915. Crossing to the south bank of the Thames, bombs fell in Deptford on the Foreign Cattle Market, home to the Army Service Corps' No. 1 Reserve Depot. They also caused severe damage to the London Electric Supply Company and the Deptford Dry Dock. Mathy continued, following the south bank of the Thames back to the east until, over Norway Street in Greenwich, he turned south and dropped bombs on the railway station. The following morning the stationmaster turned up for work proudly displaying 'a wonderful black eye' and a face covered with scores of minute cuts, caused by a shower of

The 24/25 August 1916 raid on London: L.31 (Kptlt Heinrich Mathy)

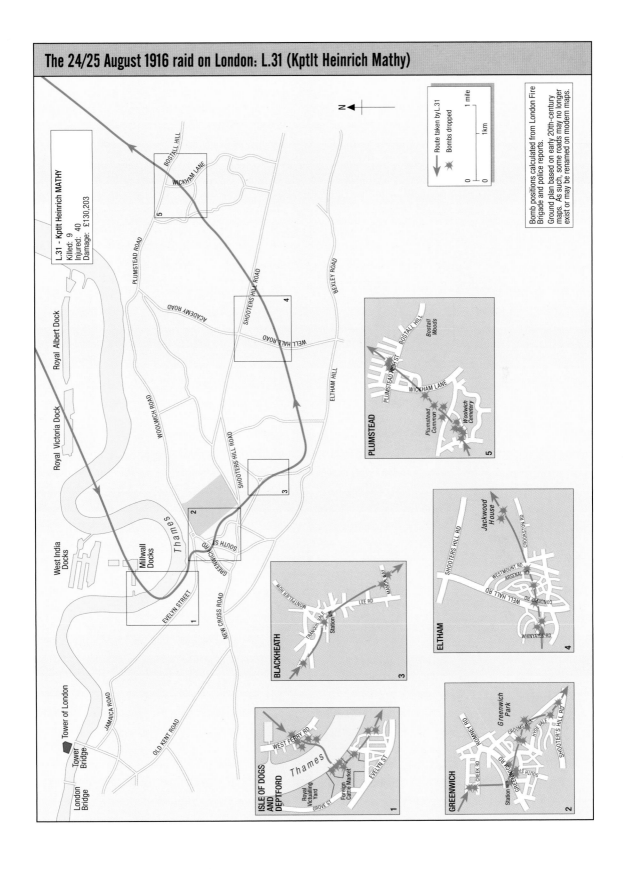

L.31 - Kptlt Heinrich MATHY
Killed: 9
Injured: 40
Damage: £130,203

→ Route taken by L.31
✳ Bombs dropped

N◀

0 ___ 1 mile
0 ___ 1km

Bomb positions calculated from London Fire Brigade and police reports. Ground plan based on early 20th-century maps. As such, some roads may no longer exist or may be renamed on modern maps.

Tower of London
Tower Bridge
London Bridge
West India Docks
Millwall Docks
Royal Victoria Dock
Royal Albert Dock
Thames
Jamaica Road
Old Kent Road
New Cross Road
Evelyn Street
Greenwich Rd
South St
Woolwich Road
Academy Road
Plumstead Road
Shooters Hill Road
Shooters Hill Road
Wickham Lane
Bostall Hill
Well Hall Road
Eltham Hill
Bexley Road

BLACKHEATH 3
Station
Tranquil Vale
Montpelier Row
Lee Rd
Manor Way

ISLE OF DOGS AND DEPTFORD 1
West Ferry Rd
Thames
Royal Victualling Yard
Foreign Cattle Market
Grove St
Evelyn St

ELTHAM 4
Shooters Hill Rd
Jackwood House
Crookston Rd
Westmount Rd
Arsenal Rd
Congreve Rd
Well Hall Rd
Whinyates Rd

GREENWICH 2
Romney Rd
Greenwich Park
Croom's Hill
Hyde Vale
Shooter's Hill Rd
Greenwich High Rd
South St
Station
Creek Rd

PLUMSTEAD 5
Plumstead High St
Bostall Hill
Bostall Woods
Wickham Lane
Plumstead Common
Woolwich Cemetery

stone and shell fragments from when the bomb had exploded. Besides causing much damage to the station, the bomb also blasted a hole in the wall of the public house opposite and inflicted superficial damage on a cluster of almshouses. Other houses in Greenwich suffered too as L.31 passed over towards Blackheath; there, an explosive bomb partly demolished a shop and house in the inappropriately named Tranquil Vale. Three other explosive bombs and an incendiary fell on the Horse Reserve Depot of the Army Service Corps, injuring 14 soldiers. From Blackheath L.31 continued to Eltham, where a bomb blasted a house in Well Hall Road, killing the occupants. Mathy then steered a north-east course, dropping bombs on Plumstead, where one demolished a house at 3 Bostall Hill, killing a family of three.

The raid commenced just after 1.30am on the morning of 25 August and was over about ten minutes later, during which time 36 explosive and eight incendiary bombs rained down. The low cloud made it very difficult for the ground defences to home in on L.31 and it appears that no searchlights located her until she passed over Eltham. Only after L.31 had completed its path of destruction across south-east London did the anti-aircraft guns begin to blast the first of 120 rounds skywards. However, one observer reported that all shells were bursting over the target. Second-Lieutenant J.I. MacKay of No. 39 Squadron was the only RFC pilot to catch even a brief glimpse of L.31 that night, before Mathy headed for home; he was pursued out to sea by two RNAS pilots from Eastchurch and Manston.

Although the raid of 24/25 August had successfully reached London, it failed to penetrate to the heart of the city. Instead, the bombs fell largely on poor housing on the south-east outskirts, although the damage was estimated at £130,000 – the greatest single damage was caused by the bombs dropping on the workshops, offices and stores of Le Bas & Co, an industrial company based in West Ferry Road. Altogether nine civilians died and about 40 soldiers and civilians were injured. As far as Strasser was concerned, this marked the start of a big effort for the raiding period planned between 20 August and 6 September. However, L.31 would not be available for service again for another month, as a rough landing necessitated extensive repairs.

Another raid had come and gone. While the increased gunfire offered the public some comfort, what they really wanted to see was a Zeppelin, one of the 'baby-killers', brought down before their own eyes. Wealthy industrialists and newspaper editors offered up monetary rewards for the first Zeppelin brought down over Britain, but that goal remained elusive.

THE TIDE TURNS – THE LOSS OF SL.11

Strasser's next big raid, aimed at London on 2/3 September, coincided with one planned by the army. That night, a total of 12 navy airships (11 Zeppelin and a

Schütte-Lanz) and four army airships (three Zeppelin and a Schütte-Lanz) set out to bomb the capital. It was the largest single raid of the war, but it ended in disaster for the Army Airship Division.

In fact the whole raid turned out badly. The naval Zeppelins encountered rain, hail and snowstorms over the North Sea, widely dispersing their attack. One bombed the East Retford gasworks in Nottinghamshire and another caused most of the night's casualties when bombing Boston in Lincolnshire, while at least six others wandered largely ineffectively over East Anglia. Only three reached Hertfordshire, north of the capital, and these were preparing to strike London when events forced them to change course and make for home. That night the army airships found themselves centre stage.

Heavy rain squalls over the North Sea forced one of the army Zeppelins, LZ.97, to turn back before crossing the coast. Another, LZ.90, came inland at Frinton on the Essex coast, penetrating as far as Haverhill in Suffolk, where it dropped six bombs before turning away and flying out north of Yarmouth.

Oberleutnant Ernst Lehmann, commanding LZ.98, came inland over New Romney on the Kent coast. Lehmann had almost reached London during the

This is believed to be the wooden-framed SL.11 under construction at Leipzig between April and August 1916. SL.11, commanded by Hptmn Wilhelm Schramm, officially entered service on 12 August. The raid of 2/3 September was its first over Britain.

raid of 2/3 April earlier in the year, but the Waltham Abbey guns forced him to turn back on that occasion. This time he approached London across Kent, passing Ashford, Maidstone and Sevenoaks, bearing towards Woolwich. The other army airship to penetrate inland was SL.11. Making landfall over Foulness, Essex, at about 10.40pm, she steered north-west across Essex into Hertfordshire, with the intention of sweeping around London and approaching the capital from the north-west. The newly commissioned SL.11 was on her first mission; her commander, London-born Hptmn Wilhelm Schramm, had previously led LZ.93 on two unsuccessful raids against the capital in April.

The British authorities, intercepting a great volume of radio traffic, were aware that a raid was imminent. No. 39 Squadron received orders to commence patrolling at about 11.00pm. Second-Lieutenant William Leefe Robinson, now commanding B Flight, was first up from Suttons Farm at 11.08pm in a BE2c. He began the long climb to 10,000ft to patrol the line from his home base to the airfield at Joyce Green. Within the next five minutes, Lt C.S. Ross took off from North Weald in a BE12, flying the line to Hainault Farm, while 2nd Lt A. de Bathe Brandon, flying a BE2c from Hainault Farm, covered the line to Suttons Farm. Neither Ross nor Brandon saw any sign of enemy airships and returned to their home airfields, where Ross made an emergency landing and crashed. Second-Lieutenant J.I. MacKay took over his patrol from North Weald and 2nd Lt B.H. Hunt replaced Brandon in the air. At 1.07am, 2nd Lt F. Sowrey ascended from Suttons Farm to take up Robinson's patrol, but Robinson had not yet started to descend. At 1.10am, flying at 12,900ft, he noticed searchlights attempting to hold a Zeppelin in their beams to the south-east of Woolwich. The airship was Lehmann's LZ.98. Anti-aircraft guns opened on the airship, turning it away to the east where it dropped bombs near Gravesend. Robinson estimated he was flying about 800ft above the Zeppelin and, preferring to maintain this advantage, closed only slowly on his target for the next ten minutes. However, his quarry steered into clouds and disappeared from view. Having lost his target Robinson turned away and, sighting the landing flares at Suttons Farm in the distance, headed for home.

At about 1.50am, some 15 minutes into his homeward flight, Robinson noticed a red glow over north-east London. Although well overdue back at Suttons Farm, he thought the glow could be the result of bombing and flew on to investigate. He was correct. After a circuitous route, Wilhelm Schramm in SL.11 set his course for the centre of London and, passing to the south of St Albans, he released a string of bombs between London Colney and South Mimms at about 1.20am. Schramm then continued towards Enfield before heading south in the direction of Southgate, dropping a few bombs as he went, before changing course again, heading west towards Hadley Wood where he dropped two bombs at about 1.45am. Schramm then set course for the centre of London once more, but as he passed over Hornsey a searchlight picked him

The 2/3 September 1916 raid on London: SL.11 (Hptmn Wilhelm Schramm)

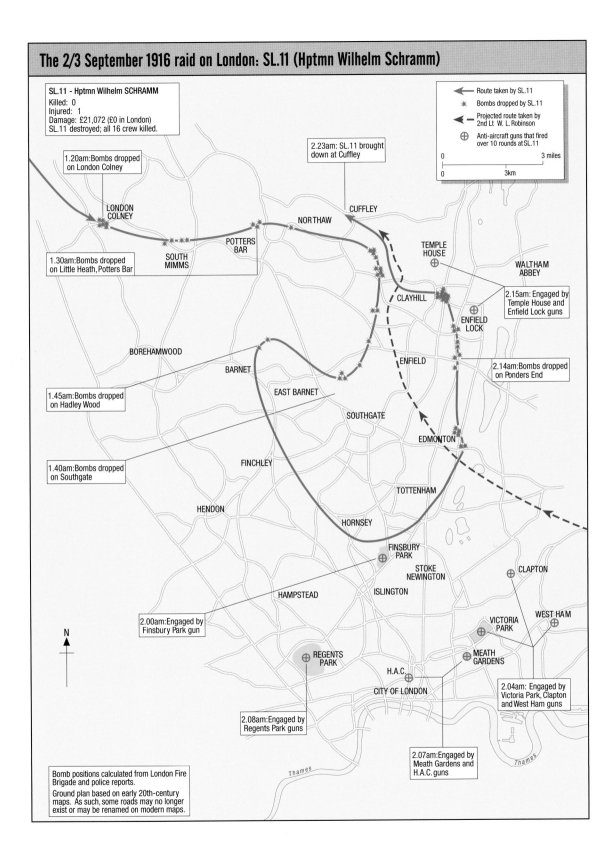

SL.11 - Hptmn Wilhelm SCHRAMM
Killed: 0
Injured: 1
Damage: £21,072 (£0 in London)
SL.11 destroyed; all 16 crew killed.

→ Route taken by SL.11
✳ Bombs dropped by SL.11
◄--- Projected route taken by 2nd Lt W. L. Robinson
⊕ Anti-aircraft guns that fired over 10 rounds at SL.11

0   3 miles
0   3km

1.20am: Bombs dropped on London Colney

2.23am: SL.11 brought down at Cuffley

1.30am: Bombs dropped on Little Heath, Potters Bar

2.15am: Engaged by Temple House and Enfield Lock guns

2.14am: Bombs dropped on Ponders End

1.45am: Bombs dropped on Hadley Wood

1.40am: Bombs dropped on Southgate

2.00am: Engaged by Finsbury Park gun

2.04am: Engaged by Victoria Park, Clapton and West Ham guns

2.08am: Engaged by Regents Park guns

2.07am: Engaged by Meath Gardens and H.A.C. guns

N

Bomb positions calculated from London Fire Brigade and police reports.

Ground plan based on early 20th-century maps. As such, some roads may no longer exist or may be renamed on modern maps.

LONDON COLNEY
NORTHAW
CUFFLEY
POTTERS BAR
SOUTH MIMMS
TEMPLE HOUSE
WALTHAM ABBEY
CLAYHILL
ENFIELD LOCK
BOREHAMWOOD
BARNET
EAST BARNET
ENFIELD
SOUTHGATE
FINCHLEY
TOTTENHAM
HENDON
HORNSEY
EDMONTON
FINSBURY PARK
STOKE NEWINGTON
CLAPTON
HAMPSTEAD
ISLINGTON
VICTORIA PARK
WEST HAM
REGENTS PARK
MEATH GARDENS
H.A.C.
CITY OF LONDON
Thames
Thames

LEFT: A postcard issued at the time supposedly showing SL.11 over London (possibly suggesting Bruce Castle, Tottenham). However, keen to cash in on the popularity of postcards such as this, they were often reproduced as depicting different raids. This picture later appeared as L.31 approaching London on the night of 1/2 October.

RIGHT: Another contemporary postcard depicting SL.11 held by searchlights and attacked by anti-aircraft guns. An earlier version of this card depicted the September 8/9 September 1915 raid over London.

out and the anti-aircraft gun in Finsbury Park immediately opened fire. The central London guns soon joined in and then, as SL.11 veered away from the immediate danger and headed towards Tottenham, the east London guns opened up too, adding to the great crescendo of noise over the city. Londoners in their thousands, awoken by the storm of shot and shell the like of which they had never heard before, tumbled from their beds, peering up at the drama being enacted in the night sky. Over Wood Green the searchlights lost Schramm's ship in clouds and, now free of their hold, he resumed bombing as he passed over Edmonton; but, when a searchlight caught him again, the crowds gathering all over London cheered vociferously. Now, flying at around 11,000ft, SL.11 released more bombs over Ponders End and Enfield Highway at about 2.14am, before the ever-vigilant Waltham Abbey area searchlights and guns locked on to her. Unknown to the crew they had but ten minutes to live.

Robinson already had SL.11 in his sights. Elsewhere, MacKay and Hunt had also turned their aircraft towards this illuminated target. Following his earlier experience with LZ.98, Robinson decided to abandon height advantage and put

his nose down to close with the airship as quickly as possible, while SL.11 attempted to gain height and shrug off the net of light beams that held her tight. At only 27ft in length, Robinson's BE2c was dwarfed by the 570ft bulk of SL.11 looming above him, yet some of those watching from below momentarily glimpsed him as he flitted through the searchlight beams. Turning some 800ft below SL.11, Robinson flew a path from bow to stern directly under the airship and emptied a drum of mixed Brock and Pomeroy ammunition into her from his upward-firing Lewis gun. To his dismay the burst of fire made no impact other than to alert the airship crew to his proximity. They immediately opened fire, their Parabellum and Maxim machine guns spitting out 'flickering red stabs of light' in the dark. Undeterred, Robinson returned to the attack, this time firing off another ammunition drum all along one side of SL.11, but again with no effect. As he prepared to make a third attack a shell from the anti-aircraft gun at Temple House exploded very close to SL.11 and may have damaged one of the engine gondolas, but then the searchlights lost her again, causing the guns to cease firing as Robinson swung in to the attack.

With the airship now at 12,000ft he took up a position behind her and about 500ft below, before emptying a third drum of mixed ammunition into one point of the rear underside. For a moment nothing happened, and then Robinson reported: 'I had hardly finished the drum before I saw the part fired at glow. In a few seconds the whole rear part was blazing.' SL.11 was doomed. Taking urgent evasive action, Robinson avoided the rapidly blazing airship as it started to fall. Lieutenant MacKay saw SL.11 burst into flames while still a mile from the target, but Lt Hunt had closed to 200 yards and was preparing to commence his own attack when she exploded. In the sudden flare of light Hunt

Members of the local fire brigade douse the smouldering remains of SL.11 while RFC men recover what they can from the wreckage. One fireman, asked for his opinion of Robinson, commented: 'He's given us plenty to do this night, he have, but us don't begrudge it. Us'd turn out any durned night for a month if us had a working job like this afore us.'

THE ATTACK ON SL.11

In the early hours of 3 September 1916, a BE2c, piloted by 2nd Lt William Leefe Robinson, attacked German Army airship SL.11. It became one of the most celebrated aerial duels of the Zeppelin war. Robinson's first two passes were unsuccessful. Because the Lewis gun on the BE2c was fitted to fire upwards, pilots would attempt to make their attack from beneath the target. Observers on the ground noted Robinson's aircraft flitting through the searchlight beams, banking 'as it turned almost on its beam ends in wheeling round, in its efforts to secure an advantage over its gigantic foe.' As Robinson manoeuvred into position the crew of SL.11 opened up with their machine guns.

The top gun platform, merely a shallow recess in the outer envelope, was the most exposed position on any airship. It was normal for at least one man to remain here on lookout throughout the flight. This could involve endless hours in freezing temperatures, the only shelter from the buffeting winds provided by a small canvas screen that shielded the guns. Access to the gun platform was via a hatch at the top of a ladder that ascended through the structure of the airship. The favoured gun was the air-cooled Parabellum MG.14, firing a 7.92mm bullet.

Robinson's third attack destroyed SL.11, the first airship to be brought down on British soil.

caught a glimpse of another airship less than a mile away but lost her in the glare. This was L.16, and her commander, Kptlt E. Sommerfeldt, reported that 'a large number of searchlights … had seized an airship travelling from south to north, which was being fired on from all sides with shrapnel and incendiary ammunition … It caught fire at the stern, burned with an enormous flame and fell.' At least five other scattered naval airships saw the destruction of SL.11 from a distance and turned for home.

The burning wreckage of SL.11 came to earth at the village of Cuffley, Hertfordshire. There were no survivors. A vast crowd of Londoners watched the flaming descent of the stricken airship, its flames illuminating the darkness 30 miles away. As it plummeted to earth the crowds erupted, giving vent to 'defiant, hard, merciless cheers.' It was as though the threat of the Zeppelins, under which Londoners had lived since the war began, had disappeared in that blinding flash of burning hydrogen. People danced in the streets, hooters sounded, bells rang and trains blew their whistles; in the morning thousands upon thousands celebrated 'Zepp Sunday' by joining the great exodus to Cuffley to see the charred remains of the once-mighty airship for themselves.

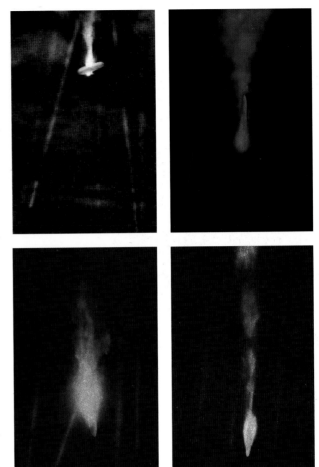

TOP LEFT: The first in a series of four postcards depicting the final moments of SL.11. The original given caption was 'Airman Attacks – 2.18am'.

TOP RIGHT: The second postcard in the sequence, titled, 'Well Alight – 2.20am'.

BOTTOM LEFT: The third card, 'Nearing the End – 2.22am'.

BOTTOM RIGHT: The final card in the series, 'Final Rapid Fall – 2.25am'. An eyewitness described the plummeting airship as 'an incandescent mantle at white heat and enveloped in flame.'

Although the authorities were aware that the destroyed airship was a Schütte-Lanz, they saw a benefit in doing nothing to dispel the belief that the wreckage was that of a Zeppelin. To the public the name Schütte-Lanz meant little, but everyone knew and hated the Zeppelins, the despised and feared 'baby-killers'. Accordingly, the victim became known as Zeppelin L.21.

Five days later, an instant celebrity, William Leefe Robinson received the Victoria Cross from King George V in a ceremony at Windsor Castle – and from the various substantial financial rewards he received, he bought himself a new car.

The loss of SL.11 struck at the failing heart of the Army Airship Service and they never raided Britain again. Disbanded within a year, the army turned its attention to the Gotha bomber. Strasser, however, was determined to continue the offensive as soon as the moon entered its next dark cycle towards the end of September, still convinced that his airships could strike an effective blow against Britain.

Part of the mass of wire from SL.11 that remained after the wooden framework was devoured in the fire. The Red Cross sold off pieces of the wire for a shilling each to raise money for the war-wounded. (Colin Ablett)

Kptlt Alois Böcker. Previously commander of L.5 and L.14, Böcker took command of the new L.33 on 2 September 1916. The raid on London in the early hours of 24 September was L.33's first and last.

THE END APPROACHES

Although Strasser remained confident, morale took a further blow with the destruction on 16 September of L.6 and L.9, now serving as training ships, following an explosion in their Fuhlsbüttel shed. In the meantime, the naval crews appeared happy to accept that the wooden construction of SL.11 may in some way have contributed to her demise, for at this time no one in Germany knew that explosive/incendiary bullets igniting the hydrogen had been the cause of her destruction.

On the night of 23/24 September, Strasser was ready to launch his airships against Britain once more. In all, 12 were detailed for the raid. Eight of the older airships were detailed to strike against the Midlands and North, while four Super Zeppelins – L.30, L.31, L.32 and L.33 – received orders for London. The only significant action by the northern group was the bombing of Nottingham by L.17; the rest made little or no impact.

The Super Zeppelins took off from their bases at Ahlhorn and Nordholz around lunchtime on 23 September. Von Buttlar in L.30 and Böcker in L.33 were to approach along the more traditional eastern routes, while Mathy in L.31 and Peterson in L.32 came in on the less anticipated southern route over Kent and Surrey.

The first to claim a successful bombing run over London was von Buttlar in L.30. He had previously filed false reports detailing raids on the capital in August and October 1915, and this appears to be another. It seems more likely that L.30 never crossed the coastline and dropped her bombs at sea. Kapitänleutnant Alois Böcker, having previously commanded L.5 and L.14, was now at the helm of the navy's latest Zeppelin, L.33, on her first raid. Böcker crossed the coast at Foulness at about 10.40pm and steered a familiar course. Fifty minutes later he passed Billericay and then, turning south over Brentwood, he flew close to Upminster and dropped four sighting incendiary bombs prior to releasing six explosive bombs close to 39 Squadron's Suttons Farm airfield at 11.50pm. Word of the approaching Zeppelin reached the airfields late and only two pilots got aloft at 11.30am; both were still climbing when L.33 passed over and out of sight.

Still undetected, Böcker dropped a parachute flare at 11.55pm south of Chadwell Heath as he attempted to determine his position. A searchlight caught L.33 briefly, but lost contact before any guns could engage. However, the flare does not seem to have aided Böcker in establishing his location, for after continuing to Wanstead he turned away from London. Then, at 12.06am, he changed direction again. Now heading south-west, he passed between the guns at Beckton and North Woolwich, before twisting to the north-west and steering towards West Ham. At 12.10am the West Ham gun opened fire as L.33 began unloading bombs on the unsuspecting streets of East London.

Böcker reported that his first bomb fell close to Tower Bridge, but he was actually approaching Bromley, just over 2 miles away, where a bomb on St Leonard's Street severely damaged four houses and killed six of the occupants. Steering westwards, he continued his bombing run but suddenly L.33 shuddered. As the first bombs fell, the guns at Victoria Park, Beckton and Wanstead opened up on L.33. The volume and accuracy of their fire shook the Zeppelin, even though it was flying close to 13,000ft. It was probably a shell from either Beckton or Wanstead that exploded close to L.33 at about 12.12am, smashing into one of the gas cells behind the forward engine gondola, while other shell splinters slashed their way through another four cells. Böcker immediately released water ballast in an attempt to gain height and turned back to the north-east, dropping bombs as he went. These caused serious damage to a Baptist chapel

The Black Swan public house in Bow Road, destroyed by one of L.33's bombs. The landlord, E.J. Reynolds escaped injury, as did his wife, but the bomb killed two adult daughters, his mother-in-law and a 1-year-old granddaughter.

A contemporary postcard showing L.33, viewed from outside London, being hit by an anti-aircraft shell while over Bromley-by-Bow. The original caption reads: 'A nasty jar for the Baby Killers'.

and a great number of houses in Botolph Road, while a direct hit on the Black Swan public house in Bow Road claimed four lives, including two of the landlord's children. Böcker steered away over the industrial buildings of Stratford Marsh, where his final bombs caused severe damage to a match factory and the depot of an oil company.

The wounded Zeppelin passed over Buckhurst Hill at 12.19am before continuing towards Chelmsford. In spite of the frantic efforts of the crew to repair the shell damage, L.33 began to lose height. As she approached Kelvedon Hatch, flying at about 9,000ft, the searchlight picked her up and the gun there opened fire, possibly inflicting further damage.

Having been in the air for almost an hour, 2nd Lt Alfred de Bathe Brandon spotted L.33 from some distance away as she bombed East London. Brandon, the same pilot who had come close to bringing down L.15 six months earlier, was unlucky this time too. As he closed with the target, his automatic petrol pump failed, requiring him to pump by hand while loading a drum of ammunition on his Lewis gun and controlling the aircraft at the same time.

During his attack on L.15 six months earlier, he ended up with an incendiary bomb resting in his lap. This time, as he raised the gun it jerked out of its mounting and fell, coming to rest across the cockpit. By the time he fitted it back into position, while still pumping fuel, he realized he had flown under and past the Zeppelin. He turned to attack, but, approaching from the bow this time, the two aircraft closed so quickly that Brandon was unable to take aim before the target flashed past. Undeterred, he turned again and approached from the rear port side, firing a whole drum of mixed Brock, Pomeroy and Sparklet ammunition. Frustratingly, he saw the Brock rounds bursting all along the side of L.33 but without apparent effect. Loading another drum of ammunition, he turned again, but after firing just nine rounds his Lewis gun jammed. He then attempted to climb above her but lost her in the clouds. His pursuit and attack had lasted 20 minutes.

On board L.33 the crew were making every effort to keep her aloft. Close to Chelmsford, the crew began throwing any removable objects overboard, including guns and ammunition, but this did not arrest the descent. Böcker hoped at least to get to the coast where he could sink his ship, but already close to the ground a gust of wind forced him down. Shortly after 1.15am, L.33 landed in a field close to the village of Little Wigborough. All 21 of the crew survived the landing; whereupon they set fire to L.33 before forming up and marching off down a country lane in a half-hearted attempt to reach the coast.

The glow of the fire attracted the attention of Special Constable Edgar Nicholas, who, cycling to the scene, discovered Böcker and his men marching towards him. In a somewhat surreal situation, Böcker asked Nicholas in English

2nd Lt Alfred de Bathe Brandon. A New Zealander, Brandon qualified as a lawyer in England in 1906. When war broke out he left his father's legal firm in New Zealand, returned to England, learnt to fly and qualified as an RFC pilot in December 1915. (Colin Ablett)

A dramatic reconstruction of Brandon's attack on L.33.

how far it was to Colchester. The constable told him, but recognizing a foreign accent decided to cycle along behind them, chatting with one of the crew. Another 'Special' and a police officer on leave appeared as the group approached the village of Peldon and the three men decided to escort the crew to the post office where they found Constable Charles Smith of the Essex Police. Smith formally arrested Böcker and the crew. He then received instructions to escort the prisoners towards Mersea Island and, calling in another eight special constables, this strange group set off and led the crew of L.33 into captivity.

L.32 – A SUPER ZEPPELIN DESTROYED

Meanwhile, Mathy in L.31 and Peterson in L.32 came in from the south. The experienced Mathy crossed the coastline over Rye at about 11.00pm and pursued a direct course for London, passing Tunbridge Wells at 11.35pm and Caterham at 12.15am. Ten minutes later, over Kenley, he released four high-explosive bombs. All fell in a line, probably intended as sighting bombs to allow the crew to judge their ground speed, but they still caused damage to three houses and injured two people. The Croydon searchlight located L.31 at about 12.30am but parachute flares, dropped to illuminate the ground below, effectively blinded the crew. About six minutes later lights picked up L.31 once more and the Croydon anti-aircraft gun opened fire, but another parachute flare caused the searchlight to lose contact again. Mathy flew on for just over 5 miles before dropping four bombs over open land near Mitcham. Then, over Streatham, he unleashed a murderous salvo of 17 explosive and 24 incendiary bombs. These fell between Streatham Common Station and Tierney Road, to the north of Streatham Hill Station; the blasts killed seven, including the driver, conductor and four passengers of a tram, and wounded another 27. From Streatham, L.31 followed the line of Brixton Hill, unloading another 16 bombs (eight explosive and eight incendiary) on Brixton, killing seven and injuring 17. Mathy dropped just one more bomb south of the Thames, which landed in Kennington Park, then ceased as he crossed the river near London Bridge. He flew right across the city, the prime target area, and only resumed bombing at 12.46am along the Lea Bridge Road, Leyton, seven and a half miles from Kennington, dropping ten explosive bombs. Another eight people died here with 31 injured; many houses and shops were damaged. It seems likely that Mathy

The 23/24 September 1916 raid on London: L.31 (Kptlt Heinrich Mathy) and L.33 (Kptlt Alois Böcker)

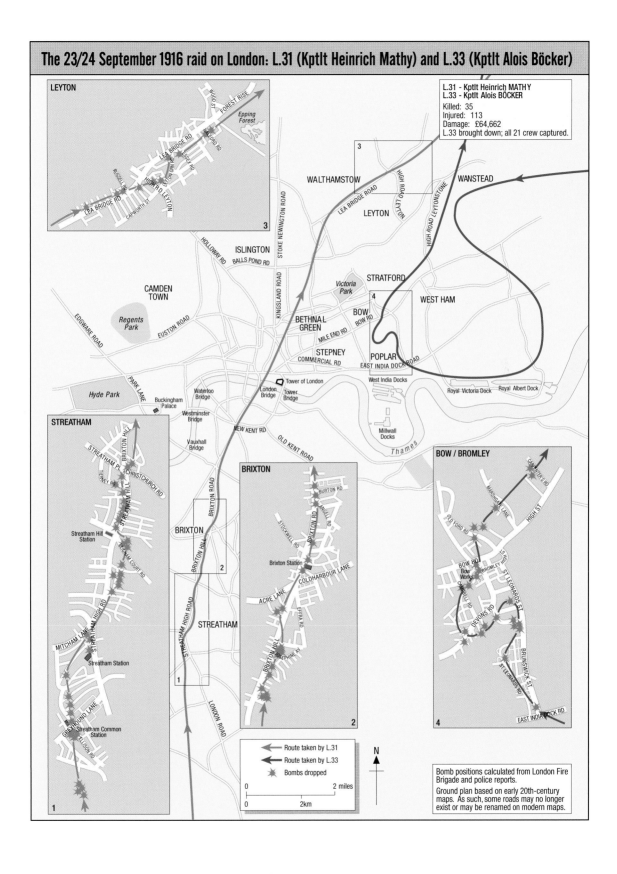

LEYTON

Wood St · Forest Rise · Epping Forest · Lea Bridge Rd · Seaford Rd · Essex Rd · Russell Rd · Leyton Grn Rd · High Rd Leyton · Canworth St · Lea Bridge Rd

3

L.31 - Kptlt Heinrich MATHY
L.33 - Kptlt Alois BÖCKER
Killed: 35
Injured: 113
Damage: £64,662
L.33 brought down; all 21 crew captured.

WALTHAMSTOW · High Road Leyton · WANSTEAD · Lea Bridge Road · LEYTON · High Road Leytonstone

3

STOKE NEWINGTON ROAD · HOLLOWAY RD · ISLINGTON · BALLS POND RD · KINGSLAND ROAD

CAMDEN TOWN

Regents Park · EDGWARE ROAD · EUSTON ROAD · PARK LANE

Hyde Park · Buckingham Palace · Waterloo Bridge · Westminster Bridge · Vauxhall Bridge

Victoria Park · STRATFORD · BETHNAL GREEN · BOW · BOW RD · WEST HAM · 4 · MILE END RD · STEPNEY · COMMERCIAL RD · POPLAR · EAST INDIA DOCK ROAD

Tower of London · London Bridge · Tower Bridge · NEW KENT RD · OLD KENT ROAD

West India Docks · Royal Victoria Dock · Royal Albert Dock · Millwall Docks · Thames

STREATHAM

STREATHAM PL · BRIXTON HILL · CHRISTCHURCH RD · TIERNEY RD · STREATHAM HILL · Streatham Hill Station · TRENHAM COURT RD · MITCHAM LANE · STREATHAM HIGH RD · Streatham Station · GREYHOUND LANE · ELLISON RD · Streatham Common Station

1

BRIXTON · BRIXTON ROAD · BRIXTON HILL · 2 · STREATHAM HIGH ROAD · STREATHAM · 1 · LONDON ROAD

BRIXTON

BURTON RD · STOCKWELL RD · BRIXTON RD · ANGEL TOWN · Brixton Station · COLDHARBOUR LANE · ACRE LANE · EFFRA RD · BRIXTON HILL · JOSEPHINE AV

2

BOW / BROMLEY

CARPENTER'S RD · MARSHGATE LANE · HIGH ST · OLD FORD RD · BOW BD · Bow Works · BROMLEY HIGH ST · ST LEONARD'S ST · CAMPBELL RD · DEVONS RD · BRUNSWICK ST · ST LEONARD'S RD · EAST INDIA DOCK RD

4

Route taken by L.31
Route taken by L.33
Bombs dropped

0 — 2 miles
0 — 2km

N

Bomb positions calculated from London Fire Brigade and police reports.

Ground plan based on early 20th-century maps. As such, some roads may no longer exist or may be renamed on modern maps.

had miscalculated his position, for in his report he claimed to have bombed Pimlico and Chelsea, then the City and Islington. Flying at 13,000ft (about two and a half miles), he may have mistaken Streatham/Brixton for Pimlico/Chelsea, with this confusion extended as he bombed Leyton. Despite this destruction, local anti-aircraft guns were unable to locate L.31; a mist had risen and smoke from fires in East London caused by L.33's bombs contributed to greatly reduced visibility. Mathy steered for home, passing close to Waltham Abbey at 1.00am before turning towards Harlow and following an unhindered course for Norfolk and the North Sea. The pursuit of L.33 across Essex held the attention away from L.31 – and then at about 1.10am, as Mathy passed Bishop's Stortford, a vast explosion filled the sky some 20 miles away to the south-east.

Oberleutnant-zur-See Werner Peterson, commanding L.32, had approached the Kent coast with Mathy, but encountered engine problems. While L.31 headed inland, L.32 remained circling slowly over the coast for about an hour. Finally, at about 11.45pm, Peterson steered inland, observed from Tunbridge Wells at 12.10am. About 20 minutes later L.32 dropped a single incendiary over Ide Hill near Sevenoaks. However, as Peterson approached Swanley a searchlight illuminated his ship. To distract the light he dropped seven explosive bombs, which only succeeded in smashing a number of windows in the town. However, a light mist south of the Thames helped shroud his movements and no gun

Special Constable Edgar Nicholas. When one of the crew asked him in English if he thought the war was nearly over, Nicholas gave the now-clichéd reply, 'It's over for you anyway'. (Colin Ablett)

The London Fire Brigade report on the bomb dropped by L.31 on Estreham Road, by Streatham Common Station, states that three houses were demolished, one partly demolished and one severely damaged.
A 74-year-old woman was killed, with nine adults and five children injured.

The looming skeleton of L.33 by New Hall Cottages, Little Wigborough, Essex. There was so little hydrogen left in the gas cells that the attempt to destroy the ship by fire left the framework almost intact, providing a useful source of information for the British authorities.

engaged him as, flying at about 13,000ft, he moved away and crossed the river east of Purfleet at about 1.00am. North of the Thames the mist cleared, and, as L.32 flew on, the searchlights at Beacon Hill and Belhus Park caught her almost immediately. The guns at Tunnel Farm were first to open fire at 1.03am, then, as L.32 dropped five explosive and six incendiary bombs on the village of Aveley, the guns at Belhus Park, engaged her too. At 1.08am, over South Ockendon, Peterson released ten explosive and 19 incendiary bombs, but the damage they caused was slight. At about the same time another five searchlights locked on and more guns opened fire. Inevitably, all this action in the sky attracted the attention of the pilots of No. 39 Squadron.

Still in the air following his unsuccessful attack on L.33, 2nd Lt Brandon caught sight of L.32 held in the searchlights and turned towards her. Second-Lieutenant J.I. MacKay had taken off from North Weald later than Brandon, and was about 35 minutes into his patrol when he also saw L.32. However, as they both homed in, a blinding light filled the sky as the raider exploded in a roaring inferno.

Second-Lieutenant Frederick Sowrey took off in his BE2c from Suttons Farm at 11.30pm, with orders to patrol between there and Joyce Green. At about 12.45am and from a height of 13,000ft he observed a Zeppelin south of

The bomb that landed on Baytree Road, Brixton, demolished No. 19 and partly demolished those on either side. The house was the home of music hall artist Jack Lorimer. The bomb killed his housekeeper-cum-nanny and the youngest of his three sons. Rescuers pulled the two other sons from the wreckage; one, 8-year-old Maxwell Lorimer, went on to earn fame as the entertainer Max Wall.

Oblt-z-S Werner Peterson. Peterson took command of L.32 on 7 August 1916, having previously commanded L.7, L.12 and L.16. On L.32's first raid on 24/25 August, she got no further than the Kent coast; on 2/3 September Peterson bombed Ware in Hertfordshire.

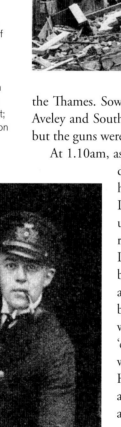

the Thames. Sowrey turned towards it and gradually closed, as bombs fell on Aveley and South Ockendon. As Sowrey swept in, searchlights still held L.32, but the guns were no longer firing.

At 1.10am, as Peterson was heading for home, Sowrey appeared out of the darkness, positioned himself below L.32 and, throttling down his engine to keep pace with the airship, opened fire with his Lewis gun. A whole drum of mixed bullets sprayed along the underside of the vast airship with no effect. As he turned to reposition himself for a second attack the machine guns on L.32 spat out their bullets in response. Undeterred, Sowrey slid back into a position beneath her and fired off a second drum of ammunition, traversing the belly of the craft, but again his bullets failed to set her alight. Second-Lieutenant Brandon, who had been closing on L.32, wrote in his report that he 'could see the Brock bullets bursting. It looked as if the Zepp was being hosed with a stream of fire.' MacKay closed in too. He saw Sowrey empty his first two drums and, although he was at long range, fired a few shots himself. Then he saw Sowrey fire a third drum. This time Sowrey concentrated his fire in one area and a fire took hold inside, possibly caused by a burning petrol tank, for bullet holes riddled one of those recovered from the wreckage. Flames swiftly spread throughout the airship, bursting through the outer envelope in several places. An eye-witness recalled that 'the flames crept along the back of the

A contemporary postcard originally captioned 'Hot Stuff' showing L.32 in flames over Essex after the attack by Frederick Sowrey in his BE2c.

Zeppelin, which appeared to light up in sections … until it was burning from end to end.' Then, as at Cuffley three weeks earlier, 'the people cheered, sirens started screeching, factory whistles commenced to blow, and in a moment all was pandemonium.' L.32 sagged in the middle, forming a V-shape before plummeting to earth in an incandescent mass. Another eyewitness described the demise of L.32 as it fell:

Those few moments afforded a wonderful spectacle. Flames were bursting out from the sides and behind, and, as the gasbag continued to fall, there trailed away long tongues of flame, which became more and more fantastic as the falling monster gained impetus.

The burning wreckage finally crashed to earth at Snail's Hall Farm in Great Burstead, just south of Billericay, Essex. Like the Cuffley wreck, thousands made a pilgrimage to see it. The bodies of the crew were collected together in a nearby barn – many horribly burnt. Oberleutnant Peterson, however, had jumped to his death.

Back in Germany there could be no hiding from the fact that this was a serious setback for the Naval Airship Division. With two of his new Super Zeppelins lost, Strasser ordered another raid the following day, but stressed that his commanders should exercise caution if the sky over Britain was clear. Only two, L.30 and L.31, headed for London, but a cloudless sky spelt danger and they unsuccessfully sought other targets. For the next few days bad weather kept the airship crews at home.

2nd Lt Frederick Sowrey. Aged 23, Sowrey had received a commission in the Royal Fusiliers and was wounded at the Battle of Loos in 1915. Having recovered, he transferred to the RFC and was eventually posted to No. 39 Squadron on 17 June 1916.

L.31 AND THE DEATH OF HEINRICH MATHY

The next test came on 1 October 1916. Eleven naval Zeppelins received orders to attack Britain that night, with targets specified as London and the Midlands. Strong winds and thick cloud over the North Sea prevented four airships from passing inland. Once over Britain the remaining raiders encountered cloud,

The wreckage of L.32 at Snail's Hall Farm, Great Bursted, near Billericay, Essex. There were no survivors. A medical officer reported that all but three of the bodies of the crew were 'very much burned … Several had their hands and feet burned off, nearly all had broken limbs.'

rain, snow, ice, hail and mist, and this seriously hampered navigation. Only one, Mathy's L.31, approached London.

L.31 came in over the Suffolk coast near Lowestoft at about 8.00pm and followed a course for London. As he approached Chelmsford at about 9.45pm, the searchlight at Kelvedon Hatch locked on to Mathy's ship. Turning away to the north-west, he made a wide sweeping detour, passing Harlow, Stevenage and Hatfield before turning east. At about 11.10pm, as he closed on Hertford, he silenced his engines and drifted silently with the wind towards Ware, presumably hoping to avoid the attention of London's northern defences. However, about 20 minutes later as he approached Cheshunt with the engines back on, the Enfield Lock searchlight picked up L.31, quickly attracting another five beams. At 11.38pm the Newmans anti-aircraft gun opened fire, followed a minute later by the Temple House gun.

This sudden outbreak of gunfire attracted the ever-alert pilots of No. 39 Squadron. Orders to commence patrolling only arrived a little before 10.00pm and the first three pilots were still climbing to operational height as L.31 approached and passed their patrol lines unseen. As the lights caught the

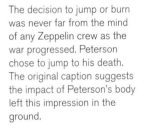

The decision to jump or burn was never far from the mind of any Zeppelin crew as the war progressed. Peterson chose to jump to his death. The original caption suggests the impact of Peterson's body left this impression in the ground.

A contemporary postcard showing a Zeppelin held by searchlights. The scene would have been similar when the searchlights caught L.31 over Cheshunt as the guns at Newmans and Temple House opened fire.

Royal Flying Corps Home Defence squadrons, November 1916

Squadron No.	Official formation date
33	March 1916
36	March 1916
39	April 1916
50	May 1916
51	May 1916
38	July 1916
37	September 1916
76	September 1916
75	October 1916
77	October 1916
78	November 1916

Turnhouse
Whiteburn
77 H.D.S. Edinburgh
New Haggerston
Dumfries
Carlisle
Ashington
36 H.D.S. Newcastle
Hylton
Seaton Carew
Catterick
76 H.D.S. Ripon
Helperby
Lancaster
York
Bradford
Copmanthorpe
Leeds
Manchester
Elsham
Liverpool
Kirton Lindsey
Sheffield
33 H.D.S. Gainsborough
Brattleby
Lincoln
Leadenham
38 H.D.S. Melton Mowbray
Buckminster
Mattishall
Marham
Norwich
Stamford
51 H.D.S. Hingham
Great Yarmouth
Leicester
Birmingham
Harling Road
Old Weston
Northampton
Yelling
Cambridge
75 H.D.S. Goldington
Ipswich
Therfield
Harwich
37 H.D.S. Woodham Mortimer
Gloucester
Oxford
Hertford
Goldhanger
North Weald Bassett
Stow Maries
39 H.D.S. Woodford
Hainault Fm
Rochford
Cardiff
Bristol
London
Suttons Farm
Reading
50 H.D.S. Harrietsham
Throwley
Bekesbourne
Chiddingstone Causeway
Tunbridge Wells
Dover
Dunkirk
Calais
Southampton
78 H.D.S. Hove
Gosport
Telscombe Cliffs

NORTH SEA

ENGLISH CHANNEL

N

● RFC Home Defence Squadron headquarters
● RFC Squadron airfield

0 — 50 miles
0 — 100km

TO BURN OR TO JUMP – THE DEATH OF HEINRICH MATHY

On the night of 1 October 1916, 2nd Lt Wulstan Tempest, in a BE2c, attacked and shot down Zeppelin L.31, commanded by Kptlt Heinrich Mathy, the most revered of all the Zeppelin commanders.

Since the introduction of explosive and incendiary bullets for use with the Lewis gun, the advantage in aerial combat had swung to the pilots of the RFC and RNAS. With the realization that they were now extremely vulnerable, German aircrew began to dwell on the last great question – if your Zeppelin is on fire and there is no hope of survival, do you jump to your death or burn in the wreckage? When Heinrich Mathy was asked this question he replied, 'I won't know until it happens.'

Elsewhere, one of his crew confessed that the old cheerfulness had disappeared:

'We discuss our heavy losses … Our nerves are on edge, and even the most energetic and determined cannot shake off the gloomy atmosphere … It is only a question of time before we join the rest. Everyone admits that they feel it … If anyone should say that he was not haunted by visions of burning airships, then he would be a braggart.'

When the time came, with the fire spreading rapidly through the gas cells contained within the outer envelope of L.31, Mathy chose to jump to his death.

2nd Lt Wulstan Tempest. Aged 25, Tempest joined the army in November 1914 and, as an officer in the King's Own Yorkshire Light Infantry, was wounded at Second Ypres in May 1915. In June 1916 he qualified as a RFC pilot and joined B Flight, No. 39 Squadron at Suttons Farm.

beleaguered airship, lieutenants MacKay, Payne and Tempest all turned towards it. Another pilot, P. McGuinness, who had taken off at 11.25pm to patrol a line from North Weald to Hendon, also saw L.31 in the searchlights about 20 minutes later and joined the chase. But it was 2nd Lt Wulstan Tempest who caught her first.

Tempest estimates he was about 15 miles away when the guns opened fire. As he closed to within 5 miles of the target, Tempest realized he was at a height well above the Zeppelin and found the anti-aircraft shells bursting uncomfortably close to his BE2c. Then, as he passed through one of the searchlights, someone on board L.31 saw his approach and Mathy immediately ordered the release of 24 explosive and 26 incendiary bombs to lighten the ship and gain height. The bombs landed on Cheshunt, seriously damaging four houses and breaking windows and doors in 343 others as well as destroying 40 horticultural glasshouses. Fortunately for the residents of the town, casualties were restricted to one woman slightly cut by flying glass. L.31 zigzagged away westwards, rapidly gaining height.

As he closed to launch his attack, Tempest's pressure petrol pump failed and he had to hand-pump furiously prior to making his attack before L.31 could climb out of reach. He recorded, thankfully, that he was now beyond the range of the anti-aircraft guns – the last gun ceased firing at 11.50pm. Flying straight at the oncoming airship, Tempest flew under its belly, firing off a short burst of mixed Pomeroy, Buckingham and standard ammunition with

The tangle of wreckage that was once Heinrich Mathy's L.31. The burning ship broke up and fell in two main sections a few hundred feet apart. This section, guarded by a cordon of soldiers, lies impaled on an oak tree in a misty Oakmere Park, Potters Bar.

no effect. He quickly turned until he was flying underneath in the same direction as L.31 and gave her another burst, but again there was no result other than to draw machine-gun fire from the crew. He banked and then sat under her tail, from where the machine guns were unable to reach him. Although he had almost begun to despair of bringing her down, he attacked again and, in his words, 'pumped lead into her for all I was worth.'

As this third burst penetrated the outer skin of L.31, Tempest recalled: 'I noticed her begin to go red inside like an enormous Chinese lantern and then a flame shot out of the front part of her and I realized she was on fire.'

L.31 shot about 200ft up in the air then began to fall, 'roaring like a furnace', directly towards Tempest who dived as hard as he could to get out of the way of the burning wreck. Tempest returned to Hainault Farm, but, feeling 'sick, giddy and exhausted', wrecked his own aircraft on landing although he only suffered minor injuries to himself. L.31 crashed to earth at Potters Bar in Hertfordshire, only a few miles from the scene of William Leefe Robinson's victory at Cuffley.

All 19 of the crew of L.31 perished. Many, including Heinrich Mathy – the most respected and successful of all the Zeppelin commanders – jumped to their deaths rather than be burnt alive. This had been his 15th raid over England and his death struck like a dagger to the heart of the Naval Airship Division. In a letter to Mathy's widow, Peter Strasser described his fallen comrade as a man of 'daring, of tireless energy … and at the same time a cheerful, helpful and true comrade and friend, high in the estimation of his superiors, his equals and his subordinates.'

ZEPPELIN LOSSES MOUNT

Zeppelins did not return to England again until the night of 27/28 November 1916, when, avoiding London, they selected targets in the industrial Midlands and the North. Yet the result was much the same. L.34, commanded by Kptlt Max Dietrich, was shot down in flames by 2nd Lt I.V. Pyott of No. 36 Squadron, based at Seaton Carew, and crashed into the sea near the mouth of the River Tees. Further south, about 10 miles off the coast from Lowestoft, the joint efforts of two aircraft piloted by Flt Lt Egbert Cadbury and Flight Sub-Lt Edward Pulling, RNAS, shot down L.21 commanded by Kptlt Kurt Frankenburg. There were no survivors from either wreck. It was this Zeppelin the authorities had already claimed was shot down at Cuffley.

On that same day – 28 November - largely unnoticed, a single German LVG C.IV aircraft appeared over London in broad daylight, dropping six 10kg bombs between Brompton Road and Victoria. The bombs injured ten. It was a sign of things to come, although few realized it at the time.

An already bad end to 1916 got even worse when the Naval Airship Division lost three more airships on 28 December. First, SL.12, although damaged,

One of many postcards produced to supply public demand for souvenirs to commemorate the destruction of four airships between 3 September and 1 October 1916. This one was titled, 'The End of the Baby-Killer'.

survived a bad landing at the Ahlhorn base, but strong overnight winds destroyed her. Then, at Tondern an equipment failure caused the ground crew to lose control of L.24 as she came in to land, whereupon she smashed against the shed and burst into flames, which also engulfed the neighbouring L.17.

Although the army had lost faith in the airship's ability to carry the war to Britain, Strasser, driven by his unshakeable belief and now appointed Führer der Luftschiffe, remained positive. He insisted on new airships of improved performance for the navy, demanding a greater ceiling to enable the airships to operate above the range of the now-lethal British aircraft. Indeed, while the overall material effect of the airship raids was limited, by the end of 1916 they resulted in the commitment of some 17,000 British servicemen to home defence duty. The army, meanwhile, began to look again at bomber aircraft as a means of striking more effectively against London.

THE 1917 ZEPPELIN RAIDS

THE ARRIVAL OF THE 'HEIGHT CLIMBERS'

The first of the new S-Class Zeppelins (in the form of L.42) entered naval service on 28 February 1917. She had an operational ceiling of 16,500ft and the ability to climb to about 21,000ft (4 miles high), way beyond the reach of the anti-aircraft guns and aircraft allocated to home defence. However, to attain these great heights the new models traded against a reduction in power, fitting five engines instead of six. With existing Super Zeppelins also altered to fulfil these new requirements, the British dubbed this new class of airship the 'Height Climbers'.

The first raid of 1917 took place on the night of 16/17 March, with London as its target. The force, made up of L.42 and four converted Super Zeppelins, encountered fierce 45mph winds from the north-west that blew them south and none penetrated further inland than Ashford in Kent.

On the night of 23/24 May, six Height Climbers targeted London again. Adverse winds at high altitude disrupted the raid and no airships reached the city. The closest, L.42, turned back over Braintree in Essex, some 40 miles away. All the crews suffered badly from the intense cold and experienced the debilitating effects of altitude sickness encountered at these great heights. Two days after this raid Germany launched its first major aeroplane raid on London, with 21 twin-engine Gotha bombers crossing the Essex coastline in daylight. Only a heavy cloud build-up over the capital prevented them from reaching London, but it marked a dramatic change in the air war over the city.

Having studied the report of the 23/24 May Zeppelin raid, the Kaiser voiced the opinion that 'the day of the airship is past for attacks on London.' However, strong representations from the naval authorities persuaded him to approve their continuation, but only 'when the circumstances seem favourable.' Strasser decided they were favourable on 16/17 June 1917. Three days earlier the Army's Gotha bombers had made a highly destructive raid on London in broad daylight.

L.48 – DEATH THROES

Strong winds and engine problems prevented all but two of the six Zeppelins detailed for the 16/17 June raid from reaching England. These winds held L.42 over Kent, where she bombed Ramsgate before heading for home, but not before one of her bombs struck lucky, hitting a naval ammunition store. The other raider, L.48, commanded by Kptlt Franz Eichler, but with Kvtkpt Viktor Schütze (the new commander of the Naval Airship Division since Strasser's appointment as Führer der Luftschiffe) on board, experienced serious engine problems and her compass froze. Unable to reach London, L.48 attempted to bomb Harwich naval base then turned north, dropping to 13,000ft to take advantage of tailwinds to compensate for the lack of engine power. At this height, and in a lightening summer sky, the air defences easily located L.48. Three aircraft from Orfordness Experimental Station, as well as a BE12 of No. 37 Squadron, all saw L.48 heading towards the coast and gave chase. Three of the aircraft scored hits as they swarmed around the lone airship. Minutes later L.48, the most recent addition to the navy's airship fleet, commissioned only 26 days earlier, crashed in flames in a field at Holly Tree Farm, Theberton, Suffolk. Miraculously, three members of the crew survived the crash, but Viktor Schütze was not one of them.

L.48, one of the new type dubbed 'Height Climbers' by the British, entered service on 23 May 1917, based at Nordholz. To hinder searchlights, the undersides were painted black. Commanded by Kptlt Franz Eichler, the raid of 16/17 June was her first time over England. (IWM, Q.58467)

The Naval Airship Division never directly targeted London again. However, in one of its most disastrous raids of the war for the Division, when high winds played havoc with the raiders, the last bombs dropped on London from a Zeppelin struck the capital on the night of 19/20 October 1917.

RNAS personnel sifting through the wreckage of L.48 at Holly Tree Farm, Theberton, Suffolk in 1917. The site again came under close scrutiny between April and June 2006 when an archaeological dig of the crash site took place.

THE SILENT RAID

The naval airships had already undertaken raids against northern England on 21/22 August and the Midlands and the North again on 24/25 September 1917 without great success. During this period, the twin-engine Gotha bombers were now attacking London, joined at the end of September by the massive Staaken 'Giants', designed by the Zeppelin Company. Then, on 19 October, 13 airships set out to attack targets in industrial northern cities such as Sheffield, Manchester and Liverpool; it was the last large-scale airship raid of the war. Two vessels failed to take off, while the other 11 encountered vicious headwinds once they had climbed over 16,000ft. The high winds battered the airships off course and reduced their ground speed to a crawl, making it almost impossible for the commanders to ascertain their positions.

Kapitänleutnant Waldemar Kölle, commanding L.45, aimed for Sheffield but found himself moving rapidly southwards and reported that 'precise orientation from the ground was impossible ... no fixed points could be discerned.' He dropped a number of bombs that fell on Northampton. Then, just before 11.30pm, the crew became aware of a large concentration of dim lights extending before them for some distance. Kölle's second-in-command, Lt Schütz, shouted 'London!' and for the first time Kölle realized how far off course L.45 had travelled. Wasting no time, he immediately released a number of bombs that fell in north-west London, causing damage to the Grahame-White Aviation Company at Hendon Aerodrome and on cottages nearby. Hendon experienced more damage before L.45, continuing on a south-east course, dropped two explosive bombs near Cricklewood Station.

The great height of L.45, coupled with a thin veil of cloud, meant Kölle's progress towards the centre of the capital remained unseen and unheard by those on the ground. Therefore no guns opened fire, and the attack became known as the 'silent raid'. One of the crew described their experience over London:

> The Thames we just dimly saw from the outline of the lights; two great railway stations I thought I saw, but the speed of the ship running almost before the gale was such that we could not distinguish much. We were half frozen, too, and the excitement was great. It was all over in a flash. The last bomb was gone and we were once more over the darkness and rushing onwards.

Members of the crew of L.45, the last to bomb London. After dropping bombs on London, strong winds carried it over France and, with only two engines still working, its commander, Kptlt Waldemar Kölle, brought her down near Sisteron, where the crew surrendered.

The 19/20 October 1917 raid on London: L.45 (Kptlt Waldemar Kölle)

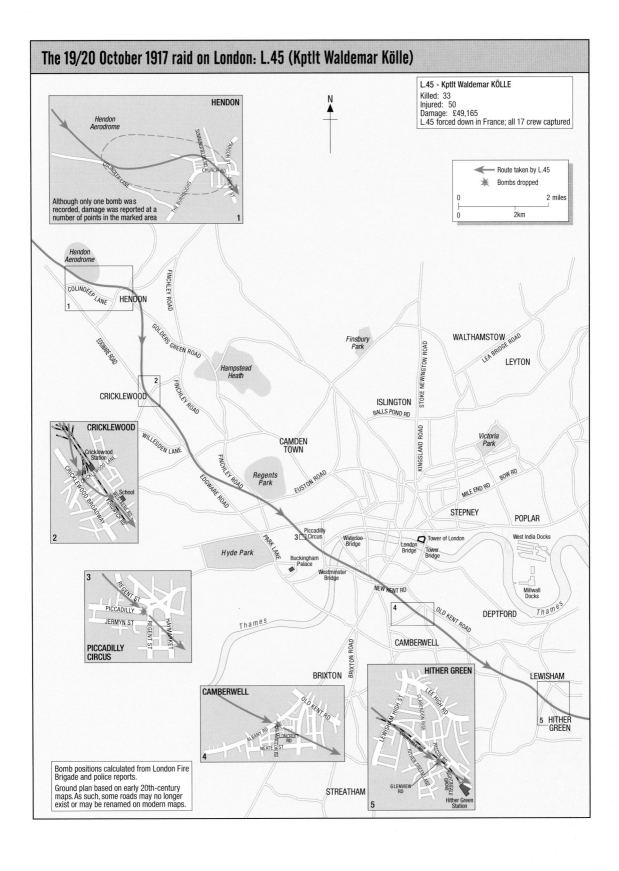

HENDON

Hendon Aerodrome

Although only one bomb was recorded, damage was reported at a number of points in the marked area

1

N

L.45 - Kptlt Waldemar KÖLLE
Killed: 33
Injured: 50
Damage: £49,165
L.45 forced down in France; all 17 crew captured

Route taken by L.45
Bombs dropped

0 ——— 2 miles
0 ——— 2km

Hendon Aerodrome

COLINDEEP LANE
HENDON
1

SUNNINGFIELDS RD
PARSON ST
CHURCH RD
BRENT ST
THE BURROUGHS

FINCHLEY ROAD
GOLDERS GREEN ROAD

EDGWARE ROAD

CRICKLEWOOD
2

FINCHLEY ROAD

WILLESDEN LANE

Hampstead Heath

Finsbury Park

WALTHAMSTOW

LEA BRIDGE ROAD

LEYTON

STOKE NEWINGTON ROAD

ISLINGTON
BALLS POND RD

KINGSLAND ROAD

Victoria Park

CRICKLEWOOD
Cricklewood Station
CRICKLEWOOD LANE
CRICKLEWOOD BROADWAY
WESTBERE RD
ASHFORD RD
School

2

EDGWARE ROAD

CAMDEN TOWN

Regents Park

EUSTON ROAD

MILE END RD
BOW RD

STEPNEY

POPLAR

West India Docks

3
Piccadilly Circus

Waterloo Bridge

London Bridge

Tower of London
Tower Bridge

Millwall Docks

Thames

3
REGENT ST
PICCADILLY
JERMYN ST
REGENT ST
HAYMARKET

PICCADILLY CIRCUS

Hyde Park

PARK LANE

Buckingham Palace
Westminster Bridge

NEW KENT RD

4

OLD KENT ROAD

DEPTFORD

Thames

CAMBERWELL

Thames

BRIXTON

BRIXTON ROAD

CAMBERWELL
4
ALBANY RD
SALISBURY RD
LONCROFT RD
NEATE ST
OLD KENT RD

HITHER GREEN

LEE HIGH RD
CLAREDON RISE
LEWISHAM HIGH ST
HITHER GREEN LANE
PASCOE RD
NIGHTINGALE GROVE
G.LENVIEW RD
Hither Green Station

5

LEWISHAM

5 HITHER GREEN

STREATHAM

Bomb positions calculated from London Fire Brigade and police reports.

Ground plan based on early 20th-century maps. As such, some roads may no longer exist or may be renamed on modern maps.

Although L.45 dropped only a few bombs on the London area, their effect was devastating. The 300kg bomb that fell in Camberwell demolished 101 and 103 Albany Road and 1 Calmington Road, and severely damaged a great number of others in the area. The bomb killed ten, including Emma, Alice, Stephen and Emily Glass, and injured 23.

In fact, these randomly dropped bombs proved devastating. The first fell without warning in Piccadilly, close to Piccadilly Circus in the heart of London's West End. The massive 300kg bomb blasted a hole in the road about 12ft in diameter, fracturing two gas mains and pipes carrying telephone cables. The blast smashed the whole of the front of the fashionable department store Swan & Edgar's, with damage extending into Regent Street, Jermyn Street and Shaftesbury Avenue amongst others. Many people were in the streets, unaware of the impending danger, and were caught in the explosion. Flying shrapnel, debris and glass scythed down 25, of whom seven died, including three soldiers on leave. One woman, so disfigured by the blast, was eventually only identified by her clothes and jewellery.

L.45 careered on. The next bomb fell in Camberwell, on the corner of Albany Road and Calmington Road, demolishing three homes as well as a doctor's surgery and a fish and chip shop. Many other buildings were seriously damaged. The blast killed ten, including four children; another ten children were amongst the 24 injured.

The final bomb dropped by L.45 landed in Glenview Road, Hither Green, demolishing three houses and inflicting less serious damage on other houses in the surrounding roads, but it claimed a high cost in human life. The bomb killed another ten children – seven of these from one family – and five women, while six people needed treatment for their injuries.

However, for the crew of L.45, their rather precarious position was just about to get worse. Having dropped to 15,000ft to get below the fierce winds at high altitude, Kölle managed to make some headway eastwards. However, near Chatham shortly after midnight, L.45 encountered 2nd Lt Thomas Pritchard of No. 39 Squadron, flying his BE2e from North Weald. Only able to get his aircraft up to 13,000ft, Pritchard fired at L.45 anyway. He missed the target, but Kölle climbed rapidly to escape the pursuer and was caught again in the gales; once more, the wind swept L.45 southwards. One engine then broke down, and in the intense cold it proved impossible to repair. One member of the crew retired with frostbite while many others suffered altitude sickness. The winds drove L.45 across France where she lost another two engines and was fortunate to survive an encounter with French anti-aircraft guns. With fuel almost exhausted and only two engines still working, L.45 had no chance of getting back to Germany, and so Kölle brought her down in a riverbed near Sisteron in southern France. The crew set fire to their ship and surrendered to a group of French soldiers.

Other ships of the attacking force suffered similar fates. L.44 came down in flames, destroyed by anti-aircraft guns while attempting to cross the front-line trenches in an effort to get back to Germany. Kapitänleutnant Hans-Karl Gayer brought L.49 down in a wood in France, where soldiers captured her before the crew could destroy her. Having lost two engines, the commander of L.50, Kptlt Roderich Schwonder, attempted to ground his ship, but a rough landing tore off the forward control gondola before she took back to the air. Most of the crew leapt to safety but the wind carried L.50 away and she was last seen drifting over the Mediterranean with four men still on board. Of the seven airships that did limp back to Germany, one of those, L.55, sustained serious damage during a forced landing and had to be dismantled. In a disastrous raid the Naval Airship Division lost five Zeppelins. But if the gale-force winds had not taken a hand, it may have been one of the most successful of the war, for some 78 British aircraft took to the skies in defensive sorties but not one was able to climb high enough to engage the attacking force.

THE END OF THE ZEPPELIN WAR

Even the overtly confident Strasser saw the disastrous outcome of the 19/20 October raid as a major setback. However, the following month engines became available – designed specifically to combat the strong winds encountered at high altitude – and Strasser's confidence returned. All new airships were to be equipped with the new engine and existing vessels re-fitted. However, before the re-equipped fleet could even contemplate returning to Britain, another disaster struck. On 5 January 1918 a fire broke out at the Ahlhorn airship base – the headquarters of the Naval Airship Division – in one of the massive sheds housing L.47 and L.51. In the great conflagration that followed, the flames engulfed four Zeppelins and one Schütte-Lanz, along with four of the all-important double-sheds – effectively putting the base out of service.

Strasser launched only four raids against Britain in 1918, the last year of the war. None of these attempted to target London, choosing instead targets in the Midlands and northern England. The final airship raid took place on 5 August 1918. Led by Strasser in person aboard the navy's latest zeppelin, L.70, five airships approached the Norfolk coast. Caught at only 13,000 feet, two aircraft of the new amalgamated Royal Air Force pounced on L.70. Moments later she 'plunged seaward a blazing mass.' Strasser, the life and soul of Naval Airship Division, and the driving force behind the airship raids on Britain, died in action with the rest of the crew.

At the start of the war, both in Germany and in Britain, belief in the danger of the threat posed to London by the German airships was great. In the early months of the war, London lay exposed, with only a limited defensive capability, but the airship fleet was not in a position to expose this weakness. From May 1915 to the end of the year, the airship raids on London faced little significant opposition but gradually the defences of the city improved. During 1916, the network of searchlights, anti-aircraft guns and observation posts increased dramatically while the escalation in aircraft production further strengthened the defence. Now organized into home defence squadrons with night-flying-trained pilots and with the introduction of explosive and incendiary bullets, from September 1916 the advantage swung dramatically away from the airships. That they kept flying over Britain after this change of circumstances says much for the courage of their officers and crews.

Although the Zeppelins had failed to achieve the goals set for them, the effect on morale of bombing London remained a great prize for Germany. Despite its losses, the Navy remained committed to the development of airships to counter Britain's improved defences almost to the end of the war, but the army, disillusioned, from September 1916 turned its attention to the potential offered by aeroplanes to carry an effective bomb load to London. It was a change of direction that signalled an escalation in London's first Blitz.

THE COMING OF
THE BOMBERS

The shelving of Wilhelm Siegert's 1914 plan for aeroplane raids on London saw the activities of the squadron he created refocused on objectives closer at hand, bombing targets behind the Allied lines, until the spring of 1915 when it briefly redeployed to the Eastern Front before returning in July 1915.

In December 1915 the squadron became Kampfgeschwader 1 der OHL – Battle Squadron 1 of the Army High Command – generally abbreviated to Kagohl 1. For the next eight months Kagohl 1 flew bombing missions, reconnaissance patrols and escort duties over Verdun and later the Somme until, in August 1916, its six *Kampfstaffeln* (flights) – abbreviated to *Kasta* – were split into two separate *Halbgeschwader* (half squadrons). Halbgeschwader 1 remained on the Somme while Halbgeschwader 2 redeployed to the Balkans.

A reorganization of Germany's army air service in late 1916 saw the appointment of Ernst von Hoeppner as its supreme commander. At the same time, the doubts the army had in the ability of its airships to carry the war to London were confirmed by the loss of SL.11 in early September. But a new weapon was now available, one that allowed Hoeppner to confidently resurrect Siegert's 1914 plan for an aeroplane bombing campaign against London – the G-type bomber. And the unit selected to carry out this mission, Kampfgeschwader 3 der OHL (Kagohl 3), he formed on a nucleus of Halbgeschwader 1. At just this time, as Germany was planning this new means of striking at the morale of the British population, Britain, convinced that the menace of the Zeppelin raids was largely over, began reducing its home defences to support the growing demands for manpower on the Western Front and in other theatres. A few months later, largely unopposed, German bombers were flying over the streets of London in broad daylight, trailing death and destruction in their wake.

THE BOMBER RAIDS — THE MEN THAT MATTERED

Generalleutnant Ernst Wilhelm von Hoeppner

Born in January 1860, Ernst Wilhelm von Hoeppner joined the army as a junior officer in a dragoon regiment in 1879 at the beginning of an impressive military career that saw him hold a number of high-profile regimental, field and staff commands. At the outbreak of war in 1914 Hoeppner was chief of the general staff of III Armee, and over the next two years he held various other senior field and staff commands. Then, the OHL, having emerged battered from the maelstrom of the Verdun and Somme campaigns, decided that the *Fliegertruppen* – the army aviation arm – needed re-forming under a general officer with command over all aspects of army aviation. The outcome was the creation of the Luftstreitkräfte and, on the recommendation of Erich Ludendorff, Generalquartiermeister of the German Army, Hoeppner, with no aviation background, was appointed Kommandierender General der Luftstreitkräfte – conveniently abbreviated to Kogenluft – on 12 November 1916.

Kogenluft Ernst Wilhelm von Hoeppner (left) meeting one of his airmen. His decision to end the Army Zeppelin raids on London opened the way for the launch of Operation *Türkenkreuz*, the Gotha bomber raids on the city.

Warming to his new role, shortly after his appointment, Hoeppner issued a memorandum. It stated that he considered airship raids on London no longer viable and as such he planned to open bombing raids against the city with aeroplanes as soon as possible. The aims of such raids were to strike at the morale of the British population, the disruption of war industry and communications, and to impede the cross-Channel supply routes. He stated – a little optimistically – that the G-type bomber aircraft were ready and soon the massive R-type would join them. However, he ended his memorandum on a cautionary note. He stated that raids by the G-type aircraft ' … can only succeed provided every detail is carefully prepared, the crews are practised in long-distance overseas flight and the squadron is made up of especially good aeroplane crews. Any negligence and undue haste will only entail heavy losses for us, and defeat our ends.'

The man given the task of carrying out these orders was Ernst Brandenburg.

Hauptmann Ernst Brandenburg

Born in West Prussia in June 1883, Brandenburg joined the infantry as a young man, becoming a Leutnant in 1908. Three years later he attended an aviation training course before returning to his regiment, 6. Westpreussischen Infanterie-Regiment Nr. 149, with whom he went to war in 1914. Promoted to Hauptmann in November 1914, Brandenburg received a severe wound the following year while serving in the trenches. After his recovery, in November 1915, like so many other soldiers no longer fit to return to the front line, he joined the army's air service. He adapted well to his new role as an observer, flying in two-seater aircraft over the front line and his abilities as an organizer and administrator shone through, quickly bringing him to the attention of his superiors. Following his appointment as Kogenluft in late 1916, Hoeppner personally selected Brandenburg to command the squadron destined to lead the strategic air campaign against London – Kagohl 3. He took up his new command on 5 March 1917, aged 33, and started with a blank piece of paper; there were no guidelines. Brandenburg created an intensive training programme for the crews that would form his squadron; he sent his crews to learn the skills needed for navigation over large expanses of open sea, while the technicalities of formation flying, a tactic considered necessary for the defensive strength of the raiding squadron over hostile territory, were absorbed. Brandenburg also insisted that all aircraft allocated to his squadron were test-flown for at least 25 hours and that his crews all carried out

Hauptmann Ernst Brandenburg. Personally selected for the task by Hoeppner, he became commander of Kagohl 3, the *Englandgeschwader,* in March 1917. Brandenburg's calm and calculating manner made him an ideal choice. (David Marks)

20 landings, half in daylight and half after dark. Finally, in May 1917, Brandenburg was ready to lead his squadron – now unofficially known as the *Englandgeschwader* (England squadron) – into battle.

Hauptmann Richard von Bentivegni

Born in Rendsburg in Schleswig-Holstein in August 1889, Bentivegni joined the army in March 1905, in 8. Thüringisches Infanterie-Regiment Nr. 153. In August 1906, two days before his 17th birthday he became a Leutnant and remained so until he volunteered to join the *Schutztruppe* in German East Africa in 1911. He returned to his regiment at the beginning of August 1914 when he became a company commander, then, in November 1914, while serving on the Western Front, he received promotion to Oberleutnant. However, in September 1915 he transferred to Flieger Ersatz Abteilung Nr. 9 at Darmstadt where he trained as an airman. He completed training in December 1915 and moved to Armeeflugpark Nr. 13 where he awaited an active appointment. Then, in January 1916 he joined Feldflieger Abteilung Nr. 28 at the front. Two months later he was promoted to Hauptmann and then, in September 1915, transferred to the Reisenflieger Abteilung to train on the giant R-type aircraft before joining Riesenflugzeug Abteilung (Rfa) 501 on the Eastern Front in October 1916, becoming commander of the squadron the following month. In July 1917 Rfa 501 relocated to Berlin where it trained on the new Staaken R.VI 'Giant' before arriving in Belgium in September 1917, when Bentivegni prepared to join the *Englandgeschwader* in the air assault on London.

Major-General Edward Ashmore

Edward Bailey Ashmore, born in London in 1872, joined the Royal Artillery in 1891, having passed through the Royal Military Academy. Having seen action in the Anglo-Boer War, Ashmore attended Staff College before joining the general staff in 1908. An interest in aviation saw him take flying lessons in 1912 and, after passing the course at the RFC's Central Flying School, he joined the reserve of the RFC in January 1913. As a staff officer with the RFC when war broke out the following year, Ashmore held a home administrative posting before taking command of 5th Wing based at Gosport in April 1915. Four months later he found himself in France in command of 1st Wing, followed by command of 1st Brigade, RFC, then later 4th Brigade, during the Somme campaign.

Maj Gen Edward Ashmore was a very single-minded and determined character. When taking flying lessons in 1912 he would arrive at the airfield at dawn, push his way to the front of the queue and stay up in the air over his allotted time, before dashing to the War Office to start work at the normal time.

At the end of 1916 Ashmore returned to his roots, transferring back to the Royal Artillery.

Following the poor showing offered up by the home defences during the daylight raids on London in the summer of 1917, an official review took steps towards revitalizing London's defences. One of its recommendations called for 'a senior officer of first-rate ability and practical air experience' to command the whole defence of London: aircraft, anti-aircraft guns, searchlights and observation posts.

Ashmore, described as 'a brilliant combination of airman and artillery officer' fitted the bill perfectly. Recalled from Flanders, where he commanded the artillery of 29th Division, he became commander of the newly created London Air Defence Area (LADA) on 5 August 1917. He later commented sardonically, 'The fact that I was exchanging the comparative safety of the Front for the probability of being hanged in the streets of London did not worry me.'

Lieutenant-Colonel Thomas Charles Reginald Higgins

Thomas Higgins, born in Buckinghamshire in July 1880, attended Dartmouth Naval College before joining HMS *Camperdown* as a midshipman in 1897. However, in 1900 Higgins transferred to the Army, serving as a lieutenant in the King's Own Royal Regiment in the Anglo-Boer War. He went on to serve in Nigeria with the West African Frontier Force, 1904–13, during which time, in 1911, he was one of an early batch of army officers to gain his flying certificate. Higgins applied to join the RFC shortly after its formation, but with the officer complement full, he found himself fighting in France until wounded early in the war.

In 1915 Higgins did transfer to the RFC, quickly becoming a flight commander before his appointment as commander of the newly created No. 19 Reserve Aeroplane Squadron in England in February 1916, with responsibility for all the widely distributed aircraft committed to the defence of London. In April 1916 the squadron was renamed No. 39 (Home Defence) squadron, which he commanded until June 1916 when he became Inspector of Home Defence. Then, in February 1917, with the rank of lieutenant-colonel, Higgins took command of Home Defence Wing which became Home Defence Group (11 squadrons and one depot squadron) in March 1917. Later, as the Home Defence organization expanded in response to the German bomber offensive, the group reorganized as Home Defence Brigade (14 squadrons and one depot squadron) and eventually became VI Brigade in October 1917.

Lieutenant-Colonel Maximilian St Leger Simon

Simon, the son of a physician/surgeon, was born in Malacca, Straits Settlement (now Malaysia), in 1876 and entered the Royal Military Academy in 1893. Two years later he received a commission in the Royal Engineers where he specialized

in submarine mining and studied coastal searchlights. He served in Singapore, England and Canada before returning to England in 1910. The following year Simon became a staff officer at the War Office, where he remained until he received a brevet lieutenant-colonelcy in late 1915 and headed for France with the 197th (Land Drainage) Company, RE. Then, in February 1916, when the War Office took over responsibility for London's defence from the Admiralty, they recalled Simon and placed him in a position to supervise the construction of gun and searchlight positions around the city. Later, in December 1916, he became Anti-Aircraft Defence Commander, London.

A British aerial reconnaissance photograph of the Kagohl 3 airfield at Sint-Denijs-Westrem, the home airfield of Kasta 13 and 14. Later, in September 1917, the 'Giants' of Rfa 501 shared the airfield.

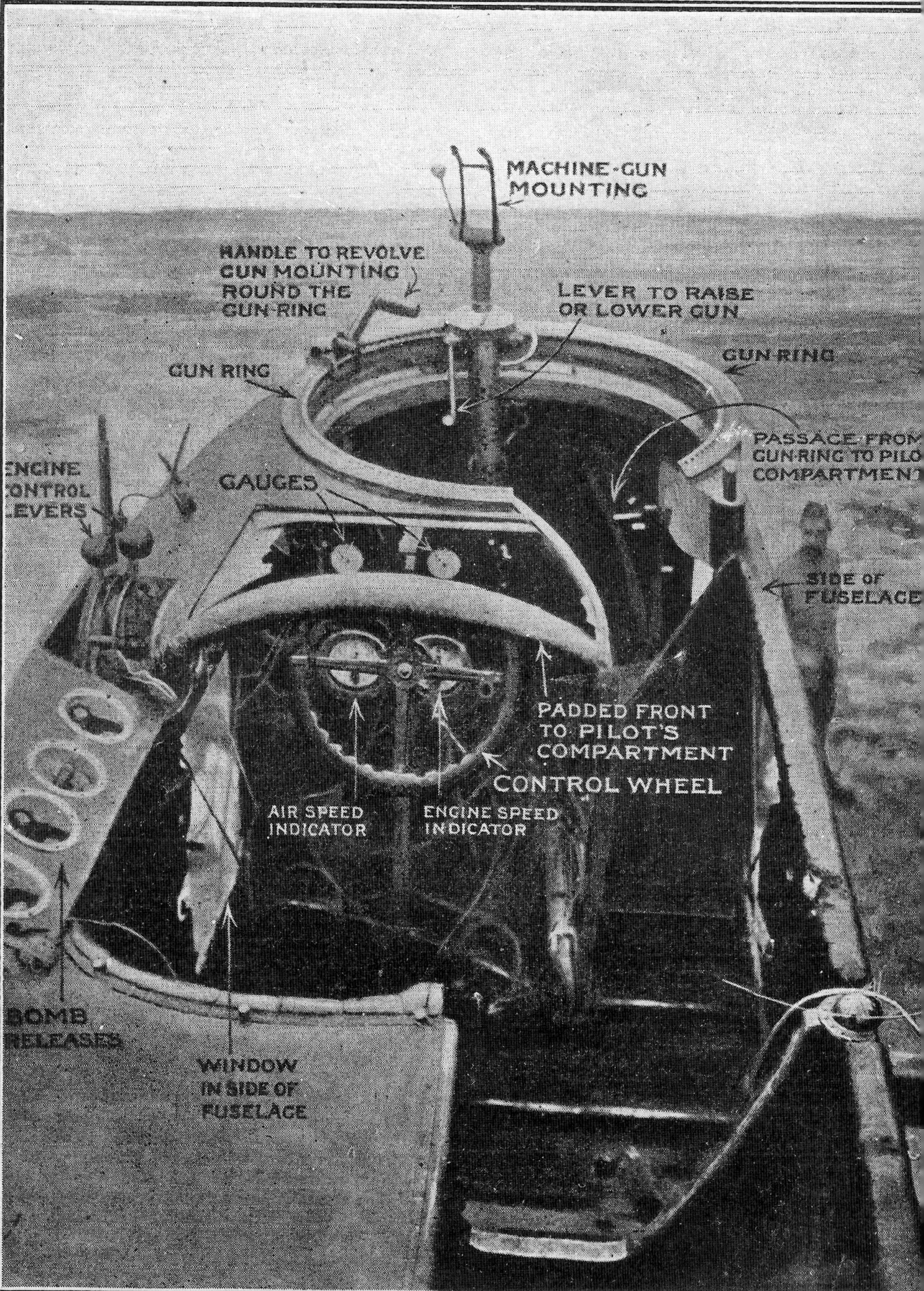

MACHINE-GUN MOUNTING

HANDLE TO REVOLVE GUN MOUNTING ROUND THE GUN-RING

LEVER TO RAISE OR LOWER GUN

GUN-RING

GUN RING

PASSAGE FROM GUN-RING TO PILOT COMPARTMENT

ENGINE CONTROL LEVERS

GAUGES

SIDE OF FUSELAGE

PADDED FRONT TO PILOT'S COMPARTMENT

CONTROL WHEEL

AIR SPEED INDICATOR

ENGINE SPEED INDICATOR

BOMB RELEASES

WINDOW IN SIDE OF FUSELAGE

PREPARING FOR THE BOMBER BLITZ

GERMAN PLANS

With the appointment of Hoeppner as Kogenluft in November 1916, the plan to commence an aeroplane bombing campaign began to take shape, based on the new G-type *Grosskampfflugzeug* (large battle aeroplane) series. In September 1916 the Gothaer Waggonfabrik AG, formerly a builder of railway carriages, received approval for production to commence on their latest aircraft design, the G.IV. Developed from the earlier G.II and G.III, the G.IV, generally known as the Gotha, was the aircraft the army had been waiting for.

Powered by two 260hp Mercedes engines, the Gotha G.IV could maintain a speed of 80mph in favourable conditions with an impressive ceiling of around 18,000ft. Despite its uncomfortable open cockpits and 78ft wingspan, it flew well, was manoeuvrable and could carry a bomb load of between 300 and 400kg and two or three 7.92mm Parabellum machine guns for defence. Most importantly, it had the range to reach London and return to bases in occupied Belgium. Its weak point was its instability when coming in to land without the ballast of bombs and fuel.

The three-man crew consisted of the commander, pilot and rear-gunner. The commander, an officer, occupied the front nose position. He was responsible for navigation and acted as observer, bomb-aimer and front-gunner. The pilot could be either an officer or senior NCO, while the rear-gunner was often a junior NCO. An innovation on the G.IV was a slanting 'tunnel' built through the fuselage, which gave the rear-gunner the added advantage of being able to fire

A view of a Gotha pilot's cockpit and the forward gun position occupied by the aircraft commander. The passage to the right of the pilot allowed the commander to move within the aircraft.

downwards at attacking aircraft taking advantage of the traditional blind spot below the tail.

Initially the load of the Gotha G.IV in the daylight raids on London consisted of a mixture of 50kg explosive bombs and 12.5kg explosive or incendiary bombs. The larger bomb was about 5ft long with a diameter of 7in and either armed for detonation on impact or with a delay fuse which allowed the bomb to penetrate through a building before exploding. However, estimates indicate that up to a third of 50kg bombs failed to explode and another 10 per cent detonated in mid-air. The actual bomb load varied but on the early daylight raids a typical load of 300kg would be four 50kg and eight 12.5kg bombs. Later in the campaign the Gothas mainly utilized the 50kg explosive bomb with a limited number of the 100kg type, as well as incendiaries.

Diagram showing evolution of the *Englandgeschwader*.

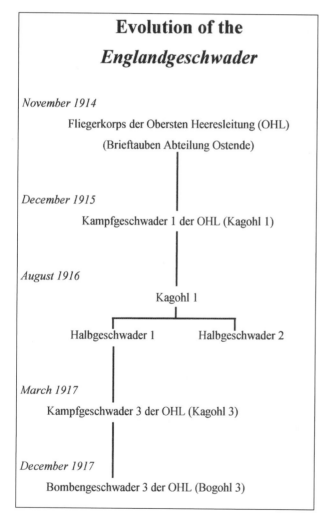

Evolution of the
Englandgeschwader

November 1914

Fliegerkorps der Obersten Heeresleitung (OHL)

(Brieftauben Abteilung Ostende)

December 1915

Kampfgeschwader 1 der OHL (Kagohl 1)

August 1916

Kagohl 1

Halbgeschwader 1   Halbgeschwader 2

March 1917

Kampfgeschwader 3 der OHL (Kagohl 3)

December 1917

Bombengeschwader 3 der OHL (Bogohl 3)

When he first took office, Hoeppner anticipated that 30 Gotha G.IVs would be available to begin attacks on London by 1 February 1917 and he further noted that development of the *Riesenflugzeug* (giant aeroplane), or the R-type, was progressing well, anticipating that these even larger and more powerful aircraft would soon be added to the weapons at his disposal.

Halbgeschwader 1 returned to Ghistelles and reformed as Kagohl 3. The three existing Kasta, 1, 4 and 6, became Kasta 13, 14 and 15 of the new squadron and were boosted by three more; Kasta 16 joined immediately, 17 and 18 in place by July 1917. Each *Kasta* consisted of six aircraft, giving a squadron strength of 36 aircraft, plus three allocated to the HQ. New airfields were under construction for the squadron around Ghent. But there were delays; the first airfields, Melle-Gontrode and Sint-Denijs-Westrem, were not ready until April 1917, followed in July by Mariakerke and Oostakker.

Although anticipated in February the first of the squadron's aircraft did not arrive at Ghistelles until March 1917. The following month Kasta 13 and 14 transferred to their new airfield at Sint-Denijs-Westrem, while Kasta 15 and 16, along with the HQ, moved to Melle-Gontrode. Yet Kagohl 3 was still not ready to begin its work. Throughout the training period the crews experienced engine problems with their new aircraft, requiring the rest of April to improve though not completely rectify these problems. And then there was the fuel issue. Tests proved that the engines would consume their full capacity of 175 gallons of petrol on even the most direct return flight to London. Any deviation or evasion tactics would exhaust the onboard supply and imperil a safe return. Therefore reserve fuel tanks were authorized for all the squadron's aircraft, their fitting causing further delay.

But by mid-May Brandenburg announced that his squadron was ready to make its first attack on London. There were ongoing delays fitting the reserve fuel tanks but he reasoned that a refuelling stop near the coast would allow the topping up of the existing tanks thus granting a little leeway. So all was ready, the crews of the *Englandgeschwader* now just waited impatiently for the advent of good weather before launching Operation *Türkenkreuz* (*Turk's Cross*) – the code-name for the attack on London.

BRITISH PLANS

There was a genuine belief in Britain that, after the successes against Zeppelin raiders in the autumn of 1916, the aerial threat was over. Even that audacious raid by a single aeroplane on 28 November, ending close to Victoria station, failed to cause any undue concern amongst the military and prompted little comment, but the press issued a cautionary warning about future aeroplane attacks. But when no more Zeppelins – or aeroplanes – appeared over the capital for the rest of 1916 or in the early weeks of 1917, the fear of aerial raids largely evaporated.

At the opening of 1917 the home defences were those instigated and developed since the War Office had taken over the responsibility for the defence of London from the Admiralty in February 1916. It was a defence system designed to oppose the night-time raids by German airships. The Home Defence Wing of the Royal Flying Corps (RFC) contained 11 squadrons assigned to the defence of Britain, of which four defended the approaches to London: Nos. 37, 39, 50 and 78. The four 'London' squadrons each had an establishment of 24 aircraft, the rest set at 18. However, as a snapshot, a report dated 7 March 1917 showed that the 'London' squadrons could muster only 64 aircraft out of an establishment of 96, and ten of those were undergoing repairs. And because of the nature of night-time defence against airships, the aircraft allocated to these squadrons were older, slower, more stable aircraft, such as the BE2c, BE12 and FE2b. The tactics were simple; each aircraft operated individually, flying along pre-set patrol lines hunting for Zeppelins caught in searchlights as they approached the city. The aircraft did not carry radios as the Admiralty opposed their introduction

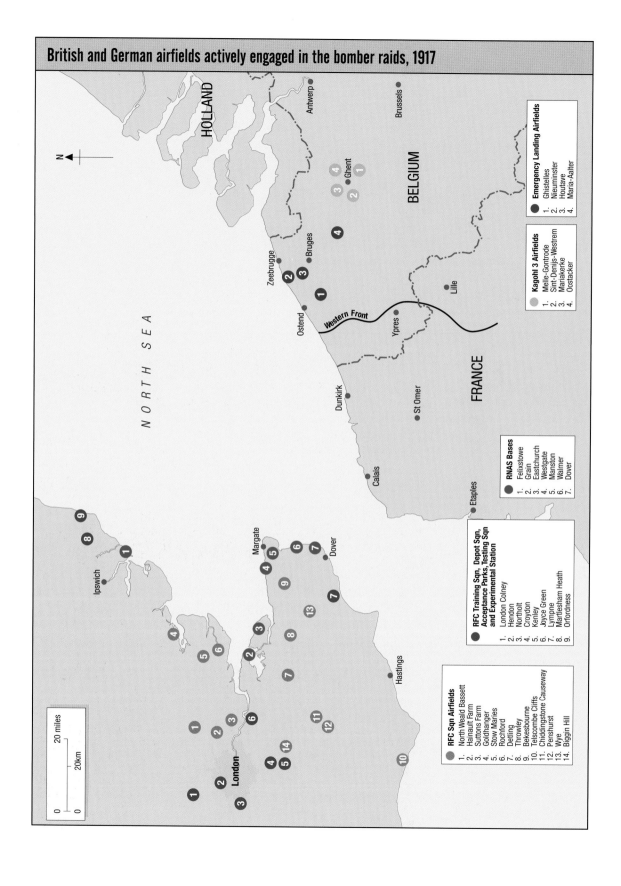

British and German airfields actively engaged in the bomber raids, 1917

HOLLAND

Antwerp

Brussels

BELGIUM

Ghent
4
3 2 1

4

Bruges
2 3
Zeebrugge
1

Ostend

Lille

Western Front

Ypres

FRANCE

Dunkirk

St Omer

Calais

Etaples

N O R T H   S E A

Emergency Landing Airfields
1. Ghistelles
2. Nieuminster
3. Houtave
4. Maria-Aalter

Kagohl 3 Airfields
1. Melle-Gontrode
2. Sint-Denijs-Westrem
3. Mariakerke
4. Oostacker

RNAS Bases
1. Felixstowe
2. Grain
3. Eastchurch
4. Westgate
5. Manston
6. Walmer
7. Dover

RFC Training Sqn, Depot Sqn, Acceptance Parks, Testing Sqn and Experimental Station
1. London Colney
2. Hendon
3. Northolt
4. Croydon
5. Kenley
6. Joyce Green
7. Lympne
8. Martlesham Heath
9. Orfordness

RFC Sqn Airfields
1. North Weald Bassett
2. Hainault Farm
3. Suttons Farm
4. Goldhanger
5. Stow Maries
6. Rochford
7. Detling
8. Throwley
9. Bekesbourne
10. Telscombe Cliffs
11. Chiddingstone Causeway
12. Penshurst
13. Wye
14. Biggin Hill

9
8
1
Ipswich

Margate
4 5
6 7
Dover

9
7
13
8
3
5 6
4
2
7
Hastings

1 2 3
6
11
12

1 2 3
4 5 14
10

2
London
1
3

20 miles
20km
0
0

claiming they would interfere with Navy signals. It was one of many flashpoints between the Admiralty and the War Office in their troubled relationship in the field of aviation.

However, stretched as the Home Defence squadrons were, with the diminishing threat from enemy airships and an ever-growing demand for aircraft and personnel on the Western Front, moves were afoot to reduce the number even more. Early in February 1917, Lt Gen David Henderson, commander of the RFC, advised that he urgently required two new night-flying squadrons for service in France. While the aircraft would be available at the beginning of March, Henderson now asked for the transfer of 36 trained pilots from the Home Defence squadrons to fly them, with an additional nine pilots each month as replacements, adding that, 'the diminished risk from Zeppelin attack amply justifies this temporary reduction'. Three days later the War Cabinet approved the transfer.

Control of the anti-aircraft gun defences of London had rested with Lt Col M. St L. Simon, RE, from December 1916. Almost immediately Simon found his command reduced. The plan of his predecessor, Admiral Sir Percy Scott, included two gun rings around London, one 5 miles out and the other 9 miles

The 3in 20cwt anti-aircraft gun, the standard weapon of the London air defences. Here it is shown on a 'trailer' mount designed and constructed by the Royal Navy Anti-Aircraft Mobile Brigade.

from the centre, each gun position mounted with twin guns, supported by an outer ring of searchlights – 'aeroplane lights'. The plan required 84 guns in 42 gun positions, but in January 1917 cuts reduced the total available to 65 following the Admiralty's demand for guns to arm merchant ships in the battle against the German U-boats. As a result Simon abandoned the original plan. Only three double-gun stations remained, the other 39 downgraded to single-gun positions and the remaining 20 guns relocated to bolster the defences on north and eastern approaches to the capital.

In December 1915, replaced as commander of the BEF, Field Marshal Lord French returned to Britain as Commander-in-Chief, British Home Forces. He presided over the gradual reduction in Britain's aerial defence capability, which left it exposed when Germany began aeroplane raids in 1917.

And then one final dramatic decision reduced London's effective defence further. At a high-ranking meeting on 6 March 1917, attention focused on further Home Defence cuts to allow redeployment of manpower to the Western Front. Field Marshal Lord French, commander-in-chief of British Home Forces, then made a remarkable recommendation, one that received immediate approval: 'No aeroplanes or seaplanes, even if recognized as hostile, will be fired at, either by day or night, except by those anti-aircraft guns situated near the Restricted Coast Area which are specially detailed for the purpose.'

With AA guns no longer on 24-hour alert, big reductions in manning levels followed. However, Lt Col Simon, who had been working on a plan to oppose future aeroplane attacks, remained unconvinced about the end of the aerial threat and, without official approval, completed his defence plan before filing it away for possible future use.

It was against this scaled-down defence system that the *Englandgeschwader* was about to open its campaign.

THE 1917 BOMBER RAIDS

THE CAMPAIGN BEGINS

Having informed Hoeppner in mid-May that he was ready to launch his first attack on London, Brandenburg then faced the frustration of a period of bad weather which prevented him from carrying out the plan. In fact the British weather, which had proved an implacable opponent to the Zeppelin raids, continued to dog the bomber raids too. Weather forecasting in the early years of the 20th century was simplistic in comparison with modern satellite systems, and in 1917 weather systems approaching Britain over the Atlantic remained unknown to German forces. Good weather, wind speeds and directions over the North Sea could be predicted with some accuracy, but what was to come over England could not.

In fact, before Brandenburg could launch his first raid, another daring attack by a single aircraft, an Albatross C VII of Feldflieger Abteilung Nr. 19, on the night of 6/7 May did reach London. The crew dropped five 10kg bombs between Hackney and Holloway, killing one man and causing two injuries, before returning unmolested to Belgium. However, on 24 May 1917, Brandenburg received a positive forecast for the following day and with that he issued orders for the first bomber squadron raid on London. Twenty-three Gotha G.IVs set off for London, but thick cloud cover blanketing the city forced Brandenburg to turn away and head home via secondary targets in Kent. The bombs intended for London caused casualties of an unprecedented level, mainly on the unsuspecting population of Folkestone and the military camp at Shorncliffe; 95 were killed and 195 injured. The defensive response was confused, uncoordinated

Damage caused during the raid of 24 September 1917 – the first raid of the Harvest Moon offensive. The bomb here, at 144a King's Cross Road, killed 13-year-old James Sharpe and injured seven others. Having helped his mother carry his brothers and sisters across the road to a shelter, James returned to help his invalid grandfather just as the bomb exploded, burying him under the rubble of the building. He died from a fractured skull. (IWM HO 72)

Gotha G.IV aircraft of Kagohl 3 preparing for a raid on England in 1917. Bad weather caused Brandenburg to abort the first two planned raids on London, but the third, on 13 June, delivered a devastating blow against the city. (Colin Ablett)

and ineffective. Only specified coastal anti-aircraft batteries opened fire – as ordered on 7 March – and despite over 70 aircraft taking to the air, only one got close enough to engage. The stiffest opposition came from RNAS aircraft based in the Dunkirk area, who encountered the returning raiders and claimed one Gotha shot down over the sea, while another crashed on landing near Bruges, killing the crew.

The raid caused a public outcry. Makeshift arrangements called for training squadrons, aircraft acceptance parks and experimental stations to make aircraft available for patrols and another 20 aircraft were drafted into the Home Defence squadrons. A conference then followed to 'report upon the defence of the United Kingdom against attack by aeroplanes', yet it achieved little. To speed up the transmission of accurate information, 24 trained anti-aircraft observers were withdrawn from France and redeployed on lightships anchored in the approaches to the Thames estuary, but other than that it was felt anything else would have a detrimental effect on front-line aircraft requirements. The question of fitting wireless transmitters into RFC aircraft again foundered in the face of Admiralty opposition. Inconclusive discussions also took place at the conference about the practicality of a public air raid warning system. No warning system had been used in London during the Zeppelin raids.

A second raid followed on 5 June with similar results. Weather conditions forced Brandenburg to turn away and head for secondary targets along the Thames estuary. His bombs were hitting home as Home Defence pilots still struggled up to operational height. There was, however, one beacon of light for the defenders; the eight coastal AA guns around Shoeburyness and Sheerness opened on the raiders and brought down one of the Gothas, which crashed into the estuary. Then, three days later, on 7 June, an order cancelled the three-month-old restriction on general anti-aircraft fire. Lieutenant-Colonel Simon immediately dusted off his plan, pigeon-holed since March, and prepared for the inevitable raid on London that everyone knew must follow. It came on the morning of Wednesday 13 June 1917.

LONDON'S FIRST DAYTIME RAID

With a good forecast from his weather officer, Brandenburg prepared his crews for a third attempt on London. All aircraft now had the reserve fuel tanks fitted so it would be a direct flight – he chose a morning departure as there was a possibility of thunderstorms later. On 13 June, 20 aircraft took off from the two airfields near Ghent, but very quickly two turned back with engine problems. The rest continued on course; the mood was buoyant. One later wrote, 'We can recognise the men in the machine flying nearest us, and signals and greetings are exchanged. A feeling of absolute security and indomitable confidence in our success are our predominant emotions.'

Shortly after, one Gotha left the formation and turned southwards towards the Kent coastal town of Margate on which it dropped five bombs; moments later it was gone. Word of the raid reached Home Forces GHQ, followed swiftly by news of a large formation of aircraft approaching the Essex coast. At this point three more Gothas left the formation, two peeling off towards Shoeburyness, where they dropped six bombs before heading home while the other crossed to the south of the Thames and followed a course towards Greenwich, believed to be on a photo-reconnaissance mission. Brandenburg continued towards London with the

The recovery of the wreckage of Gotha G.IV /660/16, shot down by anti-aircraft guns along the Thames estuary on 5 June. Only the Gotha's gunner, Uffz Georg Schumacher, survived.

THE FIRST DAYLIGHT RAID, 25 MAY 1917

This illustration shows a Gotha G.IV about to take part in the first attempt by Kagohl 3 to bomb London on Friday 25 May 1917. Twenty-three Gothas set out for London that day. However, thick cloud cover over the city forced the formation to seek secondary targets in Kent. The bombs intended for London caused casualties of an unprecedented level, mainly on the unsuspecting population of Folkestone and at the Shorncliffe military camp.

The aircraft shows the standard pale blue finish used on daylight bombing raids, with pale grey engine compartments. Defensive armament generally consisted of two 7.92mm Parabellum machine guns, one in the front cockpit and one in the rear (hidden behind rear wing struts). Mesh guards fitted to prevent the rear gunner shooting off the rear-mounted propeller blades resulted in a limited lateral field of fire. The usual bomb load on daylight raids amounted to 300kg, typically made up of six 50kg bombs or a combination of four 50kg and eight 12.5kg bombs.

The senior crew member occupied the cockpit in the nose, from where he controlled navigation, observation, bomb-aiming and also operated a front machine gun. All of the three-man crew were seated in the open, making long flights uncomfortable and requiring them to be well protected from the wind and cold.

The Gotha was a reliable aircraft in flight, it had good manoeuvrability and its two 260hp Mercedes engines gave a maximum speed of 87mph. However, the great flaw in the Gotha design was its instability when landing at the completion of a mission without the ballast provided by bombs and fuel, which resulted in a high percentage of losses in landing accidents.

remaining 14 aircraft in two formations flying abreast on a wide front. The noise they created was so great that those on the ground claimed they heard it ten minutes before the aircraft came into view. Yet most who came out into their gardens on this warm, hazy, summer's morning to watch these 'silver specks' flying overhead, presumed them to be friendly aircraft and watched in admiration as they passed.

News of the approach of the Gothas reached Nos. 37, 39 and 50 squadrons at 10.53am. Twenty minutes later the additional formations instructed to assist in defence received orders to take off. At 11.24am the 3in 20cwt AA gun at Romford became the first of the London guns to open fire, followed by the Rainham gun at 11.30am – but others struggled to locate the target in the hazy sky. One of the Gotha commanders described the moment: 'Suddenly there stand, as if by magic here and there in our course, little clouds of cotton, the greetings of enemy guns. They multiply with astonishing rapidity. We fly through them and leave the suburbs behind us. It is the heart of London that must be hit.'

Moments later the first bomb dropped, harmlessly, on an allotment in North Street, Barking, immediately followed by another seven that fell in East Ham. Two in Alexandra Road damaged 42 houses, killing four and injuring 11. Another bomb fell on the Royal Albert Docks, where it killed eight dockworkers and damaged buildings, vehicles and a railway truck.

The City of London was now clearly in view directly ahead and Kagohl 3 closed up into a wide-diamond formation. One of the commanders looked out entranced as though a tourist, 'We see the bridges, the Tower of London, Liverpool [Street] Station, the Bank of England, the Admiralty's palace – everything sharply outlined in the glaring sunlight'.

At 11.35am, over Regent's Park, Brandenburg fired a signal flare and the whole formation turned to the east, back towards the City. Once over their target 72 bombs rained down in the space of two minutes within a 1-mile radius of Liverpool Street Station – stretching from Clerkenwell in the west to Stepney in the east and from Dalston in the north to Bermondsey in the south. Even as the bombs fell people rushed outside or grabbed a vantage point to see this bewildering, confusing spectacle. An American journalist, travelling across the City on a bus observed that:

> From every office and warehouse and tea shop men and women strangely stood still, gazing up into the air. The conductor mounted the stairs to suggest that outside passengers should seek safety inside. Some of them did so.
>
> 'I'm not a religious man,' remarked the conductor, 'but what I say is, we are all in God's hands and if we are going to die we may as well die quiet.'
>
> But some inside passengers were determined that if they had to die quiet they might as well see something first and they climbed on top and with wonderstruck eyes watched the amazing drama of the skies.

Three bombs hit Liverpool Street Station. One fell on the edge of platform No. 9, blasting apart a passenger carriage and causing two others to burn ferociously just as the train was about to depart for Hunstanton. A second bomb fell close by, striking carriages used by military doctors. Casualties in the station rapidly mounted to 16 killed and 15 injured. Siegfried Sassoon, the war poet, was at the station that day while on leave and considered, 'In a trench one was acclimatized to the notion of being exterminated and there was a sense of organized retaliation. But here one was helpless; an invisible enemy sent destruction spinning down from a fine weather sky.'

Other bombs fell all around. At 65 Fenchurch Street two bombs partially demolished the five-storey office building while claiming 19 lives and injuring another 13. Thomas Burke, working in his third-floor office, heard 'ominous rumbles' and then:

> … came two deafening crashes. The building swayed and trembled. Two big plate-glass windows came smashing through. Deep fissures appeared in the walls, and I was thrown to my knees … Looking out of my window on to a street that seemed enveloped by a thick mist … a girl, who had been standing in a doorway of a provision shop, next door, having now lost both her legs … a certified accountant, who had offices near mine, lying dead beside his daughter, who had tried to help him.

Damage to the Mechanics Shop at the Royal Mint, Tower Hill, on 13 June 1917. The blast, at 11.38am, killed four men and injured 30 others.

Of nine men working on the roof of a brass foundry just to the west of Liverpool Street station, eight were killed and, not far away in Central Street, a policeman just prevented a number of female factory workers dashing into the street as a bomb exploded and killed him. Countless other dramatic and tragic stories emerged from the few minutes of horror that descended on London that summer's morning – but there was one above all others that left an indelible mark

Having passed over the city, those aircraft still carrying bombs unloaded them on east London as they departed. Tragically one fell on the Upper North Street School in Poplar. The 50kg bomb smashed through three floors of the building, killing two children in its path, before exploding on the ground floor in a classroom crammed full with 64 infants. Once the dust and debris had settled, rescuers pulled the mangled bodies of 14 children from the wreckage, along with 30 more injured by the blast, two of whom later died. Another bomb landed on a school in City Road but failed to detonate.

Yet, as Kagohl 3 completed their mission, they were still largely unmolested. Although some 94 individual defensive sorties were flown by the RFC and RNAS, the time it took to gain the Gotha's operating height, and the short time the enemy formation was over the city meant that only 11 got close enough to the departing raiders to open fire – all without serious effect. One of these, a Bristol Fighter from No. 35 (Training) squadron, finally caught up with three straggling Gothas over Ilford, Essex. Flown by Capt C.W.E. Cole-Hamilton, with Capt C.H. Keevil as observer, it closed to attack, but in the exchange that followed a bullet pierced Keevil's neck and killed him. Defenceless, Cole-Hamilton turned sharply away and headed for home. Eleven of the London AA guns opened fire on the raiders but scored no success. All the Gothas returned safely to their bases, having caused £125,953 worth of material damage in London, killing 162 and injuring 426 – this raid inflicting the highest single casualty total of the campaign on the city – and leaving the Home Defence organization exposed and largely powerless in its wake.

REACTION AND RESPONSE

The feeling of outrage amongst the public was great and the clamour for reprisal raids on German towns gained voice. Zeppelins had approached under the cloak of darkness, but the Gothas appeared brazenly in broad daylight. In addition, the

A newspaper photograph taken four days after the first Gotha raid on London, which killed 18 schoolchildren in Poplar. The original caption reads, 'School children practice what to do in an air raid – at a given signal all lie down flat'.

The 13 June 1917 raid

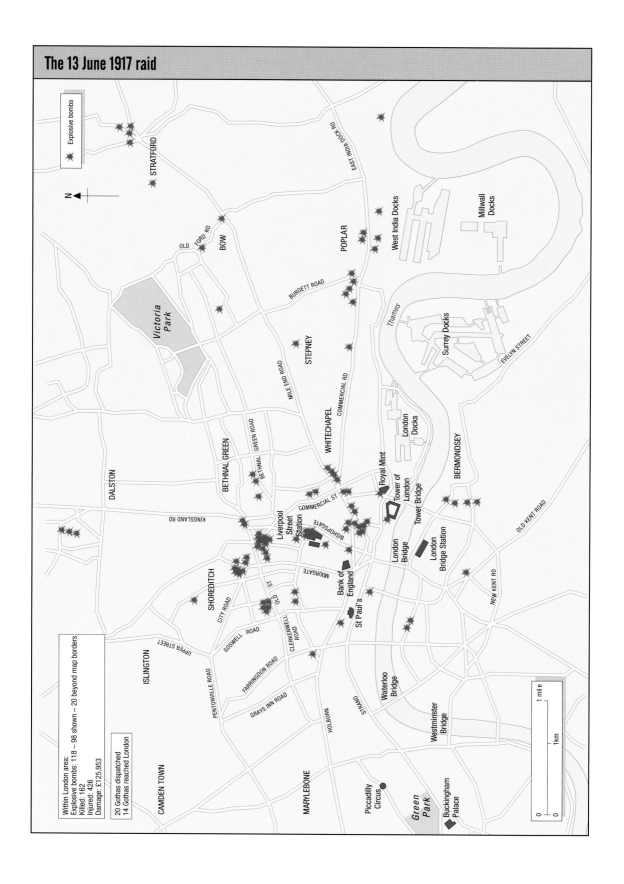

Explosive bombs

Within London area:
Explosive bombs: 118 – 98 shown – 20 beyond map borders
Killed: 162
Injured: 426
Damage: £125,953

20 Gothas dispatched
14 Gothas reached London

N

STRATFORD

OLD FORD RD

EAST INDIA DOCK RD

BOW

Victoria Park

POPLAR

West India Docks

Millwall Docks

BURDETT ROAD

STEPNEY

Thames

MILE END ROAD

Surrey Docks

COMMERCIAL RD

EVELYN STREET

BETHNAL GREEN

BETHNAL GREEN ROAD

WHITECHAPEL

DALSTON

KINGSLAND RD

COMMERCIAL ST

Royal Mint

Tower of London

London Docks

BERMONDSEY

Liverpool Street Station

BISHOPSGATE

Tower Bridge

OLD KENT ROAD

SHOREDITCH

CITY ROAD

OLD ST

MOORGATE

Bank of England

London Bridge

London Bridge Station

NEW KENT RD

ISLINGTON

UPPER STREET

GOSWELL ROAD

CLERKENWELL ROAD

FARRINGDON ROAD

St Paul's

PENTONVILLE ROAD

GRAYS INN ROAD

HOLBORN

STRAND

Waterloo Bridge

CAMDEN TOWN

MARYLEBONE

Westminster Bridge

Piccadilly Circus

Green Park

Buckingham Palace

1 mile

1km

0

0

question of the lack of public air raid warnings was also the subject of much debate – one that the government struggled to decide upon. It was clear that being out in the streets during a raid was more dangerous than being under cover, yet when enemy aircraft appeared people ran out into the streets to watch them. Would even more of the curious go into the streets, the government considered, if they knew a raid was imminent, risking their own safety and hindering the movement of the emergency services?

The following day Brandenburg flew to Germany, ordered to report to Supreme Headquarters to relate the details of the raid to the Kaiser; he received the Pour le Mérite (the 'Blue Max') for his achievement. But on his homeward journey on 19 June disaster struck. The engine of his two-seater Albatross stalled and the aircraft crashed, killing his pilot and, although Brandenburg was dragged alive from the wreckage, it proved necessary to amputate one of his legs. The news stunned the previously jubilant crews of Kagohl 3.

In London the War Cabinet met on the afternoon of the raid and again the following day to consider this new threat. A demand for a dramatic increase in the strength of the RFC was, after discussion, finally approved in July, but this was long term. In the meantime, a further

The monument to those killed at Upper North Street School, in Poplar Recreation Ground, paid for by public subscription. The monument bears the names of all 18 victims, the majority of whom were under six years old.

meeting already planned for 15 June took place with Field-Marshal Sir Douglas Haig and Maj Gen Hugh Trenchard present, respectively commanding the Army and RFC on the Western Front. Reluctantly Trenchard approved the temporary detachment of two front-line squadrons to take part in enhanced patrols on each side of the English Channel; No. 56 Squadron (equipped with the SE5a) moved to Bekesbourne near Canterbury and No. 66 Squadron (Sopwith Pups) relocated to Calais. But Trenchard stressed the importance of the return of both squadrons to him by 5 July. Haig needed the RFC at full strength to support his major attack at Ypres, intended to push through and clear the Germans from the Belgian coast.

Meanwhile, Higgins, commanding Home Defence Brigade, RFC, was beginning to receive new, more efficient aircraft for his squadrons, as Sopwith Pups, Sopwith 1½ Strutters, SE5as and Armstrong-Whitworth FK8s joined his roster. This meant that pilots familiar only with the BE types needed a period of retraining. At the same time the RNAS at Eastchurch received a batch of new Sopwith Camels previously earmarked for France. However, Lt Col Simon's request for an additional 45 AA guns, to bolster the thin defences on the eastern approaches to the capital and complete his previously shelved plans, failed because neither the guns nor the men to crew them were available. Further meetings also took place regarding the implementation of public air raid warnings but again the government blocked their introduction – citing this time, amongst other reasons, evidence that munitions workers alerted to air raids had left their work place and often did not return after the threat had passed – having a negative effect on war production.

Back in Belgium a new man arrived at Melle-Gontrode, the headquarters of Kagohl 3. Hauptmann Rudolph Kleine took up his position as Brandenburg's replacement in late June and waited, like his predecessor, for a suitable break in the weather. With no option presenting itself for London, Kleine ordered an attack on the naval town of Harwich on 4 July, which proved successful. But by now Trenchard's loan of two squadrons was over. The day after the Harwich raid No. 56 Squadron headed back to France, having, as one of their pilots put it, 'stood by, perfectly idle'. No. 66 Squadron left Calais a day later, and then, inevitably, the day following their departure, Kagohl 3 launched its next attack on London.

THE SECOND DAYLIGHT RAID – SATURDAY 7 JULY

A Bristol Fighter on display at the Shuttleworth Collection. The addition of the 'Brisfit', far superior to old BE-types that formed the bulk of the defence force in June 1917, gave Home Defence pilots a chance to engage the Gothas on equal terms.

Kleine chose an early take-off again, and reduced each aircraft's bomb load, to allow his formation to fly faster and higher. Word of the approach of the formation of 22 Gothas, transmitted early by observers on the Kentish Knock lightship, meant that 15 minutes later defence aircraft were taking off, enabling some to engage Kagohl 3 on the way to London. One Gotha wheeled away with engine problems, making a brief bombing run over Margate before heading home. The main body crossed the coastline near the mouth of the

river Crouch, flying in close formation at about 12,000ft, heading west towards the landmark of Epping Forest before beginning to climb for their bombing run. No. 37 Squadron, directly in the Gotha's flight path, had at least 11 aircraft in the air, but realistically only its four Sopwith Pups could hope to engage the Gothas. Three of them attacked the formation: one pilot gave up his attack when his guns jammed, another suffered engine problems and a third abandoned his attack because of a combination of both.

Other pilots with high-performance aircraft closed to engage but many suffered problems with guns jamming that day. Despite this increased attention and the fire of AA guns along their route, the Gothas continued on their course without significant distraction and, as they got closer to their target, Kleine tightened up the formation. Kleine led, then behind came two flights of eight aircraft, side by side, extended for about a mile, with the remaining four bringing up the rear. Once over Epping Forest, Kleine signalled the formation to begin its turn towards the city.

The morning was bright and sunny with a light haze in the eastern sky. Before the guns opened and the bombs began to drop many onlookers, watching the approaching flight, described it in picturesque terms, likening it to a flock of birds, while a journalist wrote:

Following the injury to Brandenburg, command of Kagohl 3 passed to Hptmn Rudolph Kleine (left) on 23 June. Here Kleine is with his adjutant, Oblt Gerlich. Whereas Brandenburg was calm and calculating, Kleine proved to be impatient and rash at times.

> To the spectator, in the midst of a quiet orderly London suburb, busily engaged in its Saturday shopping, it seemed ludicrously incredible that this swarm of black specks moving across the summer sky was a squadron of enemy aircraft, laden with explosive bombs waiting to be dropped into 'the brown' of London's vast expanse of brick and mortar.

Moments later the peace of that Saturday morning was broken. At 10.21am the AA gun at Higham Hill opened fire, followed by Wanstead two minutes later. The guns at Palmers Green, Finchley, Highbury and Parliament Hill then opened up too. As the Gothas banked the formation appeared to open out into two groups, that on the left passing south over Tottenham while those to the right continued westwards before turning south-east as they approached Hendon. The first guns of the Western AA district opened fire at 10.26am, the guns at Tower Bridge and Hyde Park joined in at 10.30am. Another journalist takes up the story, '... for five minutes the noise was deafening. Shells bursting in the air left puffs of black smoke, which expanded and drifted into one another.

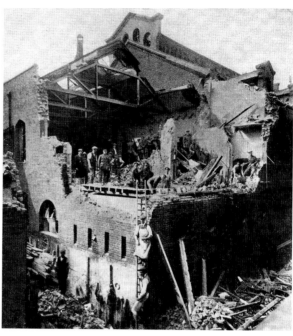

LEFT: Members of the public and a policeman seek shelter during the raid on Saturday 7 July. A newspaper reported that buses stopped while the passengers and crew got off and dashed into buildings before retaking their seats when the Gothas had passed.

RIGHT: Bomb damage caused on 7 July to the German Gymnasium in Pancras Road, between King's Cross and St Pancras stations. Built in 1864–65 by the German Gymnastics Society, it is believed to be the first purpose-built gymnasium in the country.

It seemed impossible that the raiders could escape being hit. Machines were often hidden in the smoke, but always they came through safely.'

With the increase in gunfire the Gotha formations opened out and began evasive tactics. The first bomb fell on Chingford, followed by a handful more falling in Tottenham and Edmonton inflicting limited damage to property. Then, in Stoke Newington – the scene of the first London Zeppelin raid – the human tragedies began. Four bombs fell close together, in Cowper Road, Wordsworth Road and two in Boleyn Road. In Cowper and Wordsworth roads the bombs severely damaged three houses and another 60 suffered lesser damage, but the bomb that exploded in Boleyn Road delivered a more deadly effect. William Stanton was in the road when the bomb fell: 'About 10.30am someone shouted in the street, "The Germans!" I looked up and saw the aeroplanes. People were running everywhere. There was a terrible explosion, and a hundred yards away three houses were blown to the ground.'

The explosion killed a 12-year-old grocer's delivery boy as he cycled past and a naturalized German baker and his wife died while working in their shop; seven other lives were lost in the blast and nine injured. Over 50 buildings, many let out as tenements, also suffered damage.

The raiding aircraft continued southwards over Dalston, Hoxton and Shoreditch before reaching the City where they turned to the east and continued bombing as they set course for home. Meanwhile the western part of the formation was now closing in on the City too. Bombs fell close to King's Cross Station and

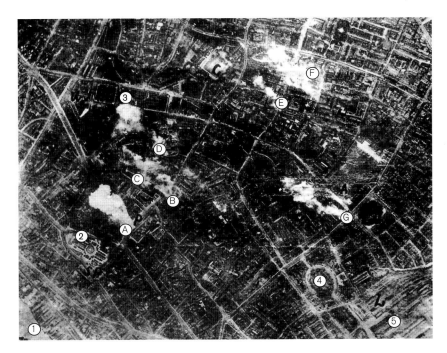

Aerial view of London taken at 14,200ft during the raid of 7 July. **Geographic key**: **1**: River Thames. **2**: St Paul's Cathedral. **3**: Smithfield Market. **4**: Finsbury Circus. **5**: Liverpool Street Station. Bomb key: **A**: Central Telegraph Office. **B**: Aldersgate Street. **C**: Little Britain. **D**: Bartholomew Close. **E**: Golden Lane. **F**: Whitecross Street. **G**: Chiswell Street. (IWM Q 108954)

around Bartholomew Close, Little Britain, Aldersgate Street and Barbican, causing significant destruction, while a number of fires also broke out. One bomb, falling on the roof of the Central Telegraph Office in St Martins Le Grand, caused significant damage to the two top floors of this large building. More bombs fell in and around Fenchurch Street, Leadenhall Street and Billingsgate Fish Market, while another landed in Tower Hill, close to the Tower of London.

The Tower Hill bomb exploded outside offices where some 80 people were sheltering. Those inside heard a deafening crash followed by 'a blinding flash, a chaos of breaking glass' then dust, soot and fumes filled the air. The blast killed eight and injured 15 of those taking shelter, while outside, the explosion left 'three horses lying badly wounded and bleeding'. A fireman used his axe to put the horses out of their misery.

The sound of the raid caused shoppers in neighbouring Lower Thames Street to seek shelter in an alleyway to the side of The Bell public house, but a bomb brought a neighbouring house and part of the pub crashing down, burying the shoppers under the rubble. Eventually rescuers recovered the bodies of four men and dragged seven injured from the wreckage, including a child.

A few of the raiding aircraft extended across the Thames on their eastward flight dropping bombs close to London Bridge station. The final bombs fell at about 10.40am in Whitechapel, Wapping and the Isle of Dogs as Kleine led Kagohl 3 away from London.

Large crowds gather after a bomb hits the roof of the Central Telegraph Office on the morning of 7 July. The bomb damaged the top two floors, injured four and falling masonry killed a sentry in the street.

The RFC now had 79 aircraft in the air of 20 different types, while the RNAS put up 22 aircraft. As the incoming formation had headed for London, Higgins redirected individual flights to a position off the north Kent coast where he hoped they would intercept the raiders on their return journey. A series of confused individual attacks harried the Gothas who began to draw their formation together. Many reported problems with jammed guns or an inability to keep up with the raiders. One who did get into close combat, Capt J. Palethorpe, piloting a DH4 from a Testing Squadron, with Air Mechanic F. James as observer, engaged a leading Gotha as it headed across Essex towards the coast. Palethorpe's Vickers gun jammed but he kept up with the formation, allowing James to engage three enemy aircraft with his Lewis gun. James fired off seven drums of ammunition in all and closing in to within 30 or 40 yards of one, he fired into it until it began to emit smoke. But before they could see the outcome a bullet struck Palethorpe 'in the flesh of the hip' and, with blood running down to his boots, he turned sharply away and landed safely at Rochford.

Another crew, flying a No. 50 Squadron Armstrong Whitworth FK8, one of those waiting to intercept the returning Gothas, closed to engage over the North Sea. Flying at 14,000ft, the pilot, 2nd Lt F.A.D. Grace with observer, 2nd Lt G. Murray, attacked one Gotha without effect, then attacked a group of three, but turned away because of the intensity of the return fire. Spotting a straggler flying below his FK8, Grace then pounced on this new target, as he later recalled: 'We dived at it, firing our front gun, range 800 yards, as we got closer on a zig-zag course, and when between 600 and 400 yards, we got on its starboard side and above. The observer opened fire on it, with good results, as we saw black smoke coming from the centre section, and the H.A. [hostile aircraft] dived into the sea.'

The Gotha remained on the surface for a while, and although Grace and Murray circled, attempting to alert surface craft, with fuel running low, they reluctantly turned away. Neither the crew nor aircraft were recovered.

Kleine led his formation on a wider return flight in an attempt to avoid the Dunkirk squadrons and in this he was successful, but RNAS pilots from Manston pursued his formation most of the way back to Belgium. Damage from incessant

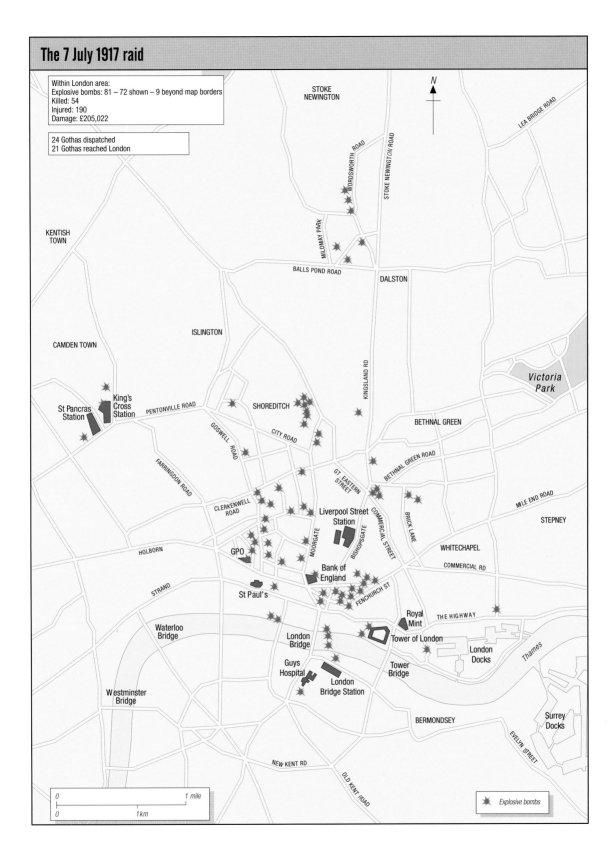

The 7 July 1917 raid

Within London area:
Explosive bombs: 81 – 72 shown – 9 beyond map borders
Killed: 54
Injured: 190
Damage: £205,022

24 Gothas dispatched
21 Gothas reached London

N

STOKE
NEWINGTON

LEA BRIDGE ROAD

WORDSWORTH ROAD

STOKE NEWINGTON ROAD

MILDMAY PARK

KENTISH
TOWN

BALLS POND ROAD

DALSTON

CAMDEN TOWN

ISLINGTON

KINGSLAND RD

Victoria
Park

St Pancras
Station

King's
Cross
Station

PENTONVILLE ROAD

SHOREDITCH

BETHNAL GREEN

GOSWELL ROAD

CITY ROAD

BETHNAL GREEN ROAD

FARRINGDON ROAD

GT EASTERN STREET

MILE END ROAD

CLERKENWELL ROAD

Liverpool Street
Station

COMMERCIAL STREET

BRICK LANE

STEPNEY

HOLBORN

MOORGATE

BISHOPSGATE

WHITECHAPEL

COMMERCIAL RD

GPO

Bank of
England

STRAND

St Paul's

FENCHURCH ST

Royal
Mint

THE HIGHWAY

Waterloo
Bridge

London
Bridge

Tower of London

London
Docks

Thames

Guys
Hospital

Tower
Bridge

Westminster
Bridge

London
Bridge Station

Surrey
Docks

BERMONDSEY

EVELYN STREET

NEW KENT RD

OLD KENT ROAD

0   1 mile
0   1km

★ Explosive bombs

attacks forced one Gotha down on the beach at Ostend and Kagohl 3 lost three others, wrecked on their airfields, a combination of many factors, including enemy action, strong winds, lack of fuel and the Gotha's inherent instability when unladen. British aircrew suffered too with two aircraft shot down.

Back in London there was concern over the number of anti-aircraft shells that had landed on the city adding to the casualties; the London Fire Brigade recorded the fall of 103 shells. Total casualties in the capital reached 54 killed and 190 injured. Of these, ten were killed and 55 injured by this 'friendly fire'.

The raid brought a wide variety of reactions. Sections of the bombed

A historic photograph showing the 21 Gothas of the *Englandgeschwader* that reached London on 7 July as they flew over Essex on their return flight.

population turned against immigrants in their midst, considering many with foreign names to be 'Germans'. Riots broke out in Hackney and Tottenham, where mobs wrecked immigrant houses and shops. Moreover, such was the anti-German feeling that four days later King George V, with the unfortunate addition of Gotha in his family name (Royal House of Saxe-Coburg-Gotha), issued a proclamation announcing a change of name to the Royal House of 'Windsor'.

Feelings of anger were rife against the Government too. The War Cabinet held a series of meetings between 7 and 11 July. Frustrations at the removal of the two 'loaned' squadrons just hours before the raid were voiced and in response a squadron currently forming for service in France was instead earmarked for home service. Another squadron, No. 46, which was operating on the Western Front received orders temporarily redeploying it to England for Home Defence (10 July–30 August). Discussions followed highlighting the limited response to the raid; these resulted in approval for the formation of a committee to consider Home Defence arrangements and the organization of aerial operations.

Lt Gen Jan Christian Smuts. The former Boer guerrilla leader came to London in 1917 as the South African delegate to the Imperial War Cabinet. Having impressed with his sharp intellect and analytical brain, Smuts was invited to join the War Cabinet.

LONDON MAKES READY

The committee was unusual in that it really revolved around just one man, the former Boer guerrilla leader, now Lt Gen Jan Christian Smuts. Having exhaustively interviewed all the senior officers involved, he produced a detailed report on the air defences eight days later. In it he highlighted the flaws in the current system of defence and recommended that a single officer 'of first-rate ability and practical air experience be placed in executive command of the air defence of the London area', bringing together the RFC, AA guns and Observation Corps under a united command. Smuts also called for additional AA guns and the rapid completion and training of three new day-fighter squadrons (Nos. 44, 61 and 112) and a general increase in aircraft committed to the defence of the capital, allowing for the creation of a reserve.

This first part of the report received swift approval leading to the creation of the London Air Defence Area (LADA) on 31 July. The command included all gun batteries in the south-east from Harwich to Dover and inland to London, the nine RFC squadrons allocated to Southern Home Defence wing (Nos. 37, 39, 44, 50, 51, 61, 75, 78 and 112) and all observation posts east of a line drawn between Grantham in Lincolnshire and Portsmouth on the Hampshire coast. The man chosen for the job was Maj Gen Edward B. Ashmore, a former senior RFC officer and currently commander of the artillery of 29th Division.

The raid of 7 July also raised the question of a public air raid warning again. This time the government felt unable to block the demand and a system of marine distress maroons would in future announce incoming daytime raids, combined with police alerts which would also extend into the evening.

Following the raid of 7 July the government authorized a system of air raid warnings. On 14 July an announcement confirmed that in future marine distress maroons fired from fire stations would alert the public of approaching enemy aircraft during daylight hours.

AN ENGLISH SUMMER

While this reorganization was under way London was free from attack. The *Englandgeschwader* waited for its next opportunity but the weather reports were not favourable for attacks on the city. However, clear skies over the coast prompted attacks on Harwich and Felixstowe on 22 July, which resulted in 13 deaths and 26 injuries.

As July passed into August the weather effectively blocked Kleine's ambition and granted Ashmore much-needed time to improve London's defences. The first three weeks of the month heralded a typical English summer – rain and high winds! It proved a disastrous month for Kleine. On 12 August, at short notice, he ordered an attack on Chatham. Strong winds delayed the formation forcing it to attack Southend and Margate instead. Engaged by AA guns and pursued by the RFC and RNAS back across the North Sea, heavy casualties followed: one Gotha shot down at sea, one forced down and crashed near Zeebrugge with four more wrecked in landing accidents.

Kleine ordered two more raids in August on south-eastern coastal towns. Both ended in disaster. On 18 August strong winds forced the formation of 28 Gothas way off course and, with fuel running low, the raid was abandoned. Driven by the wind towards neutral Holland, it appears that Kleine lost as many

In conjunction with the maroons, policemen on foot, on bicycles and in cars would tour the streets carrying placards emblazoned with 'take cover', accompanied by whistles, bells or motor horns. (Colin Ablett)

as nine aircraft to a combination of Dutch AA fire, shortage of fuel and crash landings. Certainly, when the dogged Kleine ordered the squadron airborne again four days later, he could muster only 15 aircraft. This raid, on 22 August, proved the futility of the continuance of the daylight campaign. Alerted early to the approach of Kagohl 3, the coastal AA guns were ready and RNAS aircraft in Kent were in the air and waiting. Five Gothas, including Kleine's turned back early with engine problems, the rest ran into a determined defence and turned for home after bombing Margate, Ramsgate and Dover. Three Gothas were shot down, two probably by RNAS aircraft and one by AA fire. While the weather conditions had protected the principal target, London, Kleine lost 18 of Kagohl 3's aircraft in these August daytime raids.

THE 'DAYLIGHT' DEFENCES TIGHTEN

The resolute Lt Col Simon submitted a new request for more guns in July, backed by the RFC. He asked for the construction of a new ring of gun stations 25 miles out from the centre of London, able to put up a barrage of shells to break up the attacking formations before they reached the capital, making them less formidable targets for the RFC to pick off. The scheme required 110 guns covering the north, east and south approaches to the city, but again the request failed. With no new guns available Simon implemented his plan as best he could with ten guns transferred to the eastern approaches from other London stations and a further 24 withdrawn from other duties and redeployed for the defence of London.

With the maroons initially restricted to warn of daytime raids only, the police system continued to warn the population at night – both systems incorporating the use of the police to announce the 'all clear', assisted by Boy Scouts blowing bugles.

Evidence of Kagohl 3's disastrous raid on 22 August 1917. The smouldering wreckage of a Gotha crewed by Oblt Echart Fulda, Uffz Heinrich Schildt and Vfw Eichelkamp lying on Hengrove golf course, Margate. All three died.

In an effort to stem the incidents of AA guns firing at Home Defence aircraft, Ashmore announced the creation of the 'Green Line', a fixed line drawn inside the line of the new outer barrage. Outside the Green Line guns had priority; inside the line priority switched to the defending aircraft. And while the RFC practised the intricacies of flying in formation, elsewhere four BE12 aircraft became the first to be fitted with wireless-telegraphy equipment, enabling them to transmit, but not receive, Morse messages to ground stations detailing the movements of enemy formations. Moves also commenced to improve telephone communications between Horse Guards and observer posts, airfields and AA gun positions. In addition, a new operations room was under development at Spring Gardens, by Admiralty Arch, Westminster.

August also witnessed a significant development in the history of British aviation. During this month Smuts released the second part of his report, *Air Organization and the Direction of Aerial Operations*. It considered the future of air power and with great insight stated, 'As far as can at present be foreseen, there is absolutely no limit to the scale of [the air service's] future independent war use. And the day may not be far off when aerial operations with their devastation of enemy lands and destruction of industrial and populous centers on a vast scale may become the principal operations of war.'

The report concluded by making a strong recommendation for combining the RFC and RNAS into a single air service and urging its swift implementation. It marked the birth of the Royal Air Force, which finally came into being on 1 April 1918.

THE SWITCH TO NIGHT BOMBING

However, all these plans, designed to counter daylight raids, were about to become redundant; the daylight offensive was over. The dramatic losses incurred on recent raids indicated to Kleine the futility of continuing on this course. Therefore, the *Englandgeschwader* prepared for a switch to night flying but retained a hope that the new Gotha variant, the G.V., would revitalize the daylight offensive. These hopes ended when the G.V. failed to offer any significant improvement in performance over the G.IV. After a period of intensive night-flying training, plans were ready in early September 1917 for Kagohl 3 to return to the offensive.

On the night of 3/4 September, before Ashmore's new arrangements were in place, a force of four Gothas attacked Margate, Sheerness and Chatham; it was at the last of these towns that the heaviest casualties occurred when two bombs fell on a drill hall at the naval barracks. When the dust settled 138 naval ratings lay dead amidst the rubble while colleagues dragged clear the 88 injured. The opposition that night proved negligible. With further good weather, the following day Kleine announced a return to London.

At about 8.30pm on 4 September, the first of 11 Gothas took to the air at five-minute intervals. The formations of the daylight campaign were finished, now the aircraft flew singly to avoid collisions in the dark. Inevitably two dropped out with engine problems, leaving the other nine to feel their way with difficulty to England. The first came inland at 10.40pm, the last at 12.10am. Observers struggling to interpret the engine sounds in the dark submitted numerous exaggerated claims about the strength of the incoming Gothas. Eighteen RFC aircraft took off, but only the four Sopwith Camels of No. 44 Squadron and an FK8 of No. 50 Squadron stood any real chance of interception, but no pilots effectively engaged the incoming

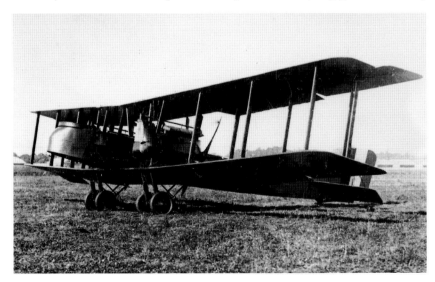

The Gotha G.V. Hopes that the G.V would deliver a superior performance to the G.IV and enable Kagohl 3 to resume daytime bombing were soon dashed. Although it offered a small increase in speed, it did so with a lower rate of climb. (IWM Q 67219)

A Sopwith Camel. During the raid on Chatham on 3 September 1917, three Sopwith Camels of No. 44 Squadron, arguably the best day-fighter possessed by the RFC, took to the air at night and confounded current opinion that they were too tricky to fly in the dark.

bombers that night. However, the AA gun at Borstal near Rochester proved more effective. Held for some minutes by a searchlight, the gun targeted a Gotha at a height estimated at 13,000ft and opened fire at 11.27pm. The gun commander, 2nd Lt C. Kendrew, RGA, reported that the Gotha 'was apparently disabled by our gun fire … A direct hit was then scored and it was observed to fall almost perpendicularly for a short distance turning over and over'. An exhaustive search discovered no wreckage, leading to the presumption that the aircraft came down in the Medway or Thames Estuary and sank. Of the remaining eight Gothas that came inland reports show that just five reached London.

The moon was two days beyond full so the sky was bright over the capital when the first Gotha arrived, although a thin haze hindered the work of the searchlight crews. The lead aircraft dropped its bombs over West Ham and Stratford at around 11.25pm. One fell on an unoccupied factory that had until recently been used as an internment camp for German nationals. Another bombed between Greenwich Park and Woolwich at about 11.45pm.

When the first AA guns in London opened fire '… many people rushed for shelter. Those nearer the tubes went to the stations in all stages of undress and were conveyed in the lifts to the underground platforms. There were hundreds of women and children and scores of men who made for these places of refuge.'

A third Gotha appeared at 11.52pm over Oxford Circus in central London and dropped a 50kg bomb, causing serious damage to Bourne and Hollingsworth's store on East Castle Street. Its next bomb fell in Agar Street, off the Strand, outside the main entrance to the Charing Cross Hospital. A man, H. Stockman, was about to take shelter in a hotel entrance opposite where two others already stood. But at that moment, 'a woman came up with terror written on her face'. Mr Stockman, realizing there was room only for three, indicated to the woman to take the place, for which she thanked him profusely. Moments later the bomb exploded and blew the gallant

The 4/5 September 1917 raid

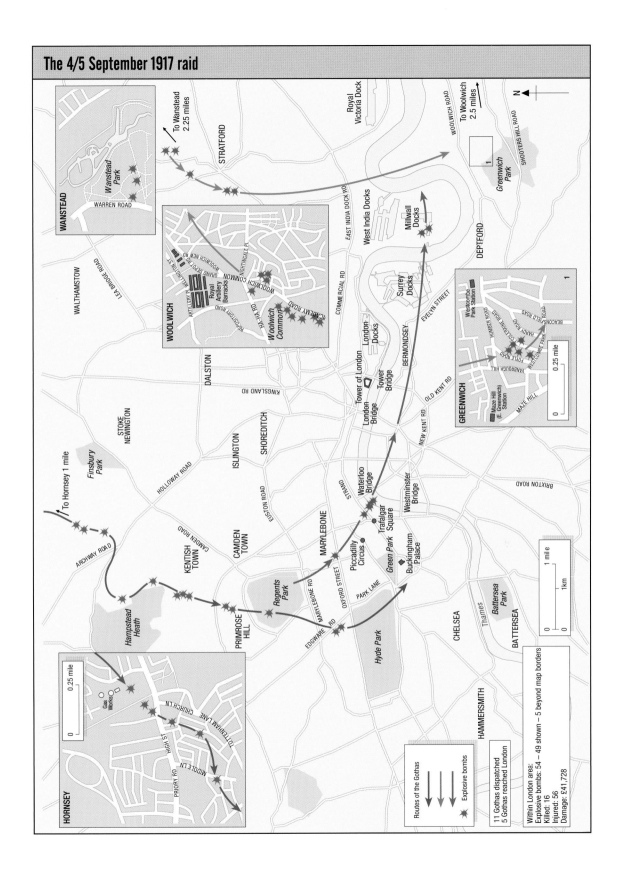

N

To Wanstead
2.25 miles

WANSTEAD

Wanstead Park

WARREN ROAD

STRATFORD

Royal Victoria Dock

WOOLWICH ROAD

To Woolwich
2.5 miles

SHOOTERS HILL ROAD

Greenwich Park

1

LEA BRIDGE ROAD

WALTHAMSTOW

EAST INDIA DOCK RD

West India Docks

Millwall Docks

DEPTFORD

WOOLWICH

Royal Artillery Barracks

NIGHTINGALE PL

GRAND DEPOT RD

WOOLWICH NEW RD

WELLINGTON ST

ARTILLERY PL

REPOSITORY ROAD

HA-HA RD

WOOLWICH ROAD

ACADEMY ROAD

Woolwich Common

COMMERCIAL RD

London Docks

Surrey Docks

Tower of London

Tower Bridge

London Bridge

BERMONDSEY

EVELYN STREET

OLD KENT RD

GREENWICH

1

Westcombe Park Station

BEACONSFIELD ROAD

HUMBER ROAD

HARDY ROAD

COLLERNE ROAD

FOYLE ROAD

VANBROUGH HILL

Maze Hill (E. Greenwich) Station

MAZE HILL

0.25 mile

0

To Hornsey 1 mile

Finsbury Park

STOKE NEWINGTON

DALSTON

KINGSLAND RD

SHOREDITCH

ISLINGTON

HOLLOWAY ROAD

EUSTON ROAD

NEW KENT RD

BRIXTON ROAD

ARCHWAY ROAD

CAMDEN ROAD

KENTISH TOWN

CAMDEN TOWN

MARYLEBONE

STRAND

Waterloo Bridge

Westminster Bridge

Regents Park

Hampstead Heath

PRIMROSE HILL

MARYLEBONE RD

EDGWARE RD

OXFORD STREET

Piccadilly Circus

Trafalgar Square

Green Park

Buckingham Palace

PARK LANE

Hyde Park

CHELSEA

Thames

Battersea Park

BATTERSEA

HAMMERSMITH

0.25 mile

0

Gas Works

TOTTENHAM LANE

CHURCH LN

HIGH ST

PRIORY RD

MIDDLE LN

HORNSEY

1 mile

0

1km

0

Routes of the Gothas

Explosive bombs

11 Gothas dispatched
5 Gothas reached London

Within London area:
Explosive bombs: 54 – 49 shown – 5 beyond map borders
Killed: 16
Injured: 56
Damage: £41,728

The former factory of Messrs. Wm. Ritchie, Jute Spinners and Weavers, in Carpenters Road, Stratford, bombed at about 11.25pm on 4 September. The factory, vacant since 1904, had been in use as an internment camp until June 1917.

Stockman to the ground. When he looked up he realized the woman was dead. An RFC officer on leave, standing on the corner of Agar Street, rushed to help and, seeing the demolished front of the hotel, stepped into the building. There he found '… two Colonial [Canadian] soldiers sitting dead in their chairs. One had been killed by a piece of the bomb, which went through the back of his head and out of the front of his Army hat, taking the cap badge with it.'

Besides these three deaths, another ten lay injured, including three soldiers, an American naval rating and a policeman. Across the Strand a bomb damaged the roof of the Little Theatre, converted into a soldiers' canteen by the Canadian YMCA, and another fell in Victoria Embankment Gardens, just missing the Hotel Cecil. Then, seconds later, a fourth 50kg bomb of this salvo exploded on the Victoria Embankment, close to Cleopatra's Needle, just as a single-decker tram passed. The blast seared through the tram, killing the driver and two passengers but the bewildered conductor, Joseph Carr, staggered clear.

A few bombs dropped on Wanstead at around 11.55pm, then, about 30 minutes later, the fifth Gotha appeared. At about 12.30am bombs dropped on Edmonton, followed by explosions in Tottenham, Hornsey, Crouch End and Upper Holloway, where a bomb demolished the laundry of the Islington Workhouse in St John's Road. Another fell harmlessly in Highgate, just east of Hampstead Heath, followed by two bombs, both of 12kg, which landed in Kentish Town. One of these, falling in Wellesley Road, damaged the doors and windows of 15 houses but also claimed lives too. A witness reported seeing '… a flash in the air, and immediately afterwards there was a tremendous explosion. A dense volume of smoke was rising from the road'.

As the smoke cleared the bodies of a soldier, home on hospital leave, and a woman with her five-year-old child were revealed, dead in the passageway of the house where they lived. The soldier had just pushed his mother clear, saving her life, when the bomb exploded. Further bombs landed in Primrose Hill and Regent's Park before the two final bombs fell close to Edgware Road at about 12.50am. One of these, in Norfolk Crescent, killed a woman, while the other exploded in the air above Titchborne Street (no longer there, it was just south of the present Sussex Gardens). The blast caught an 11-year-old girl as she walked to the end of the road to see if the 'all-clear' had sounded and bowled her along the street. Having convinced herself she was still alive, she made her way home. Only then did she realize, 'I had a hole through my knee. Also, the frock I was

A bronze sphinx guarding Cleopatra's Needle on the Victoria Embankment. At about midnight on 4 September a 50kg bomb exploded close to the ancient monument, the blast hitting a passing tram, killing the driver and two passengers. Scars from the bomb can still be seen today on the sphinx and pedestal.

THE FIRST NIGHT-TIME RAID, TUESDAY 4 SEPTEMBER 1917

The skies over London had been free of German aircraft for almost nine weeks, but that changed on the night of 4 September 1917 when a new phenomenon struck the capital – the first night-time Gotha raid.

That evening five Gothas reached the capital. One dropped its first bomb over Oxford Circus shortly before midnight and flew on towards the Thames. The next three bombs all fell close to the Strand.

Shortly before they landed, a single-decker 'G' Class tram, No. 596, had crossed Westminster Bridge and stopped before continuing along the Victoria Embankment. The driver, Alfred Buckle, felt uneasy that night and, according to his conductor, Joseph Carr, was keen to get his shift over. At Westminster Buckle asked if he could move off in front of another tram and, having shunted onto the line, as Buckle proceeded along Victoria Embankment he heard the sound of exploding bombs near the Strand. Keen to get clear he accelerated but, just as he passed Cleopatra's Needle, a 50kg bomb exploded on the pavement between the tram and the ancient monument. The blast smashed through the pavement, destroying a gas main, damaging the base of the Needle and an adjacent sphinx. The blast seared through the tram, killing Buckle, the two passengers – a man and a woman – and blew Joseph Carr from one end of the tram to the other, but he staggered out onto the street and survived. Eight passers-by were also injured by the blast. An eyewitness recalled that Buckle 'appeared to kneel down suddenly, still pulling at his controls. I saw him fall, and that his legs had been blown off: so while dying his last thoughts were to stop his tram.'

The demolished laundry of the Islington Workhouse in St John's Road (now St John's Way) in Upper Holloway. A 50kg bomb landed at around 12.30am on 5 September but there were no casualties.

wearing had 15 holes in it where I had been whirled along and struck by shrapnel.' The bomb injured 16 people caught in the blast, one of whom later died, damaged 33 houses in Titchborne Street, and blew out the windows of 12 shops in Edgware Road. That sound of smashing glass signalled the end of the raid and silence gradually returned to the skies over London.

DEFENSIVE IMPROVEMENTS

The switch to night-bombing presented Britain's defences with a new threat. The War Cabinet called again on the indefatigable Smuts and on 6 September he produced another report. Smuts doubted the ability of aircraft to engage enemy raiders at night, but recommended the use of more powerful searchlights, hoping to dazzle the incoming pilots. He also supported the idea just proposed by Ashmore for a balloon barrage, 'a wire screen suspended from balloons and intended to form a sort of barrage in which the enemy machine navigated at night will be caught'. Experiments began and approval was given for 20 of these screens, although ultimately only ten were raised, the first in October 1917.

After the first moonlit raid, the weather turned in favour of the defenders, granting them time to hone the defensive arrangements to meet this new threat. Investigations into new methods of sound-location continued and Ashmore's plan for the Green Line became operational. No British aircraft were to fly beyond the outer gun line or over London. The AA guns were now authorized to consider any aircraft in these areas as hostile. Within these cleared areas Simon developed a new system of barrage fire which directed guns to direct 'curtains' of shellfire in specific locations, with these walls of fire extending over 2,500ft from top to bottom, targeted at varying heights between 5,000 and 17,000ft.

A diagram illustrating the new barrage fire system, producing curtains of concentrated fire in the path of incoming aircraft. Barrages were fixed on map coordinates and bore code-names such as Jig-saw, Bubbly, Knave of Hearts and Cosy Corner.

With each barrage screen fixed by map reference, a coordinator directed different barrages to commence firing as an enemy aircraft progressed across the plotting table. Once held by searchlights the AA guns could switch from barrage fire to direct fire against the enemy bomber.

While grounded by the weather, Kleine received the news that a new squadron was about to join the attacks on London. In September 1917 the OHL transferred Riesenflugzeug Abteilung (Rfa) 501 from the Eastern Front, via Berlin, to Belgium. Riesenflugzeug Abteilung 501 had been flying early versions of the R-type – *Riesenflugzeug* (Giant aircraft) – since August 1916. Now the commander of Rfa 501, Hptmn Richard von Bentivegni, received R-types of the latest design, the R.VI, designed by the Zeppelin works at Staaken (as well as the single model R.IV and R.V types). Somewhat ungainly in appearance, the Staaken R.VI, with its crew of seven, was advanced for its time, boasting an enclosed cockpit for the two pilots, navigational aids including wireless telegraphy (W/T) equipment, and could carry a large bomb load, including bombs of 100, 300 and even 1,000kg. On 22 September the first aircraft of Rfa 501 arrived at Sint-Denijs-Westrem, sharing the airfield with two flights of Kagohl 3, and began to prepare their aircraft for their first raid on London. They were not yet operational when favourable weather was forecast for Monday 24 September, the start of an intense period of bombing – later known as the Harvest Moon Offensive – during which six raids took place over a period of eight days.

A Gotha G.V being loaded with two 100kg and five 50kg bombs, a total weight of 450kg – just under half a ton – a fairly typical weight for a night raid. (David Marks)

THE HARVEST MOON OFFENSIVE

Sixteen Gothas set out on the raid but three turned back with technical problems. The remaining 13 crossed the English coastline between Orfordness and Dover. The wide-ranging courses of these attacks meant the 30 RFC aircraft that took off to intercept the raid – including the first use of Biggin Hill airfield by the RFC – saw nothing, and similarly the searchlights struggled to pick out the raiders. However, only three bombers penetrated inland to London, six contented themselves with a bombardment of Dover while the remaining four dropped their bombs on coastal targets in south Essex and north Kent. Those that did battle through to London found the new AA barrage fire system in operation. The first to approach did so over the eastern suburbs and dropped its first bomb, an incendiary, on Lodore Street, just off East India Dock Road, around 8.05pm, followed quickly by a couple more on Poplar, just north of the West India Docks. Then it crossed the Thames and dropped four bombs on Rotherhithe and Deptford before turning away and heading east. The effectiveness of the new barrage impressed those watching on the ground: 'Everyone agreed that the intensity of the bombardment from the anti-aircraft guns was the greatest yet experienced … A searchlight succeeded in finding one of the raiders … Shrapnel was bursting all around, and more than once it looked as if the aeroplane would be brought crashing to earth … after a shell had burst in front of him he banked steeply and made off in the opposite direction, followed by a violent bombardment, until he disappeared from view.'

The other two Gothas came in over north London around 8.35pm, dropping a mixture of explosive and incendiary bombs on Islington before heading

OPPOSITE: 'Giant' R.33, an R.VI type, designed by the Zeppelin works at Staaken. These huge four-engine aircraft, significantly larger than any Luftwaffe aircraft that attacked London in the Second World War, had a wingspan of 138ft, not far short of twice the size of a Gotha.

towards the centre of the city. An explosive bomb that fell in King's Cross Road caused much local damage and killed 13-year-old James Sharpe.

Elsewhere a bomb exploded outside the Bedford Hotel on Southampton Row, Bloomsbury. A doctor, R.D. MacGregor, on his way to have dinner at the hotel, heard the bomb falling and, diving through the door, shouted a warning to a small group gathered there. Doctor MacGregor survived but the bomb killed 13, including three hotel staff, and injured 22. Damage nearby was extensive.

The bomb made a hole in the roadway some 4ft deep, the force of the explosion blowing out all the windows in front of the building, even to the sixth storey, and shattering the glass in most of the houses on either side of the street for several hundred yards.

Moments later another 50kg bomb crashed through the glass roof of the Royal Academy in Piccadilly, causing considerable damage to the building and, even before the dust had settled, the next bomb fell at the north-east corner of Green Park.

The tally for the night was 13 explosive bombs and 19 incendiaries, with a total of 14 killed and 49 injured. Reports showed that one Gotha crashed on landing in Belgium, possibly having suffered damage from AA guns on the homeward journey. However, the increased anti-aircraft barrage fire resulted in the police recording damage caused by 73 AA shells: one, landing in Cloudesley Road, Islington, injured five. Another dramatic change that night was the number of people who rushed to the nearest Underground station when the police gave the 'take cover' warning shortly before 8.00pm. The government estimated 100,000 Londoners went underground that night; the trend was to continue and grow.

When the warning sounded again the following night the crowding in the Underground was beginning to be a problem, with the authorities growing concerned by the exodus from the East End. *The Times* blamed it on the 'alien population of the East-end' who they claimed, arrived in family groups to camp out on the platforms 'as early as 5 o'clock in the afternoon'.

The Gothas returned the following night, Tuesday 25 September. Fifteen Gothas set out to attack London, but this time only one dropped out with technical problems. Crossing the coast between Foulness and Dover from about 7.00 to 7.45pm, most settled on targets on the north-east Kent coast, such as Margate and Folkestone, with only three penetrating to the south-eastern corner of London. One of these arrived later than the first two, dropping three bombs over Blackheath, all of which failed to explode, and one on

The blasted façade of the Bedford Hotel in Southampton Row. A 50kg bomb landed in the road outside the hotel at about 8.55pm on 24 September, killing 13 and injuring 22. All the windows in the hotel are smashed.

The 24 September 1917 raid

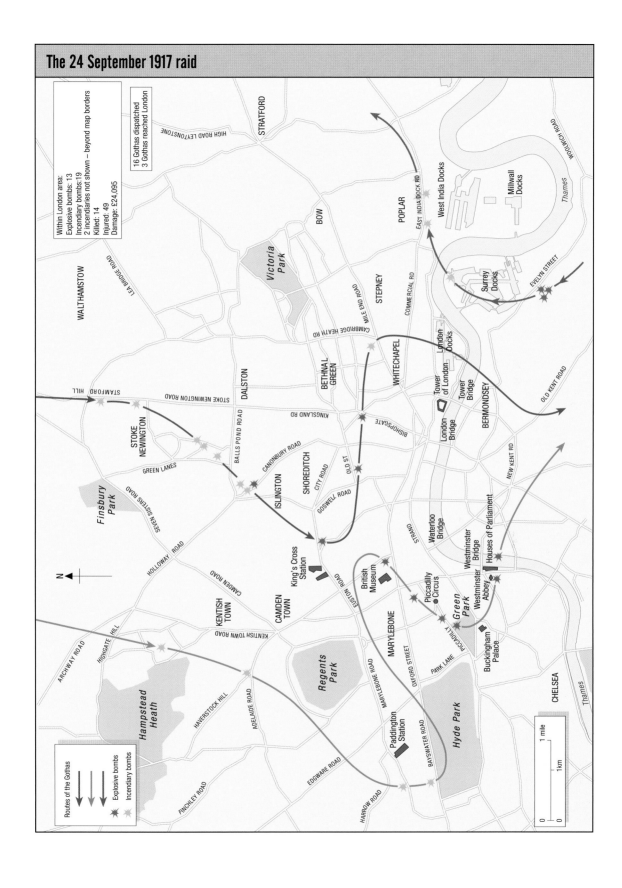

Within London area:
Explosive bombs: 13
Incendiary bombs:19
2 incendiaries not shown – beyond map borders
Killed: 14
Injured: 49
Damage: £24,095

16 Gothas dispatched
3 Gothas reached London

Routes of the Gothas

Explosive bombs

Incendiary bombs

WALTHAMSTOW

STRATFORD

HIGH ROAD LEYTONSTONE

LEA BRIDGE ROAD

Victoria Park

BOW

POPLAR

EAST INDIA DOCK RD

West India Docks

Millwall Docks

Thames

WOOLWICH ROAD

STAMFORD HILL

STOKE NEWINGTON ROAD

DALSTON

BETHNAL GREEN

STEPNEY

MILE END ROAD

CAMBRIDGE HEATH RD

COMMERCIAL RD

Surrey Docks

EVELYN STREET

STOKE NEWINGTON

GREEN LANES

BALLS POND ROAD

CANONBURY ROAD

KINGSLAND RD

SHOREDITCH

WHITECHAPEL

London Docks

Tower of London

Tower Bridge

BERMONDSEY

OLD KENT ROAD

Finsbury Park

SEVEN SISTERS ROAD

ISLINGTON

CITY ROAD

OLD ST

BISHOPSGATE

London Bridge

NEW KENT RD

GOSWELL ROAD

HOLLOWAY ROAD

CAMDEN ROAD

King's Cross Station

EUSTON ROAD

British Museum

STRAND

Waterloo Bridge

Westminster Bridge

Houses of Parliament

N

ARCHWAY ROAD

HIGHGATE HILL

KENTISH TOWN

CAMDEN TOWN

KENTISH TOWN ROAD

Piccadilly Circus

Green Park

Westminster Abbey

Hampstead Heath

HAVERSTOCK HILL

ADELAIDE ROAD

Regents Park

MARYLEBONE

MARYLEBONE ROAD

OXFORD STREET

PARK LANE

PICCADILLY

Buckingham Palace

FINCHLEY ROAD

Paddington Station

BAYSWATER ROAD

Hyde Park

CHELSEA

Thames

EDGWARE ROAD

HARROW ROAD

1 mile

1km

0

0

Charlton Park before turning away in the face of the barrage. Twenty defence aircraft took off, but again all but one failed to locate the incoming aircraft. Unfortunately for those living in the area where the other two aircraft dropped their bombs, it appears no 'take cover' warning reached them and many were out in the streets when the bombs began to fall. One of the first landed in Marcia Road, just off the Old Kent Road, shortly before 8.00pm. The bomb landed in the street, smashing a gas main and wrecking about 20 houses and 'in the whole length of it there was not a pane of glass left intact'.

A woman living on the top floor of one of the houses had rushed upstairs to turn off the gas when she saw through a window 'a great ball of flame falling towards us'. She remembered no more until, having crashed down to the ground floor, she heard her sister calling as helping hands dragged her carefully from the rubble. She survived with injuries just to her legs. Others in the street were not so lucky; three died and another 16 were injured, one of whom later died.

Just a few yards away in Old Kent Road another bomb fell directly on Tew's Bakery. The owner of the business had constructed a bunker of heavy flour sacks in the bakehouse under his shop. The family were just sitting down to supper when, as one of the baker's daughters explained, a cry went up in the street. '"They're here!" We all made a rush to our bakehouse, as did many neighbours. The moment we were there there was a terrifying crash, and we knew the house had been struck. The dreadful noise and the sudden darkness; the choking dust; the screaming; the continuous tumbling of the ruin above us, we shall always remember.'

It was a terrible experience, but all 17 people huddled in the bake-house survived uninjured to tell their story.

The Gotha dropped further 50kg bombs close by in Mina Road, Odell Street, Coburg Road and Goldie Street. The accompanying aircraft dropped a string of 16 incendiary bombs in New Cross and Deptford, with one landing uncomfortably close to the South Metropolitan Gas Company off Old Kent Road.

At about 8.15pm a Sopwith 1½ Strutter of No. 78 squadron with Capt D. J. Bell and 2nd Lt G.G. Williams on board was flying south of Brentwood when it came under attack. The enemy aircraft was flying east, presumably returning from London. The Sopwith took up the chase and for 15 minutes kept it in sight, firing frequent bursts before the target disappeared from view. The following day the press carried a story about a substantial amount of petrol falling in Essex, suggesting damage to one of the Gotha's fuel tanks. Certainly one Gotha failed to return, lost over the sea, possibly having run out of fuel.

The weather then turned against Kagohl 3 once more, with the return of rain and heavy cloud. But in London the nightly exodus to the Underground continued. In fact the skies over the Belgian airfields did not begin to clear until the afternoon of Friday 28 September. Kleine gathered 25 Gothas for the raid and this time Bentivegni had two of his R-type 'Giants' ready too. It was the largest force yet assembled against London. However, serious doubts surfaced about the weather just before take-off, forcing Kleine and Bentivegni to issue orders to their crews to turn back if they encountered solid cloud cover. Fifteen did just that and only three Gothas and the two 'Giants' claimed to have dropped any bombs, but none got close to London. The cloud cover meant few anti-aircraft guns opened fire and those that did were just firing in the general direction of the engine noise. Oberleutnant Fritz Lorenz, commanding Kasta 14 of the *Englandgeschwader*, left a rather poetic description of his flight over England on this occasion: 'Probing in vain, the searchlights painted large yellow saucers in the clouds below us. Where a devil's cauldron of bursting shrapnel had never let a machine pass without inflicting at least some hits, there prevailed this time in this silvery solitude a peace which was like something out of a fairy tale.'

But this peaceful interlude soon came to an abrupt end. The journey turned from fairy tale to nightmare for many. Three crews never returned, believed shot down by AA guns at Deal, Ramsgate and Sheppey while five Gothas crashed in Belgium and one in Holland – a third of all attacking aircraft lost.

Yet even though no aircraft reached London there were casualties in the city. Anticipating the incoming raid the 'take cover' warning went out just before 8.00pm. Suddenly there was a rush by about 200 to 300 people for the entrance of the Underground at Liverpool Street Station. Four policemen on duty there tried to stem the tide, but as one reported, 'there was a panic, they lost their heads'. By the time the police had fought their way down the crowded stairs where 'people were packed like sardines', they found a heap of eight bodies. According to a newspaper report the following day: 'Eight cases of injury were reported … chiefly of broken limbs and body injuries. One elderly woman was crushed to death and another, whose breastbone was fractured, is not expected to live. A child reported to be killed was taken away on an ambulance.'

A cutaway diagram showing a Gotha commander using his Goertz bombsight. In reality most commanders released their bombs over London without worrying too much about careful aiming.

THE ARRIVAL OF THE 'GIANTS'

Although the raid had made a large dent in the strength of Kagohl 3, the relentless Kleine ordered another attack the next evening, Saturday 29 September. He mustered just seven Gothas while Rfa 501 prepared three R.VI

'Giants' for the attack. Over England the force encountered cloud while a low ground mist hampered the Home Defence squadrons. Many observers, searchlight and gun crews were confused by the sheer noise generated by the massive four-engine 'Giants', whose existence was not yet general knowledge, submitting reports mistaking single aircraft as groups of incoming Gothas. The RNAS sent three aircraft up from the airfield at Manston while the RFC put 30 aircraft in the air, but there were only three brief sightings of hostile aircraft.

German sources report that just two Gothas and one of the R.VI 'Giants' – R.39 – reached the capital. The exact courses taken by the raiders over the capital are hard to define but one headed much further west than usual, dropping a bomb on Notting Hill and two on Putney Common (now Barnes Common) in south-west London, possibly attempting to extinguish a searchlight based there. One of these killed a married couple, 47-year-old George Lyell and his wife, who were walking on the common when the bomb landed. The blast left Lyell's body 'about six yards from where the bomb fell, and the woman on the other side of the road'. A string of five 50kg bombs landed in a line from Waterloo Station to Kennington. The bomb at Waterloo caused extensive damage around the station while another just south of the station, in Mead Row, injured five people and severely damaged 14 houses. A further bomb fell on the lawn of the Bethlem Hospital Lunatic Asylum in Lambeth (now home to the Imperial War Museum); the patients and staff had a miraculous escape as reported in the press: 'Then a remarkable thing happened. One of the patients shouted to the others to lie flat on the ground, and they did so. Immediately there was a loud report and a crashing of glass, woodwork and stone … the bomb had fallen in the grounds of the building, not fifty yards away. Hundreds of windows had been shattered … Yet there was not a single casualty.'

North of the Thames there were two main concentrations of bombs, one on an east–west line across Haggerston and Dalston where nine 12kg explosive bombs

A rare photograph of the flight crew and ground crew of 'Giant' R.39. The man in the centre of the front row is Dietrich Freiherr von Lentz, the senior pilot. The commander of R.39, von Bentivegni, is missing from the photo. (Collection DEHLA)

The 29 September 1917 raid

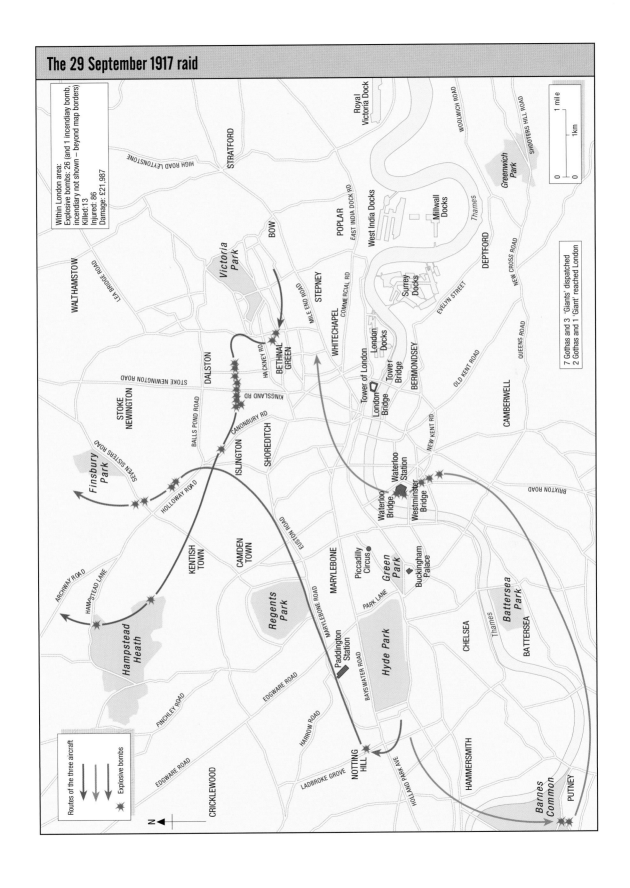

Within London area:
Explosive bombs: 26 (and 1 incendiary bomb,
incendiary not shown — beyond map borders)
Killed: 13
Injured: 86
Damage: £21,987

7 Gothas and 3 'Giants' dispatched
2 Gothas and 1 'Giant' reached London

Routes of the three aircraft
Explosive bombs

1 mile
1km

N

WALTHAMSTOW
LEA BRIDGE ROAD
STRATFORD
HIGH ROAD LEYTONSTONE
Victoria Park
BOW
STEPNEY
POPLAR
EAST INDIA DOCK RD
Royal Victoria Dock
WOOLWICH ROAD
SHOOTERS HILL ROAD
Greenwich Park
MILE END ROAD
West India Docks
Millwall Docks
Thames
DEPTFORD
NEW CROSS ROAD
STOKE NEWINGTON
DALSTON
STOKE NEWINGTON ROAD
HACKNEY RD
BETHNAL GREEN
KINGSLAND RD
WHITECHAPEL
COMMERCIAL RD
London Docks
Surrey Docks
EVELYN STREET
QUEENS ROAD
Finsbury Park
SEVEN SISTERS ROAD
BALLS POND ROAD
CANONBURY RD
ISLINGTON
SHOREDITCH
Tower of London
London Bridge
Tower Bridge
BERMONDSEY
OLD KENT ROAD
CAMBERWELL
ARCHWAY ROAD
HAMPSTEAD LANE
HOLLOWAY ROAD
KENTISH TOWN
CAMDEN TOWN
EUSTON ROAD
Waterloo Station
Waterloo Bridge
Westminster Bridge
NEW KENT RD
BRIXTON ROAD
Hampstead Heath
Regents Park
MARYLEBONE
MARYLEBONE ROAD
Piccadilly Circus
Green Park
Buckingham Palace
FINCHLEY ROAD
EDGWARE ROAD
Paddington Station
BAYSWATER ROAD
PARK LANE
Hyde Park
CHELSEA
Thames
Battersea Park
BATTERSEA
HARROW ROAD
EDGWARE ROAD
CRICKLEWOOD
NOTTING HILL
LADBROKE GROVE
HOLLAND PARK AVE
HAMMERSMITH
Barnes Common
PUTNEY

fell, and another running north-west across Islington towards Hampstead Heath.

In Dalston two bombs fell in Shrublands Road. One exploded in a back garden killing two children, William and Ethel Lee, who were in the kitchen with their parents. In another house, at 34 Mortimer Road, two women were sheltering with nine children when a bomb exploded, again in the back garden. The blast smashed through the kitchen window killing a soldier's wife, 32-year-old Mabel Ward, and her six-year-old son Percy.

However, the worst casualty list of the night came in Holloway at The Eaglet public house. On hearing the 'take cover' warning, the landlord, Edward Crouch, sent his wife and child down to the cellar to take cover. A number of customers and passers-by rushed down too but Crouch remained in the bar counting the takings. Moments later a 50kg bomb 'struck the wooden cellar flap just outside the entrance, penetrated to the cellar, and exploded forcing everything upwards'. The stunned landlord's last memory was of a terrific crash and the floor blown to pieces. The devastating explosion killed his wife and three others and injured 32.

The intense anti-aircraft barrage probably forced the raiders to turn away early. One newspaper reported that the bombardment was 'unprecedented in this country' and went on to remind its readers that 'Shrapnel cases and bullets, if fired into the air, must obviously fall somewhere, and it is utter folly for people to stand about in the streets, in open doorways, or at windows.'

This was a very real danger. That night the police recorded 276 anti-aircraft shells falling on London; two landing in Chiswick High Road injured 11, one in Goldhawk Road, Shepherd's Bush, killed a man and elsewhere across the city another 13 people were injured. That night estimates show some 300,000 people took shelter in Underground stations.

The attacking aircraft did not get away without loss either. One Gotha crashed in Holland, resulting in internment for the crew, and it appears likely that the Dover AA guns shot down another over the sea.

If the hard-pressed defenders hoped for a lull in the attacks to enable them to take stock they were to be disappointed; the following night – 30 September – the raiders returned again. It was the night of the full moon, the weather in London had been good and the population waited nervously, expecting another attack. Kleine mustered just 11 Gothas for the attack, and then, as usual, once airborne one quickly dropped out. The attacking aircraft came in between 6.45 and 8.15pm. The RFC flew 35 defensive sorties in response with the RNAS putting up two aircraft from Manston. According to an RFC report, 'Three pilots thought that they saw Hostile machines and two of these pilots opened fire', but without result. Once again the over-worked gun barrage prepared to deflect the attack. Out in the western sub-command of the London guns, Lt Col Alfred Rawlinson bleakly summed up his command: owing to cuts in personnel he had '... the very smallest number of men which would suffice to work the guns ... these men were necessarily of indifferent physique, such as did not

The Eaglet public house, on the corner of Seven Sisters Road and Hornsey Road. During the raid on 29 September a bomb exploded in the cellar causing over 30 casualties.

permit their employment at the Front … they were hurriedly and recently trained … there were no reserves, and it was therefore necessary to keep every man, however exhausted, at his post at all costs …'

On the night of 30 September Rawlinson reported that a number of his guns each fired 'over 500 rounds'. With the barrels becoming red hot, and despite pouring cold water over them, he had to call 'cease fire' at times to assist cooling. The hot barrels also caused rounds to jam. In an attempt to get the guns firing again as soon as possible he issued the extremely dangerous non-regulation order, 'Jam another round in behind it and fire it out'.

According to one newspaper account, 'it was just half past seven when the distant booming of the guns was heard' and the reporter watched and listened as, 'Closer and closer came the noise of guns until it developed into a veritable roar.' The barrage fire was intense and threatening to the attacking crews. Reports indicate that only six aircraft reached London that night and their stay over the capital was brief and generally ineffective; the police and fire service recorded only 22 explosive and 14 incendiary bombs. Most of the damage occurred in East London where bombs fell in Wanstead, Poplar, Plaistow and Barking. At Fairfoot Road, Bromley-by-Bow, 'a narrow thoroughfare of two-storeyed residences', a bomb fell on No. 3, completely demolishing it, killing an 80-year-old man, and injuring a sailor on leave, his wife, another woman and a child. It also damaged another 12 houses in the road. About three-quarters of a mile to the south, a bomb on Southill Street, Poplar, injured nine and two bombs exploded around the Midland Railway cleaning sheds at Durban Road, West Ham, damaging three locomotives. In north London a string of bombs fell across Archway and Highgate with the last three falling in Parliament Fields where they damaged a cricket pavilion. Finally, in south-east London two explosive and two incendiary bombs fell in and around the Woolwich Royal Dockyard, with most damage occurring around Trinity Road.

In spite of the intensity of the aerial barrage – just over 14,000 shells fired over London and south-east England (9,000 by LADA) at the ten raiding aircraft – and the claims of a Dover gun crew to have brought down a homeward-bound Gotha, all aircraft appear to have returned safely. Total casualties of the raid were one killed and 19 injured by bombs, with another two killed and 12 injured by AA shells.

Undeterred, Kleine ordered Kagohl 3 to attack again the next night, Monday 1 October. In London that night the weather was fine; there was good visibility with little wind and no clouds, but a ground mist increased during the night hindering German navigation and preventing some British squadrons getting airborne. Kleine dispatched 18 Gothas but it appears six turned back. The leading aircraft crossed the coast at 6.50pm, the last not until two hours later. The RFC managed to get 18 aircraft in the air but only one pilot caught a brief glimpse of a raider. The AA guns experienced problems too. The constant firing over the last few days meant many were running short of ammunition and others – with a lifespan estimated at 1,500 rounds – were coming to the end of their usefulness. To preserve them as long as possible an order restricted each burst of barrage fire that night to last no longer than one minute.

A combination of the barrage fire and ground mist meant that perhaps only six Gothas arrived over London, dropping bombs between 8.00 and 10.00pm. The first bomb fell in north London near the Edmonton Gas Works, followed by one that fell directly in the Serpentine in Hyde Park, then four 50kg bombs landed in Belgravia and Pimlico close to Victoria Station. One of these bombs, dropping in Glamorgan Street, claimed the lives of four friends sheltering from the raid. Frederick Hanton and Leo Fitzgerald, both 18, and George Fennimore and Henry Greenway, both 17, all played for the same football team and all died in the blast, killed by splinters from the bomb. A few bombs landed in the Highbury–Finsbury Park area; one in Canning Road, Highbury, killed Harriet Sears, a 78-year-old woman, and damaged 36 houses. The most damage though was concentrated within a few streets in Shoreditch, between Haggerston and Hoxton. In a matter of seconds 16 50kg bombs fell on a north–south line parallel with the Kingsland Road. The police records show that these bombs damaged about 770 houses (damage ranging from houses demolished to windows smashed); they also killed four people living in Hows Street and injured eight in Maria Street, six in Caesar Street, two in both Laburnum Street and Pearson Street, and one in Nichol Square.

Shortly after 10.00pm the last raider departed the skies over London and 'the firing practically ceased, only an occasional distant boom of the guns being heard, and all was quiet at 10.20.' It was of course anything but a quiet night for those left searching for casualties amongst the piles of rubble that had moments before been homes. Total losses in London that night amounted to 11 killed and 41 injured, with material damage in and around the capital estimated at £44,500.

Although Londoners could not know it at the time, the raid of 1 October 1917 marked the end of the Harvest Moon offensive. A dramatic change in the weather put a halt to further raids by Kagohl 3 for the next four weeks. Five raids had reached London in the eight days of the offensive, yet from a German viewpoint the results were disappointing; the authorities recorded 151 bombs in London (94 explosive and 57 incendiary) with material damage estimated at £117,773 and casualties confirmed at 50 killed and 229 injured. However, the raids were producing some of the effects outlined in the orders for Operation *Türkenkreuz*; production of munitions at Woolwich Arsenal fell significantly during the raids: on the night of 24 September the production of .303 rifle ammunition fell by 84per cent and the following night it was down by 77per cent. And many Londoners, a great number of whom now regularly slept on crowded and insanitary station platforms, were suffering from stress and shattered nerves.

Caesar Street (now Nazrul Street), near Kingsland Road, suffered badly on the night of 1 October. Three 50kg bombs fell on the street, demolishing numbers 21, 23 and 41, causing major damage to 11 houses and lesser damage to 40 others.

A BRIEF RESPITE

In this welcome lull, efforts to improve the ammunition supply to the AA guns were successful and the poor condition of the guns received attention; each month 20 worn-out guns were scheduled for relining. In addition, the production output of 3in 20cwt AA guns for October, earmarked for arming merchant ships, was reassigned to the London defences, while local authorities began requisitioning buildings with suitable basements as shelters and the press were told to moderate their reports of the bombing. The first two of the proposed balloon aprons, approved to cover the approaches to London, from Tottenham in the north around the east via Wanstead, Ilford, Barking, Plumstead to Lewisham, south-east of the city, were in operation in early October. Both were in Essex, one about a mile south-east of Barking and the other about 2 miles east of Ilford. To aid sound detection, experiments were under way with a 'sound reflector' cut into the chalk cliffs near Dover – first used during the night of the 1 October raid. Other experiments using pairs of horns fixed on vertical and horizontal arms – sound locators – proved that when accurately adjusted they could give a trained operator an indication of the height, direction and distance of incoming aircraft. And after

Balloon apron cables extended for 1,000 yards, held aloft by three balloons. From the cable 1,000ft-long steel wires hung down, 25 yards apart, their purpose being to force attacking aircraft up to a predictable height where the AA guns could concentrate their fire as well as presenting an obstacle to incoming raiders.

much public pressure the government authorized a committee to investigate retaliatory bombing of German towns and cities. The RFC and RNAS were already bombing the Kagohl 3 airfields in Belgium and at the end of September these nagging attacks on Sint-Denijs-Westrem and Melle-Gontrode forced Kleine to redistribute the *Kasta* around the Ghent airfields. On 4 October, in a brief respite from the stresses of command, Kleine received the Pour Le Mérite in recognition of his recent London raids. Meanwhile, while Kleine waited for a forecast of good weather, the pilots of the RFC continued to familiarize themselves with the complexities of flying their latest fighter aircraft at night.

THE BOMBERS RETURN

With an improvement in the weather, Kleine prepared the *Englandgeschwader* for an attack on the night of 31 October, the day after the full moon. He mustered 22 Gothas, and this time they all reached England. Kleine hoped the staggered take-off pattern would ensure a constant flow of raiders over London for a three-hour period, and with half the bombs loaded this time being incendiaries he hoped to start major fires all over the city. The first aircraft crossed the Kent coast at about 10.45pm, the rest came inland, singly or in pairs, over the next two-and-a-half hours. Many, however, were pushed north by crosswinds, abandoned London as a target and attacked towns in Kent instead. German reports claim ten continued to the capital but there were only three main areas that were bombed, suggesting that three aircraft reached south London with perhaps another two getting as far as Erith on the south-eastern approaches. Certainly some 11 explosive and 20 incendiary bombs fell on Erith and neighbouring Slade Green at around 11.45pm – of these, two of the explosive bombs and six of the incendiaries were duds.

Over London clouds began gathering at about 10,000ft, hindering the searchlights and guns – this resulted in the LADA guns firing only 2,000 shells. In the city ' … the warning was soon followed by the report of distant gunfire, heavy, rapid and muffled. Presently nearer guns joined in the bombardment, and then for nearly a couple of hours sleep was impossible.'

An attack developed over the Isle of Dogs at about 12.45am, possibly by two aircraft, when a bomb that dropped on Maria Street, just off West Ferry Road, damaged about 100 houses. Further bombs fell on Greenwich Park, where an incendiary just missed the Royal Observatory and three others fell between the entrance to the Blackwall Tunnel and South Metropolitan Gas Works, but two of them, both incendiaries, failed to ignite. Another incendiary fell on the works of a paint company based on the Thames at Charlton where it burnt out a storeroom, before eight explosive bombs dropped harmlessly over the Belvedere marshes as the aircraft headed home.

The final attack of the night developed over Tooting in south-west London at about 1.30am, marked by a steady string of 13 explosive bombs between there and Streatham. In Crockerton Road a bomb killed two people standing in an open doorway and injured two others. Half a mile further on, in Romberg Road, three died, one of them, 13-year-old Boy Scout Alfred Page, while waiting to go out and sound the 'all clear' on his bugle. The bomb also killed his father and injured a woman and two children. An eyewitness recalled that 'the roof of the house, the walls, and the furniture were reduced to a chaotic mass of brick and plaster, wood and iron'. From Streatham the aircraft appears to have headed out in a north-easterly direction, dropping bombs on Deptford, Surrey Docks, Millwall Docks and Plaistow as it went.

For Kleine, however, the results were again disappointing. Although 22 aircraft had reached England only 40 explosive and 37 incendiaries (12 of which failed to ignite) were recorded in London, amounting to damage calculated at just £9,536, of which £2,000 was on outlying Erith. Casualties were minimal too: eight killed and 19 injured (five of these by AA shells). And Kleine's disappointment did not end there. Back in Belgium the returning bomber crews found their arrival coinciding with the appearance of a rolling bank of fog. A returning Gotha circled the airfield and later one of the crew recalled that '… the fog showed no sign of thinning, but staying airborne for much longer was impossible; our fuel reserves were almost exhausted … We sank into the fog, with no feeling for our positioning in the air, dropping into the unknown … Death lurked below us, ready to pounce. Seconds lasted for eternities, then: There! The ground! We were safe!'

Other crews were not so fortunate; five crashed and wrecked their aircraft attempting landings in the fog. Bad weather meant it would be over a month before Kleine could try for London again.

While he waited for a gap in the weather, Kleine concentrated on intensive training for his crews; many new men had arrived and were struggling with the demands and stresses of the bombing campaign. In London the population settled into the rhythm of the moon cycle, linking the arrival of the full moon with a return of the raiders, and as the time of the next full moon drew closer – 28 November – Londoners turned once more to the safety of the Underground stations. But good weather did not coincide and Kleine's men did not come.

The moon was in its last quarter when Kleine received news of a break in the weather – meaning a very dark night by which to navigate. However, he grasped the opportunity and readied Kagohl 3, and for only the second time Rfa 501 joined the raid with two Staaken 'Giants'. Disappointed by the previous raid's failure to set London burning, this time the great majority of bombs loaded were incendiaries.

THE FAILURE OF THE FIRESTORM

The night of 5/6 December 1917 was freezing on the ground in London, there was frost and ice on windows, in the air the cold must have been almost unbearable. In Belgium 19 Gothas and two 'Giants' set course for England – three Gothas turned back early. The first crossed the Kent coastline at about 1.30am on 6 December and many of the raiding force targeted Kent with their bombs, including one of the 'Giants'. Later the other 'Giant' came inland but it too shied away from London. Although taken by surprise with the raid developing in the early hours of a dark morning, the RFC still put up 34 aircraft, including No. 39 Squadron's two new high-performance Bristol Fighters, but no pilots located any enemy aircraft. The first of the six Gothas to penetrate the London defences approached the outer barrage at about 4.30am. When the first bombs began to fall at around 4.45am most Londoners were still asleep in their beds. About 40 incendiaries rained down across Westminster and Chelsea but just over half caused no damage at all, while the rest caused only minor damage. Two other curving, almost parallel, lines of incendiaries were dropped: one from Shaftesbury Avenue over Bloomsbury and Clerkenwell towards Hoxton, Bethnal Green and Mile End, while the other followed a line from Somerset House in Aldwych up through Holborn, Farringdon, along Old Street, over Spitalfields and Whitechapel. These two bombing runs dropped about 90 incendiaries between them yet only three serious fires resulted. The most dramatic was just north of Liverpool Street Station, in Curtain Road at the junction with Worship Street. There a single bomb burnt out a cabinetmaker's factory and that of L. Rose and Co., producers of Rose's lime cordial. The London Fire Brigade estimated material damage caused by this fire at £45,400. A second serious conflagration occurred at 113 Whitechapel Road where the flames also engulfed a number of adjoining premises involved in the clothes trade, causing damage estimated at £16,385. The third fire was at the Acorn Works in Henry Street (now Roger Street) off Gray's Inn Road. A bomb here set alight a range of buildings, recording damage estimated at £13,500.

Other bombing runs took place over south-west London (about 54 bombs: three explosive and 51 incendiary) in Lambeth, Kennington and Battersea as well as Clapham, Brixton and Balham, while in south-east London 68 bombs (nine explosive and 59 incendiaries) fell in Lewisham, Brockley, Sydenham, Dulwich and Lee. Despite dropping over 120 bombs south of the Thames the results were extremely limited. A fire at the Sunnybank Laundry by Vauxhall

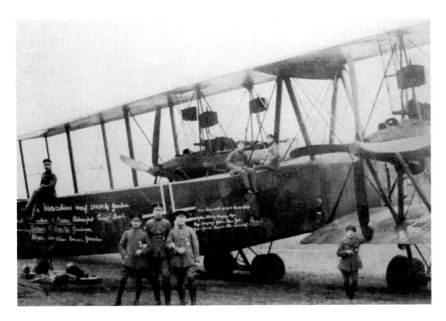

The single model R.IV-type Staaken 'Giant', the R.12, with its crew. Unlike the R.VI-type, which had four engines, the R.IV had six – two 160hp Mercedes D.III and four 220hp Benz Bz.IV – driving three propellers.

Park caused £2,000 of damage to the premises. Explosive bombs caused damage to a tenement in Burgoyne Road, Stockwell, while another landed in a garden in Paradise Road, close to Stockwell station, injuring three children. The most deadly blast took place when a 50kg explosive bomb dropped in College Road, Dulwich. Here, at a property owned by the British Red Cross Society, the bomb exploded in a room where the caretaker's wife, Edith Howie, and her 13-year-old niece were sleeping, killing both. Her husband, who was in the kitchen at the time, reported that the 'force of the bomb was such as to blow my wife and the child through the roof.'

The barrage had once again given the German crews plenty to think about and for those inexperienced in the task often proved effective in turning them from their intended course. And for the first time it appears one of the London guns inflicted critical damage to a Gotha over the city. *The Times* reported that '... a series of shell-bursts culminated in one which apparently struck a raider. Loud cheers were raised, and cries of "Got him!" The enemy machine was seen to wobble and descend slowly to the north.'

Shrapnel peppered the Gotha, crewed by Lt S.R. Schulte, Lt P.W. Barnard and Vfw B. Senf, damaging the port radiator. This gradually caused the engine to overheat and, once it caught fire, the crew knew they would have to try to land. They then came under fire from a mobile AA gun at Herne Bay and also a Lewis gun based at Bekesbourne airfield, which may have scored hits, but by then the damage was already done; the Gotha crash-landed in a field near Canterbury. The crew set fire to the wreckage of their aircraft and surrendered to a local special constable.

The types of P.u.W aerial bomb available to the German air force in 1918. From left to right: 50kg, 100kg, 300kg, 1,000kg, while the soldier in the centre holds a 12.5kg bomb.

Another aircraft, a Gotha G.V, that failed to reach London, had a propeller shot away by AA gunfire while over Canvey Island, Essex. Looking for somewhere to land the pilot, Gemeiner J. Rzechtalski, steered towards the lights of Rochford airfield but they clipped a tree on their approach and crashed on a nearby golf course. The pilot and his fellow crew members, Lt R. Wessells and Vizefeldwebel O. Jakobs, crawled from the wreckage into the arms of their surprised captors. Later, when a group of officers was inspecting the wreck they lost a valuable prize when a signal pistol picked up by one went off accidentally and set the petrol-soaked wreck ablaze. Another Gotha failed to return, presumed forced down and lost at sea, while two more limped back and crash-landed in Belgium; a final aircraft crashed as it landed at its home airfield.

Kleine lost six of his 16 attacking aircraft, yet, despite dropping over 260 incendiary and 13 explosive bombs, total damage in the London area was estimated at £92,303 of which about half occurred at one site. The bombs killed two civilians and injured seven, while falling AA shells killed a man in Wanstead and injured eight others across London. Kleine's great hope to set London ablaze had failed. The problem was that so many of the incendiary bombs fell in roadways or gardens where they burnt out and those that did ignite could be extinguished by a determined person with water or sand if they could get to them early enough; others just failed to ignite. Ten years later, Major Hilmer von Bülow, a historian of the German air force wrote:

> A great deal of time was spent over the design of these incendiary bombs, on whose effect on the densely populated London area such high hopes were based. The bomb was a complete failure. During the two night raids on England, on the 31st of October and the 6th of December, 1917, large numbers of these bombs were dropped, both times with no success. The sound idea of creating panic and disorder by numbers of fires came to nothing owing to the inadequacy of the material employed.

In Germany technicians were working on a new foolproof incendiary bomb – the Elektron bomb – although it would not be ready for deployment until August 1918. But Hptmn Rudolph Kleine was not to see it developed. Six days after the 6 December raid, Kleine led Kagohl 3 on a raid against British encampments near Ypres. Pounced upon by a patrol of No. 1 Squadron, RFC, Kleine's crew lost the battle; later a German soldier discovered Kleine's body on

Skeleton of Lower Right-hand Wing
The Remains of the Fabric can be seen

Framework of Aileron or Balancing Flap

Framework of Aileron or Balancing Flap

Framework of Aileron or Balancing Flap

Framework of Upper Left-hand Wing

the ground, his Pour le Mérite still around his neck. The loss of Kleine did nothing to help the failing morale of Kagohl 3, already struggling with the constant attrition amongst its crews. Temporary command passed to Oblt Richard Walter, Kagohl 3's senior flight commander.

A SUCCESS IN THE SKY

On Tuesday 18 December, after less than a week in command, forecasters alerted Walter to a break in the weather and, although his predecessors had relied on the light of the full moon, he took the opportunity and launched his first attack on this dark night. That night Kagohl 3 did so under a new designation: Bombengeschwader 3 der OHL (Bogohl 3).

In London a thin mist hung over the Thames, with the moon described as a 'thin sickle clear cut in an inky sky'. Fifteen Gothas set out on the raid with two dropping out before reaching England. On this occasion a lone Staaken 'Giant' – the R.12, the single R.IV type – also joined the raiding force. Reports estimate that six Gothas evaded the barrages and made it through to London, where bombing runs took place between 7.15 and 8.30pm. R.12 reached the capital later, just after 9.00pm. With the unanticipated appearance of enemy aircraft on a dark night the warning system was caught off guard and notification of the

The wreckage of one of the two Gothas shot down in the early hours of 6 December 1917. One landed at Sturry near Canterbury, the other crashed on a golf course while attempting an emergency landing at Rochford airfield. All crew members survived.

The 18 December 1917 raid

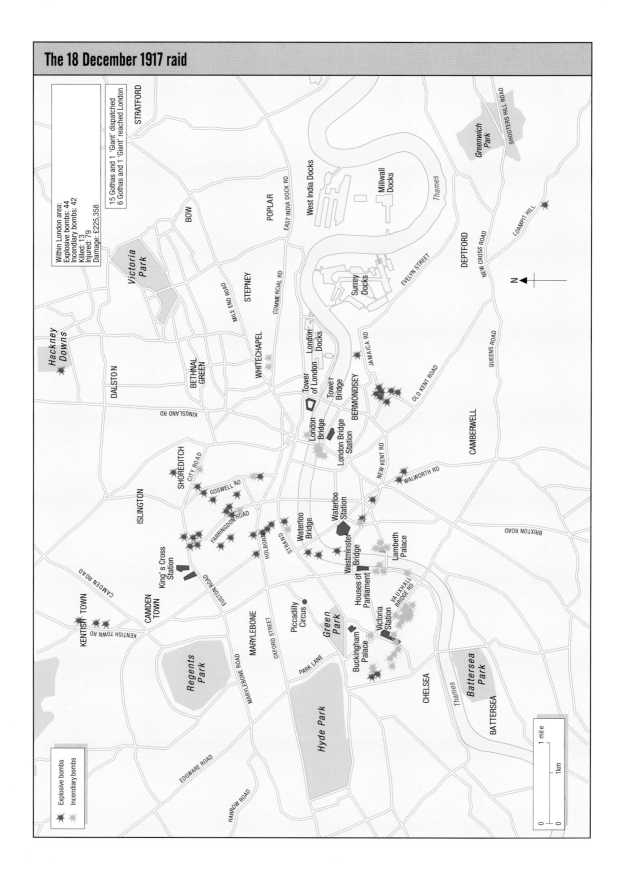

Within London area:
Explosive bombs: 44
Incendiary bombs: 42
Killed: 13
Injured: 79
Damage: £225,358

15 Gothas and 1 'Giant' dispatched
6 Gothas and 1 'Giant' reached London

Explosive bombs
Incendiary bombs

1 mile
1km

imminent raid was received too late to send out warnings. The first bomb appears to have fallen on 187 Westminster Bridge Road, followed moments later by another on the Victoria Embankment, close to Cleopatra's Needle, just a short distance from where a previous bomb fell on 4 September. The bomb killed three women and Henry King, a 38-year-old special constable, as they stood at a tram stop. An incendiary bomb landed on Murdoch's piano manufacturers at 91 Farringdon Road causing a huge fire. A further cluster fell close to the junction around King's Cross Road and Pentonville Road around 7.33pm, damaging over 120 houses, killing two children and injuring 22 civilians and a policeman before the aircraft flew out over Hackney Downs, where one final bomb dropped at about 7.45pm. A second aircraft followed a similar line, dropping bombs around Temple, Chancery Lane, Lincoln's Inn, Gray's Inn and ending the run over Kentish Town where it dropped three explosive bombs. Other bombs fell in Goswell Road, Aldersgate Street and a couple in Whitechapel. South of the Thames, a small cluster fell in Bermondsey and Walworth, with most damage occurring in Spa Road, Bermondsey, where four explosive bombs fell close together. Two of these caused extensive damage to buildings owned by the Salvation Army where people took shelter during the

The engineers' compartment in the nose of 'Giant' R.12, containing the two 160hp Mercedes engines. Unlike the R.VI-types, the R.IV had an open cockpit for the pilot which can be seen on the left.

raids. A Mrs Gibbons who lived in the road rushed there with her five children and waited until '… a loud explosion occurred and the lights went out; the suspense was awful as we waited expecting the roof to fall in. In the midst of the confusion a voice shouted, "No lights! I'll shoot the first man to light a match!" We afterwards learned that a gas main had burst.'

Commander of the Gotha that bombed Bermondsey was Oblt G. von Stachelsky, with Lt Friedrich Ketelsen and Gefreiter A. Weissmann as crew. It flew in over Essex where Capt G.W. Murlis-Green, the commanding officer of No. 44 Squadron, closed in to attack, attracted by searchlights and the Gotha's two exhaust flares. His first attack failed when the muzzle flash from his guns temporarily blinded him. Ketelsen flew on and moments later Stachelsky began releasing his bombs over Bermondsey. With his night vision restored, Murlis-Green made two more attempts to get into a position to attack, but although he reported his tracers entering the Gotha's fuselage, both times his muzzle-flash forced him away. Every time he attacked, caught in searchlights, he was targeted by Stachelsky with the front machine gun, but he commented that his adversary's 'tracers were always very wide of the mark'. He then closed in for a fourth attack, this time there was no searchlight. He emptied the rest of his ammunition drum into the Gotha at which point it dived steeply in front of him, and as he turned to get out of the way, he was caught in the slipstream, which sent his Sopwith Camel into a spin. By the time he regained control the Gotha had disappeared. But the bomber was in trouble. Bullets had damaged the starboard engine, which finally burst into flames halfway back to the coast. Ketelsen hoped to coax the Gotha back on one engine but it soon became clear that was impossible and he ditched in the sea off the coast at Folkestone at about 9.00pm. An armed trawler prepared to pick up the crew and with Stachelsky and Weissmann already safely on board, Ketelsen slipped from his precarious position on the upper wing and drowned.

While this drama played out, the final attack of the night began as 'Giant' R.12 flew across London and dropped a huge 300kg bomb on Lyall Street, Belgravia. The bomb landed in the roadway gouging a great crater 30 by 20 by 7ft deep. It damaged gas and water mains and about 20 houses close by, including breaking the windows of the Russian Embassy, but there were no casualties. It appears that the rest of the bomb load were incendiaries and these fell across Belgravia, Pimlico, Lambeth – where four bombs fell close to Lambeth Palace, residence of the Archbishop of Canterbury – and three dropped on or around Southwark Cathedral, but this resulted only in slight damage to the roof. The final incendiary bomb appears to have fallen on Billingsgate Fish Market where it caused a small fire.

A total of 43 explosive and 39 incendiary bombs were recorded falling on London, causing material damage estimated at £225,000, the largest single total since the Zeppelin raid of 8/9 September 1915 (£530,000). The final London casualty checks recorded 13 killed and 79 injured. But again, Bogohl 3 sustained heavy losses. With one Gotha confirmed shot down it was clear that the British defences were beginning to come to terms with the night-bomber raids. And back in Belgium the mournful toll continued: two Gothas were lost when they burst into flames on landing and five others sustained damage.

PREPARATIONS FOR A NEW YEAR

Yet Ashmore was not complacent and demanded improvements. The attack by Murlis-Green had been the first recognized successful aerial engagement since the night raids began – one success from countless sorties. Two new Home Defence squadrons were forming to join the roster: Nos 141 and 143. The balloon apron was extending although it never comprised the 20 sections originally envisaged; in the end there were just ten. Improvements in aerial gunnery followed: the new Neame gunsight included an illuminated ring that a Gotha filled at 100 yards' range and work was under way to eliminate the muzzle-flash causing pilots' temporary loss of night vision. A new bullet became available too for use in the Lewis gun – the RTS (Richard Threlfall and Sons) with explosive and incendiary capabilities. The aircraft available for Home Defence improved too as more high-performance types such as the Sopwith Camel, Sopwith Pup, SE5a and the two-seater Bristol F.2B – the Bristol Fighter or 'Brisfit' – joined the squadrons, all capable opponents for the Gothas and 'Giants'.

Breakdown of VI (Home Defence) Brigade, RFC.

The ground defences were overhauled too. A new system of anti-aircraft barrage fire superseded 'curtain' fire. The 'polygon' barrage aimed to surround enemy aircraft with shell bursts instead of presenting a line of fire across their path. Other improvements saw searchlights regrouped and their command system redefined while the observer posts of the Observer Corps, except those on the coast, passed to police control in December 1917. This was in reaction to concerns that those manning them consisted mainly of soldiers unfit for service overseas who in many cases lacked the alertness required for this vital role in the defence system. Demands for more aircraft followed too. At this point estimates showed that 89 day-fighters and 69 night-fighters defended London – although as some aircraft appeared in both sections the efficient strength was about 100 aircraft. Then, one final change followed. The raid on 18 December had caught the defences off guard, preventing the issue of an effective warning to the public. Angry scenes followed and

VI (Home Defence) Brigade Royal Flying Corps – February 1918
No. 46 (Northern) Wing
No. 47 (South Midlands) Wing
London Air Defence Wings
No. 49 Wing
No. 39 Squadron
No. 44 Squadron
No. 78 Squadron
No. 141 Squadron
No. 50 Wing
No. 37 Squadron
No. 61 Squadron
No. 75 Squadron
No. 198 (Night Training) Squadron
No. 53 Wing
No. 50 Squadron
No. 61 Squadron
No. 143 Squadron

London Air Defence Area (LADA), 1918

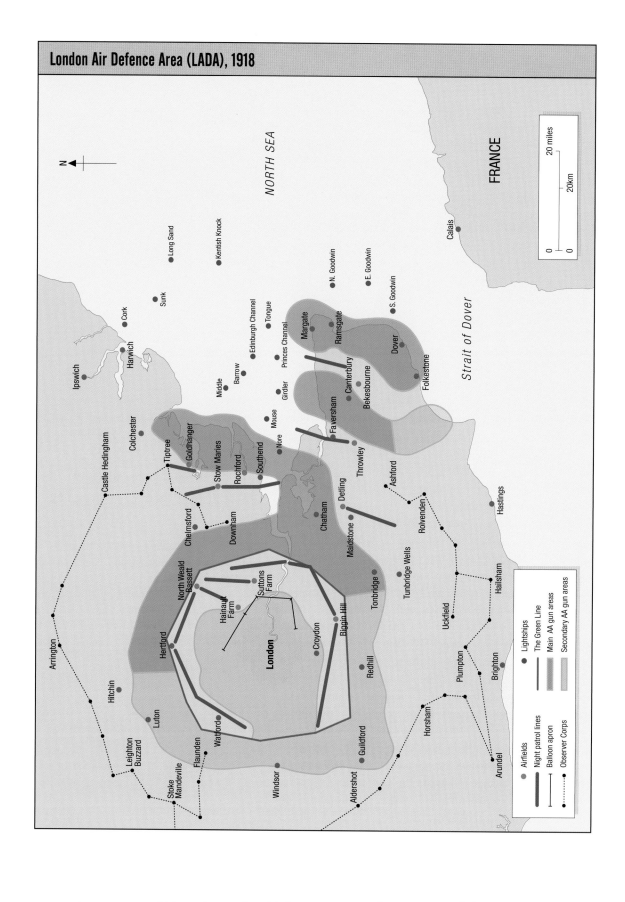

FRANCE

NORTH SEA

Strait of Dover

Calais

N

0	20 miles
0	20km

Long Sand
Kentish Knock
Sunk
Cork
Harwich
Ipswich
N. Goodwin
E. Goodwin
S. Goodwin
Margate
Ramsgate
Dover
Folkestone
Edinburgh Channel
Tongue
Princes Channel
Barrow
Middle
Girdler
Mouse
Nore
Canterbury
Bekesbourne
Faversham
Throwley
Ashford
Colchester
Castle Hedingham
Tiptree
Goldhanger
Stow Maries
Rochford
Southend
Chelmsford
Downham
Chatham
Detling
Maidstone
Hastings
Rolvenden
Tunbridge Wells
Tonbridge
North Weald Bassett
Suttons Farm
Hainault Farm
London
Croydon
Biggin Hill
Hertford
Arrington
Hitchin
Luton
Watford
Flaunden
Leighton Buzzard
Stoke Mandeville
Windsor
Aldershot
Guildford
Redhill
Uckfield
Hailsham
Plumpton
Brighton
Arundel
Horsham

Legend

- Airfields
- Lightships
- ⦿ Observer Corps
- Night patrol lines
- The Green Line
- Balloon apron
- Main AA gun areas
- Secondary AA gun areas

in response the government granted the extension of the use of warning maroons. Previously authorized to warn only of incoming daylight raids, now they could alert the public to the approach of hostile aircraft up to 11.00pm, although later alarms were permitted in instances where the police did not have enough warning to tour the streets with their placards.

While all this was under way Bogohl 3 and Rfa 501 waited impatiently for another chance to strike at London. However, London experienced an extremely cold January with thick blankets of fog wrapped protectively around the city. Back in Germany a new massive 1,000kg explosive bomb was ready, although only one 'Giant' was adapted to carry it, and intensive work continued to perfect the new Elektron incendiary bomb.

THE 1918 BOMBER RAIDS

THE LONG ACRE TRAGEDY

At last the sky looked clear again, and on Monday 28 January 1918 preparations for the first raid of the year were in full swing. But a change was coming and, after 13 Gothas had taken off in their now-usual staggered pattern, fog closed in around the Belgian airfields and prevented the rest following. The fog extended far out to sea too, forcing six of the Gothas to turn back. Two 'Giants' joined the raid, but one soon turned back with engine trouble.

The Gothas crossed the coastline between 7.55 and 8.25pm, with just three attacking London. The other four settled for the less risky option of attacking coastal towns in north-east Kent. The night sky was clear and bright over London when, at about 8.00pm, the night-time air raid warning maroons exploded in the sky for the first time. In Shoreditch big queues were building up outside two music halls and a cinema for the evening performances. These sudden aerial explosions, which many presumed to be German bombs, took the crowds by surprise, causing a rush towards Bishopsgate railway goods yard, which served as a vast air raid shelter. However, as the mass of people struggled to push through the narrow gates, panic set in. When order was finally restored the casualty list recorded 14 killed and 12 injured, crushed and trampled in the press. Another panic, at Mile End railway station, resulted in injuries to two women.

The first Gotha appeared over east London at about 8.45pm, having weaved its way through the defensive barrage and released a series of explosive bombs on Poplar, Limehouse and Stepney before passing over Shadwell and across the

Damage caused by the 100kg bomb that fell on Savoy Mansions, close to Victoria Embankment, early on 29 January. The Air Board had occupied the premises until the Air Ministry replaced that organization at the beginning of the month.

The 28/29 January 1918 raid

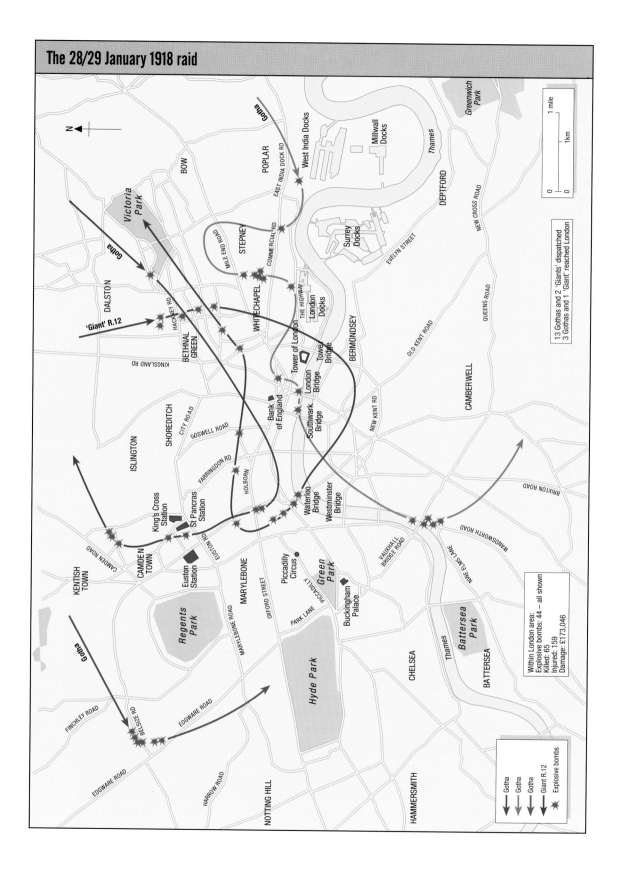

13 Gothas and 2 'Giants' dispatched
3 Gothas and 1 'Giant' reached London

Within London area:
Explosive bombs: 44 – all shown
Killed: 65
Injured: 159
Damage: £173,046

Gotha
Gotha
Gotha
Giant R.12
Explosive bombs

Thames by Cannon Street Station. It resumed bombing over Vauxhall where four bombs killed three men and injured three men, four women and three children.

Twenty minutes later a second Gotha appeared over London, dropping its first bomb at about 9.15pm in a garden in Gore Road, south Hackney, damaging eight houses. The next two bombs fell close together in Holborn causing considerable damage to a printworks before the aircraft turned northwards, dropping bombs close to Euston, King's Cross and St Pancras railway stations, with the last bomb dropping at 9.30pm.

For twenty minutes all was quiet but then, at about 9.50pm, a Gotha G.V, crewed by Lt Friedrich von Thomsen, and Unteroffiziere Karl Ziegler and Walter Heiden, appeared over north-west London and quickly unloaded six bombs on a curving line along Belsize Road towards Maida Vale, before turning eastwards and setting course for home. With a clear sky and a definite improvement in the coordination of London's defences, searchlights picked up the returning Gotha and, as it approached Romford, two No. 44 Squadron Sopwith Camels, piloted by Capt George Hackwill and 2nd Lt Charles Banks, observed its progress and turned to engage. A tremendous running battle developed between the three aircraft as the Camels swooped in to attack and then withdrew again, recovered their positions before attacking again – the whole drama watched closely from below. Then, as Banks turned away with mechanical problems, Hackwill made a fresh attack and this time he met with success – the Gotha shuddered, flames spread and the aircraft went down, crashing at Frund's Farm at Wickford in Essex.

After this last Gotha turned away from London, just before 10.00pm, the guns fell silent over the city, and, although the all-clear did not sound, many took advantage of the lull and left the safety of the shelters to make their way home. However, London's ordeal was not yet over. R.12, the single R.IV-type Staaken 'Giant', crossed the coastline at about 10.25pm and after circling over

The wreckage of Gotha G.V 938/16, brought down at Frund's Farm at Wickford in Essex on 28 January, following repeated attacks by two Sopwith Camels of No. 44 Squadron. All three of the crew died.

Suffolk for some time was now heading towards London. Near Harlow a Bristol Fighter from No. 39 Squadron, flown by Lt J.G. Goodyear and 1st AM W.T. Merchant, attacked R.12 and, after a few ineffectual exchanges, bullets from one of R.12's six or seven machine guns splattered along the Brisfit wounding Merchant in the arm and smashing the main petrol tank. With his engine stopped Goodyear turned away and expertly glided down to North Weald airfield to make a perfect landing.

Undeterred, R.12 continued towards London, approaching the city at about 12.15am. The 'Giant' encountered heavy barrage fire but dropped its first bombs on Bethnal Green and Spitalfields, killing one and injuring 18, these bombs also demolishing three houses and damaging over 300. R.12 then crossed the Thames and began turning until it recrossed the river by Waterloo Bridge where a bomb dropped in the water. The next smashed into Savoy Mansions causing considerable damage to the building; moments later bombs landed in the Flower Market at Covent Garden, Long Acre, Bedford Place and Hatton Garden before R.12 dropped two final bombs on Bethnal Green and set course for home.

But it was the bomb that fell in Long Acre that left the most traumatic mark on London that night. The basement of Odhams Printing Works, a four-storey building in Long Acre with 10in thick concrete floors on the two lower levels,

The devastation caused by the 300kg bomb dropped on Odhams Printing Works, Long Acre – an official air raid shelter. One of the huge printing presses has fallen through the floor and rolls of paper hang precariously on the upper floors. The tally of 38 killed and 85 wounded was the most caused in London by a single bomb throughout the war.

was an official air raid shelter. People started arriving just after 8.00pm when the maroons fired their warning. The bomb dropped by R.12 was a massive 300kg of high explosive; it missed the building but smashed through the pavement and exploded in one of the basement rooms. The blast shook the foundations and fire quickly spread through huge rolls of newsprint stored there. Some of those sheltering in the basement stumbled, bewildered, from the building as fire crews, policemen, ambulances and soldiers rushed to help. One woman, haunted by what she witnessed, recalled that 'there were shrieks and cries and blood and shattered walls and burning wood and bodies stretched on the floors'.

But as the rescuers began to pull people from the rubble, one of the outer walls gave way, collapsing inwards, and the weight falling on the heavy printing presses forced the floors to collapse and crush down on the basement. A boy, J. Sullivan, who had been in the shelter playing with two friends, was knocked unconscious by the first blast. His recollections tell of some of the horrors encountered by those who survived: '... when I regained my senses it was like a nightmare. Everything seemed to be alight and falling on me. I was pinned to the ground with a piece of machine across my legs. My two playmates were missing and no trace was ever found of them. I can vividly remember women and children, bleeding and burning, lying near me, and one woman with her dress blazing actually ran over me.'

The devastation was immense and the rubble so extensive that it was not until March, some six weeks later, that the last two bodies were recovered. The final toll was 38 killed (nine men, 19 women and ten children) and 85 injured (43 men, 28 women and 14 children), the most casualties caused by a single bomb on London during the war. Total casualties for the raid on the city amounted to 65 killed and 159 injured (nine of which were caused by anti-aircraft shells). As well as the Gotha shot down in Essex, Bogohl 3 also lost another four aircraft in landing accidents.

THE NIGHT OF THE 'GIANTS'

The following night, Tuesday 29 January, without support from Bogohl 3, Rfa 501 launched four of its 'Giants' against London alone. Only three – all of the R.VI-type – reached England: R.25, R.26 and R.39. The last to cross the coastline was R.26, but having developed engine problems over Essex it returned to base. The first of the two remaining aircraft, R.39, came inland at about 10.05pm and encountered Capt Arthur Dennis, No. 37 Squadron, flying a BE12b. Dennis, flying at 12,000ft moved to 'fairly close range' and attacked. But after a furious exchange of fire, his aircraft became caught up in the 'Giant's' powerful slipstream and he lost sight of his adversary.

R.39 continued towards London after the engagement but it may have lost its bearings as it was over north-west London before it eventually turned

THE FIRST GOTHA SHOT DOWN ON BRITISH SOIL, MONDAY 28 JANUARY 1918

Having completed a bombing run over north-west London, a Gotha G.V – shown in the irregular four-coloured hand-painted night camouflage pattern – crewed by Lt Friedrich von Thomsen, Uffz Karl Ziegler and Walter Heiden, turned for home. Over Essex two Sopwith Camel pilots of No. 44 Squadron, Capt George Hackwill and 2nd Lt Charles Banks, observed the Gotha and turned to attack.

Many on the ground watched the combat develop at about 10,000ft. One report told how one of the Camels swooped from above and took up a position behind and below the Gotha on its left, but probably not more than 25 yards away. The other Camel got under the Gotha's tail and a '… Tremendous machine-gun fire broke out immediately from all three machines.' The Gotha pilot tried to shake off his pursuers 'but the two British pilots kept a grip on him.'

The Gotha 'fought hard, but the British machines hung on, firing for all they were worth'. This running fight continued for about 10 miles. Banks then experienced some mechanical problems and turned away, while Hackwill continued his attack. Then, as the report concluded, a burst from Hackwill hit the Gotha critically and it started to burn.

The Gotha fell as a 'bright ball of flame' and crashed not far from a farmer's house. When the farmer reached the crash site the wreckage was ablaze and he reported that he 'could see by its light the charred body of a German, and two others were observed burning in the aeroplane.'

For their involvement in bringing down the first Gotha on British soil, both Hackwill and Banks received the Military Cross.

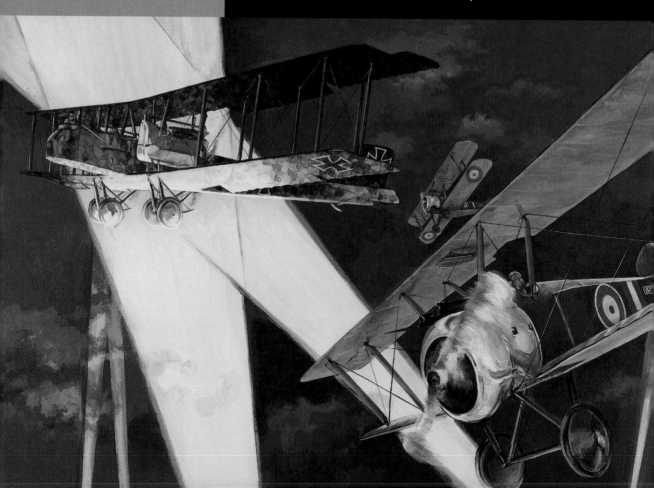

This superb photo shows Staaken 'Giant' R.39 – an R.VI-type – at Scheldewindeke, with R.25 in the background. R.39, commanded by the leader of Rfa 501, Hptmn Richard von Bentivegni, was the only aircraft raiding England adapted to carry the 1,000kg bomb. (Collection DEHLA)

southwards. Then, following a tortuous course over the south-western suburbs it appeared over the Old Deer Park, Richmond and Syon Park at about 11.30pm, dropping 16 incendiary and two explosive bombs which caused little or no damage. R.39 then turned east and began dropping an extended string of explosive bombs. The first, tragically, demolished a house in Whitestile Road, Brentford. George Bentley was on his way home when he '… saw an aeroplane caught in the beam of a searchlight. At the same moment a man a few yards in front of me dived to the ground and shouted to me to lie down, which I did … There were three deafening thuds and flashes.'

Bentley rushed to his house, which had suffered in the blast, but, finding his family were uninjured, he then ran to Whitestile Road where he discovered that the bomb had hit the house of a friend, Sgt Maj Kerley, serving with the Middlesex Regiment. As he stared at the devastation he heard a groan. Bentley clambered over the rubble, then, he later recalled: 'I pulled and wriggled my way into the cellar, which was full of gas and water, and in the darkness came across a young woman, only just alive. Most of her clothes were blown off her. With help I managed to get her to the surface, but by that time she was dead.'

By next morning the bodies of Sgt Maj Kerley's wife, May, their five children, aged three months to 12 years, a 22-year-old niece – Hilda Kerley – and an elderly woman lodger had all been recovered from the wreckage.

After the bombs on Brentford, R.39 dumped eight in close concentration on the Metropolitan Water Board Works by Kew Bridge on the north bank of the River Thames. These bombs caused considerable damage in the area and claimed the lives of two men at the waterworks. Another two dropped in Chiswick High Road, damaging 72 houses before the last fell in Park Road, Chiswick, after which R.39 crossed the Thames and took a homeward course south of the river. Three RFC pilots attempted to engage the returning 'Giant' but it shrugged off all their attacks.

The other 'Giant' to reach London, R.25, came inland at about 10.50pm. The crew brushed off an attack from a No. 37 Squadron BE2e and then, 20 minutes later, a Sopwith Camel of No. 44 Squadron observed R.25 near North Benfleet and attacked. The pilot, 2nd Lt R.N. Hall, tried to close in but every time he did his guns jammed. Another pilot from the squadron, 2nd Lt H.A. Edwardes, joined the attack and fired three bursts before his guns jammed; selflessly he then switched on his fuselage light and flew above the 'Giant' to attract other pilots. R.25 'kept turning sharply to the left and right losing height' as it continued towards London. Two more No. 44 Squadron pilots attacked: 2nd Lt T.M. O'Neill and squadron commander Major Gilbert Murlis-Green. O'Neill experienced frustrating problems with his guns as he attacked before losing R.25 in the dark, while Murlis-Green, thwarted at first by the 'short and accurate bursts' of machine-gun fire aimed at him, eventually got below the 'Giant's' tail and opened fire at what he believed was 50 yards' range. However, confusion caused by the Neame gunsight meant that he later discovered the range was far greater. Pilots knew that a Gotha filled the gunsight ring at 100 yards, but little was yet known about the 'Giants'; at almost twice the size of a Gotha, a 'Giant' was much further away when it filled the ring. Murlis-Green reported later that, '… all my R.T.S. [ammunition] looked as if it was detonating on the fuselage of the hostile machine. I kept my triggers pressed and fired one complete double drum of R.T.S. and three quarters of a drum from my second gun. At any moment I expected the hostile machine to burst into flames.'

But R.25 continued on its course. When Murlis-Green later discussed the incident with his pilots they informed him that his bullets were bursting prematurely, at about 100 yards, still short of the target.

This whole experience however must have been sobering for the crew of R.25 for next, with horror, they saw one of the balloon aprons looming up directly ahead. They turned sharply away, released their entire load of 20 explosive bombs over Wanstead shortly after midnight, where they caused negligible damage, and turned for home. Having landed safely back in Belgium the much-relieved and fortunate crew of R.25 discovered 88 bullet holes in their aircraft.

CHELSEA – THE 1,000KG BOMB

In February, Bogohl 3 welcomed back their former commander Ernst Brandenburg after a period of convalescence following his crash just over seven months earlier. Now walking with difficulty on an artificial leg, he found his former command much demoralized by the regular loses they were experiencing, particularly in landing accidents. He immediately suspended any further action by Bogohl 3 and ordered replacement aircraft to return the squadron to full strength.

Therefore, when the next air raid set out on the evening of 16 February, the pilots of Rfa 501 continued the assault on London alone. Five 'Giants' set out but, encountering strong winds, three switched to the secondary target of Dover, leaving just the more powerfully engined R.12 and R.39 to continue towards London. On board R.39 hung a single bomb; weighing 1,000kg, it was 13ft long and the heaviest type dropped from the air during the war.

The two crossed the coast around 9.40pm with R.12 flying a few minutes ahead. At about 10.15pm, R.12, commanded by Oblt Hans-Joachim von Seydlitz-Gerstenberg and piloted by Lt Götte, was approaching Woolwich in south-east London at a height of 9,500ft when suddenly before them loomed a section of the balloon apron. Götte made a desperate attempt to avoid the steel cables but his starboard wing made contact and threw R.12 dramatically to the right before it fell out of control to the left. With immense coolness Götte throttled down all engines then opened up the two port engines which allowed him, after plummeting 1,000ft, to regain control and steer away to the south-west. During those anxious moments one of the mechanics saved himself from being thrown out of his engine nacelle only by holding on to the forward exhaust manifold, severely burning his hands. The violent manoeuvres shook free two 300kg bombs which exploded in Woolwich. One demolished a building in Artillery Place, killing five and injuring two, the other blasted a great crater in the road by the parade ground of the Royal Artillery Barracks and damaged St George's Garrison Church; it also killed a nurse and an Australian soldier. A quick inspection of R.12 showed that the encounter with the balloon apron, although no doubt terrifying for the crew, had inflicted only minor damage to the aircraft so they turned over Beckenham, offloaded their remaining eight bombs and turned for home. The bombs fell in a group near Shortlands railway station causing only minor damage in the vicinity.

The leader of Rfa 501, Richard von Bentivegni, commanded R.39, now specially adapted to carry a single massive 1,000kg bomb. He believed he dropped the bomb east of the City but it actually fell in Chelsea, on the north-east wing of the Royal Hospital, home of the Chelsea Pensioners. The bomb killed an officer of the hospital staff and four of his family, but rescuers discovered three children still alive beneath the rubble and debris of the blast.

The dark moonless night aided the two 'Giants' on their way home and although 60 defensive sorties were flown that night there were only three brief sightings. All returned in one piece although R.33, one of those forced back early, limped home on one engine.

On 16 February at about 10.10pm R.39 dropped its single 1,000kg bomb on the north-east wing of the Royal Hospital, Chelsea. The bomb killed five, injured three, destroyed three buildings within the hospital grounds, severely damaged another and caused slight damage to another 200 buildings in the vicinity.

'A FINE PIECE OF SHOOTING'

Despite having only one aircraft available after the experiences of the previous night, Bentivegni ordered R.25 – one of the R.VI-types – to raid London alone on 17 February. R.25 came inland at about 9.45pm and managed to avoid the attention of the RFC on the inward journey, but encountered a stiff barrage fire from the AA guns near Gravesend, Kent. Taking evasive action, R.25 circled around before dropping an incendiary bomb on Slade Green near Erith. Then it continued over Bexley and Eltham before dropping the first of its 19 explosive bombs, on Newstead Road, Lee, and left an evenly spaced trail of destruction right across London, with bombs falling in Hither Green, Lewisham, New Cross, Peckham, Camberwell, Southwark, New Fetter Lane in the City, Holborn and ending, devastatingly, on St Pancras Station. Such was the accuracy of the bombing run that a British analysis of the raid was generous in its praise of the tight grouping of five bombs on the station, describing it as '… by far the most accurate and concentrated fire ever yet brought to bear on any target in London, either by day or night and was a fine piece of shooting by the man responsible for it.' This achievement is often attributed to Lt Max Borchers – however, the credit is due to Hans-Wolf Fleischhauer.

Yet beyond this professional appreciation lay the personal tragedies of the raid. The first 12 bombs caused varying levels of damage to hundreds of properties, killed a soldier home on leave in Searlees Road, Southwark, and injured eight other people.

However, the situation at St Pancras was entirely different. The five bombs fell within seconds of one another on the station and adjoining Midland Hotel. One of the bombs struck a tower of the hotel sending heavy masonry crashing down

On the night of 17 February 'Giant' R.25 – an R.VI type – made a solo raid on London. The accurate concentration of five bombs on St Pancras Station brought technical appreciation from a British observer who described it as 'a fine piece of shooting'

through the building and three exploded on the station. The two that claimed most casualties landed either side of an archway leading through to the platforms where the double blast killed a number of people taking shelter from the raid.

A nurse, one of the first rescuers to arrive, reached the archway that had taken the blast: 'About ten bodies lay there, terribly mutilated; and two or three soldiers must have been among the victims, for we found two caps, three swagger canes and a limb with a puttee on it – all that remained of them, so far as I could see.'

Others had lucky escapes. A family staying in the Midland Hotel sought shelter and eventually found themselves, with others, down in the coal bay of the hotel. Then a terrific crash followed by darkness. One of the family recalled that '… showers of splintering glass fell around us, and coal dust fell, it seemed, by the ton. Those of us who were not lying on the ground bleeding and groaning were practically choking … How long we stayed like that I do not know.'

Eventually rescued, as they staggered from the darkened coal bay a grisly spectacle confronted them: 'When we moved we seemed to be ankle-deep in broken glass; and as we left the ruins matches flickered, and in their light a ghastly sight met our eyes. Dead and injured lay everywhere … Picking our way carefully, we at last came out into the air, to see in the distance flames leaping up to the sky.'

Within the station and hotel the final toll reached 20 killed (including one soldier) and 22 injured (including five soldiers, a sailor and a policeman).

The RFC had 69 aircraft in the sky searching for R.25, but the great noise generated by the aircraft's engines caused wildly conflicting accounts of numbers of enemy aircraft and their position. More than one of the aircraft on patrol found themselves subject to 'friendly fire'. Captain Cecil Lewis of No. 61 Squadron, took it in his stride. In his report he wrote 'Several times I was caught

Here a Bristol Fighter and SE5a (below) take part in a flying display at the Shuttleworth Collection. Captain Cecil Lewis (author of *Sagittarius Rising*), No. 61 Squadron, was flying an SE5a on 17 February 1918 when twice attacked over Essex by 'friendly fire'.

in searchlight beams and over Benfleet was fired at. Shooting very good. Burst exactly at my height (11,000 feet) and put several holes in my machine.'

Later that patrol another RFC pilot attacked Lewis. Unfazed, he added, 'Judging the machine had made a mistake I put my machine into a spin and cleared'.

The extremely cool commander of R.25 was quick to realize the costly effect his solo raid had on the British defences. The London guns alone fired off about 3,800 shells; in his report he wrote 'An attack by a single [Giant] is sufficient to alert the entire British defence system and to cause the expenditure of vast quantities of ammunition. It is seemingly from nervousness that not only anti-aircraft guns in the vicinity of the aircraft but also some 30km distant were being fired blindly into the air.'

Such was the nervous state of the British defences that a full-scale false alarm took place on the following night – 18 February – with 55 defensive sorties flown by the RFC and thousands of shells blasted aimlessly into the sky. In fact, the raiders did not return for almost three weeks.

THE AURORA BOREALIS RAID

Up until now, the aircraft of Rfa 501 had occupied the airfield at Sint-Denijs-Westrem, formally home airfield of Kasta 13 and 14 of Kagohl 3, and still the base for Armeeflugpark Nr. 4, but on 7 March Rfa 501 moved to a new airfield at Scheldewindeke, south of Ghent. It is surprising therefore, amidst the bustle of the move and on a moonless night, that Bentivegni ordered a raid that same evening.

Six 'Giants' took off, one dropped out leaving five to carry out the raid, but only three attacked London: R.13 – the single R.V type – and two R.VI types, R.27 and R.39. Again, R.39 carried a single 1,000kg bomb. The crews found navigation difficult that night. Hauptmann Arthur Schoeller, commanding R.27, left a fascinating report of the raid: 'We approach the coast; the night is so dark that the coastline below us is but a mere suggestion. Under us is a black abyss, no waves are seen, no lights of surface vessels flicker as we head for the Thames estuary at Margate. On our right, in the distant north, is our only light, the weak pulsating glow of the aurora borealis. Ahead of us a black nothingness.'

As the aircraft progressed clouds developed and thickened and it was only when searchlights illuminated the clouds below that Schoeller realized he was over England.

Requesting wireless bearings he discovered he was south-east of London so he turned towards the city, crossed the Thames and, turning southwards over Hampstead, released his bombs just after midnight. The first two fell in the Belsize Park area, followed by three more in St John's Wood. There a bomb on New Street (now Newcourt Street) demolished two houses, killing two families, before another exploded in the road outside Lord's Cricket Ground. Here the blast killed a soldier of the Royal Horse Artillery and Lt Col F.H.A. Wollaston, Rifle Brigade, who was on leave from service in Palestine.

R.27 continued south, crossed back over the Thames, circled in the face of heavy AA fire, then, having one more devastating blow to land, dropped a 100kg bomb in Burland Road, just west of Clapham Common. A mother and daughter heard the bomb explode:

> … there was a dreadful shriek through the air and a terrible thud. A big bomb had landed in the middle of the road. It took the front of four houses clean out, ours being one. My mother had to shake me to make me speak. It just seemed as if we were waiting for the end. Mess, and pandemonium; water rushing everywhere, and the smell of gas, for it had hit the main, and there was a great flame in the road.

R.27 headed home, but with the Belgian coast in sight all four engines seized. A quick investigation revealed that the fuel lines had frozen because of 'water-contaminated gasoline'. Too late to thaw them, Schoeller realized he must crash, but thanks to the great gliding capabilities of the 'Giant' he managed to reach land. Then, using flares to illuminate the ground below, all he could see were trenches and hollows. Considering his options, Schoeller determined his best action, aware that if he hit any obstacle he risked annihilation: 'Therefore, by pulling sharply on the controls I stall the aircraft letting it fall almost vertically against the ground. With a mighty impact it hits in front of a wide ditch. The right landing gear collapses and the right lower wing shatters, but no crew member is injured.'

The terrible destruction caused by the 1,000kg bomb dropped by R.39 on Warrington Crescent, Maida Vale. Amongst the 12 killed in the blast was Lena Ford, who, in 1914, wrote the lyrics for Ivor Novello's hugely popular wartime song, 'Keep The Home Fires Burning'.

The 17 February and 7/8 March 1918 raids

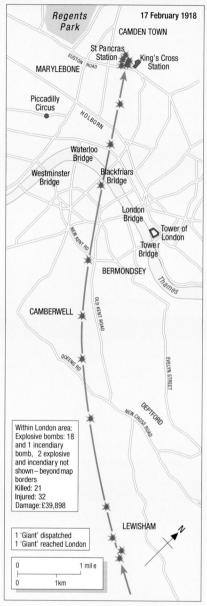

17 February 1918

Regents Park

CAMDEN TOWN

St Pancras Station

King's Cross Station

EUSTON ROAD

MARYLEBONE

Piccadilly Circus

HOLBORN

Waterloo Bridge

Westminster Bridge

Blackfriars Bridge

London Bridge

Tower of London

Tower Bridge

NEW KENT RD

BERMONDSEY

Thames

OLD KENT ROAD

CAMBERWELL

QUEENS RD

EVELYN STREET

DEPTFORD

NEW CROSS ROAD

Within London area:
Explosive bombs: 18 and 1 incendiary bomb, 2 explosive and incendiary not shown – beyond map borders
Killed: 21
Injured: 32
Damage: £39,898

LEWISHAM

1 'Giant' dispatched
1 'Giant' reached London

0		1 mile
0	1km	

LONDON

Main map area

★ Explosive bombs

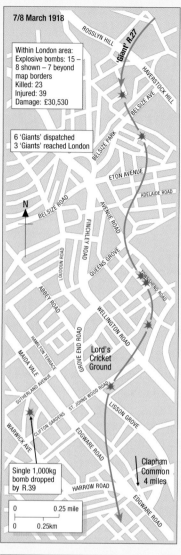

7/8 March 1918

ROSSLYN HILL

'Giant R.27'

HAVERSTOCK HILL

Within London area:
Explosive bombs: 15 – 8 shown – 7 beyond map borders
Killed: 23
Injured: 39
Damage: £30,530

BELSIZE AVE

6 'Giants' dispatched
3 'Giants' reached London

BELSIZE PARK

ETON AVENUE

ADELAIDE ROAD

N

BELSIZE ROAD

AVENUE ROAD

FINCHLEY ROAD

LONDON ROAD

QUEENS GROVE

TOWNSHEND ROAD

ABBEY ROAD

WELLINGTON ROAD

HAMILTON TERRACE

GROVE END ROAD

Lord's Cricket Ground

MAIDA VALE

SUTHERLAND AVENUE

CLIFTON GARDENS

ST JOHNS WOOD ROAD

LISSON GROVE

WARWICK AVE

EDGWARE ROAD

Single 1,000kg bomb dropped by R.39

HARROW ROAD

Clapham Common 4 miles

EDGWARE ROAD

0		0.25 mile
0	0.25km	

CLAPHAM JUNCTION

N

LAVENDER HILL

ST. JOHNS HILL

ELSPETH RD

CLAPHAM COMMON NORTH SIDE

Clapham Common

BATTERSEA RISE

NORTHCOTE ROAD

BOLINGBROKE GRO

CLAPHAM COMMON

THE AVENUE WEST SIDE

WAKEHURST ROAD

WEBB'S ROAD

CHATTO ROAD

BROOMWOOD RD

0		0.25 mile
0	0.25km	

Another aircraft, one of those that did not reach London and believed to be R.36, also made an emergency landing in Belgium and was wrecked.

Back in London, as R.27 had commenced its bombing run, R.39, carrying the single 1,000kg bomb had already completed its mission. The recipient of this steel-encased metric ton of destruction was Warrington Crescent, a quiet residential street in Maida Vale, just over half a mile from Paddington Station.

The Reverend William Kilshaw, living half a mile away, was sheltering in his basement listening to 'the barking of the anti-aircraft guns' as the clock approached midnight: 'Suddenly the darkness of the room was broken in upon by a vivid flash … and a terrific roar caused the whole house to tremble. Our top window panes fell to the ground with a shattering noise … After the bombardment we cautiously went to the window, to behold a scene reminiscent of what one reads of the Great Fire of London. The sky to the east was lurid with flames, in which dense smoke poured: the smitten district was afire.'

The bomb smashed through the roof and dividing wall between Nos. 63 and 65, four-storey Victorian houses, and detonated inside. The blast destroyed the two buildings and the two adjoining. The houses, 'all solidly built, were utterly wrecked, the four houses reduced to hideous piles of wreckage'. The bomb also caused serious damage to another 20 buildings and slight damage to 400 in the surrounding area. It took a number of days before all the bodies were accounted for, the final tally reaching 12 killed and 33 injured. Amongst those killed was an American woman, 48-year-old Lena Ford; it was she who, in 1914, wrote the lyrics to the hugely popular wartime song 'Keep The Home Fires Burning'.

The third of the 'Giants' to reach London, R.13, encountered engine problems as it approached London from the north after midnight. Bombs fell in fields north of Golders Green, at Mill Hill and Whetstone. The last of these exploded at about 12.30am in a garden in Totteridge Lane causing severe damage to houses close by, killing a man and injuring three men, six women and a child. In all, 157 buildings were damaged before R.13 turned away and the crew nursed it home on three of its five engines.

Although the RFC flew 42 defensive sorties, fewer than previous raids due to mist over some of the more eastern airfields, there were no sightings of Rfa 501's raiding aircraft. The evening ended tragically for the RFC when Capt Alex Kynoch, No. 37 Squadron, flying a BE12, and Capt Clifford Stroud, No. 61 Squadron, in an SE5a, collided over Rayleigh, Essex, resulting in the deaths of both pilots.

THE AGONY OF THE 'GIANTS'

London readied itself for the next raid, a raid that people now feared could come at any stage of the moon. However, the skies over London remained empty for the rest of the week, then the month, and the next month too. The reason for the lack of enemy activity over London was the launch of the German army's massive spring offensive, the 'Kaiserschlacht', on the Western Front on 21 March 1918; the army needed all squadrons to support the great advance. It was not until May, after the push to the Channel ports ground to a halt, that attention turned back to London. Then, the largest raid of the war set out for the capital, but not before another night of great loss for the German raiders.

Bentivegni planned a raid with Rfa 501 for the night of 9 May and Brandenburg was keen to launch Bogohl 3 too. However, Brandenburg's weather officer predicted heavy fog that night and advised against it. Brandenburg heeded the advice and duly informed Bentivegni, but the commander of Rfa 501, determined to the point of recklessness, ignored the advice and went ahead.

The weather forecast proved accurate and with fog closing in the four 'Giants' were recalled to Scheldewindeke. Although fog now completely smothered the airfield, the returning aircraft ignored advice to fly to alternate sites and all tried to land anyway. R.32 crashed and exploded on landing and all but one of the crew was killed. R.26 flew into the ground whereupon it burst into flames, again with only one survivor and R.29 was wrecked when it hit some trees; fortunately the crew survived. Only R.39, with Bentivegni on board, managed a successful landing.

THE WHITSUN RAID

The population of London was enjoying a pleasant Whitsun Bank Holiday weekend on Sunday 19 May 1918. Good weather and an absence of German bombers in the skies over the city for ten weeks promoted a relaxed mood. The skies over London that night were clear while 'a lazy breeze scarcely rustled the young leaves of the trees in the garden squares'. Into this peaceful night Germany launched its largest air raid of the war.

While Bogohl 3 focused on bombing missions on the Western Front, Brandenburg always watched for favourable weather over England. The report he wanted finally arrived on 19 May and he wasted no time in preparing 38 Gothas for the raid; this time two single-seater Rumpler aircraft led the way to check the weather ahead. Elsewhere, following the disaster earlier in the month, Bentivegni could add only three 'Giants' to this great aerial armada. Even so, it was London's largest air raid of the war.

Reassured that the weather ahead was clear, the first of the Gothas came inland over the north Kent coast just after 10.30pm, the last appeared around midnight. As with previous raids a number of aircraft were forced to turn back and it appears that 28 Gothas and the three 'Giants' made it inland. Reports from observer posts all over the south-east swamped LADA headquarters, stretching the telephone system to the limit. For the first time aircraft of the recently amalgamated Royal Air Force took off to oppose the raiders; they flew 88 sorties and soon the skies over Kent and Essex buzzed like a hornets' nest.

Captain Quintin Brand, No. 112 Squadron, took off at 11.15pm in a Sopwith Camel and, attracted by searchlight activity, quickly spotted the exhaust flares of a westbound Gotha over Faversham. The Gotha opened up with its machine guns as Brand closed to 50 yards and fired two 20-round bursts from his own guns in return, hitting and stopping the Gotha's starboard engine. The Gotha, crewed by Oblt R. Bartikowski and Vizefeldwebels F. Bloch and H. Heilgers, turned sharply to the north-east and attempted to evade the attack while losing height. Then Brand '… Followed E.A [enemy aircraft] down and closed to 25 yards and fired three bursts of about 25 rounds each. E.A. burst into flames and fell to pieces'.

Although the flames from the burning Gotha enveloped his Camel and scorched his face and moustache, Brand followed the burning wreck down to 3,000ft until he saw it crash on the Isle of Sheppey at 11.26pm. Brand had only been in the air for 11 minutes.

The AA guns along the Thames Estuary were pounding the skies too and it appears only 18 aircraft battled their way through the barrage, the rest repulsed by the onslaught. The Metropolitan Police recorded 72 explosive bombs over a wide area, with just a handful landing in the central area, roughly grouped as follows:

11.30pm Catford, Sydenham, Bexley, Bexleyheath
11.40pm Poplar, Walthamstow, Sidcup
11.45pm St James's, Bethnal Green, Tottenham, Manor Park
11.50pm Lewisham, Bromley
11.55pm Old Kent Road, Rotherhithe, Kilburn
12.00am Forest Gate, Stratford, Peckham, Bexleyheath, Chislehurst
12.10am Hither Green, Lewisham, Lee, Islington, Kentish Town
12.15am Kentish Town, Gospel Oak, Limehouse
12.20am Regent's Park, Marylebone, West Ham, East Ham, Plaistow, Canning Town
12.30am City, Shoreditch, Hackney, East Ham, Barking
12.40am Dalston

The most casualties that night caused by a single bomb were in Sydenham where a 100kg bomb fell in Sydenham Road. The bomb demolished two houses, which incorporated a dairy and bakery, as well as damaging 46 others, claiming the lives of 18 and injuring 14. These casualty figures include three soldiers killed and another 12 injured, all part of a motor transport depot billeted in buildings opposite where the bomb fell. A former soldier of the Royal Army Medical Corps, P. Leach, was one of the first on the scene and thought the scene that confronted him 'like a battlefield afterwards, with the dead and dying: and there were civilians lying dead in the gutter'. Having torn up sheets to make bandages he got to work: 'I found a Sergeant Oliver with his leg crushed to pulp, and I attended to him first. Others were getting the dead out of the shops. Then I

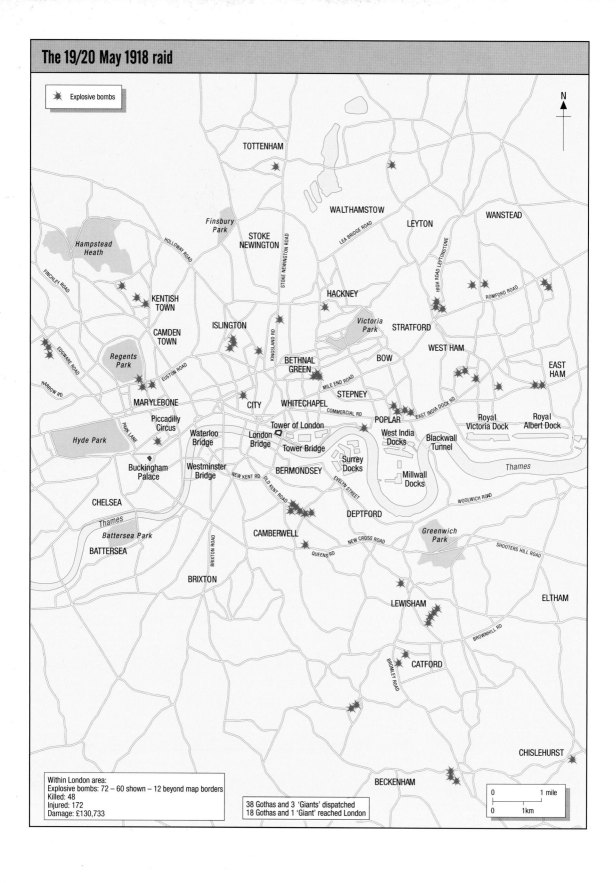

The 19/20 May 1918 raid

Explosive bombs

N

TOTTENHAM

WALTHAMSTOW

LEYTON

WANSTEAD

Finsbury Park

STOKE NEWINGTON

Hampstead Heath

HOLLOWAY ROAD

STOKE NEWINGTON ROAD

LEA BRIDGE ROAD

HIGH ROAD LEYTONSTONE

ROMFORD ROAD

FINCHLEY ROAD

HACKNEY

KENTISH TOWN

Victoria Park

STRATFORD

CAMDEN TOWN

ISLINGTON

KINGSLAND RD

BETHNAL GREEN

WEST HAM

EDGWARE ROAD

Regents Park

EUSTON ROAD

BOW

EAST HAM

HARROW RD

MILE END ROAD

STEPNEY

MARYLEBONE

CITY

WHITECHAPEL

COMMERCIAL RD

POPLAR

EAST INDIA DOCK RD

Royal Victoria Dock

Royal Albert Dock

PARK LANE

Piccadilly Circus

Hyde Park

Waterloo Bridge

Tower of London

London Bridge

Tower Bridge

West India Docks

Blackwall Tunnel

Thames

Buckingham Palace

Westminster Bridge

NEW KENT RD

OLD KENT ROAD

BERMONDSEY

Surrey Docks

EVELYN STREET

Millwall Docks

CHELSEA

Thames

DEPTFORD

WOOLWICH ROAD

Battersea Park

BATTERSEA

BRIXTON ROAD

CAMBERWELL

NEW CROSS ROAD

Greenwich Park

SHOOTERS HILL ROAD

QUEENS RD

BRIXTON

LEWISHAM

ELTHAM

BROWNHILL RD

BROMLEY ROAD

CATFORD

CHISLEHURST

BECKENHAM

Within London area:
Explosive bombs: 72 – 60 shown – 12 beyond map borders
Killed: 48
Injured: 172
Damage: £130,733

38 Gothas and 3 'Giants' dispatched
18 Gothas and 1 'Giant' reached London

0   1 mile

0   1km

THE LARGEST, AND LAST, RAID OF THE WAR, 19/20 MAY 1918

The Whitsun Bank Holiday raid proved to be the last of the war. A Bristol Fighter of No. 39 Squadron picked up one of the Gothas just after midnight, flying north of Hainault at 10,000ft.

The aircraft, flown by Lt Anthony Arkell with Air Mechanic Albert Stagg as observer/gunner, was about 1,000ft higher and dived to attack. Arkell, just 19 years old, brought the Bristol to a position about 200 yards behind the Gotha under its tail to allow Stagg to fire off half a drum. Arkell then 'zoomed up' and fired a long burst from his Vickers before dropping back down to allow Stagg to engage again. Arkell reported that 'All this time Gotha was firing back with tracer.'

Arkell then moved in closer, sitting under the Gotha's tail allowing Stagg to fire off two more drums of ammunition before he 'zoomed up again' and fired another long burst from his forward firing gun. The two aircraft were dropping all the time and, when at 1,500ft Stagg opened fire again, his bullets struck home and the Gotha's starboard engine burst into flames.

As the Gotha plummeted all three of its crew jumped to their deaths. 27-year-old Hans Thiedke's body was found on an allotment in Brooks Avenue, that of Paul Sapkowiak, also aged 27, in 'a ditch some 300 yards south of the aeroplane wreckage' and the body of the 20-year-old Wilhelm Schulte, a quarter of a mile to the south 'in the next field on the bank of a ditch'. Nearby residents crowded into the streets to witness the final moments of the London raider. The burning wreckage lay spread over 100 yards of open ground between Roman Road and Beckton Road on the outskirts of East Ham.

attended to one little mite of a girl who had lost both of her feet.'

About 15 minutes later three bombs landed close together in Bethnal Green. Two fell on the premises of Allen & Hanbury, wholesale chemist and druggist, and one in neighbouring Corfield Street. The three bombs claimed the lives of a man and two women as well as injuring seven men, eight women and two children while causing massive damage; a third of the factory was destroyed, 14 houses seriously damaged and 227 houses suffered minor damage. Total casualties in London that night amounted to 48 killed and 172 injured. But the bombers, having spent as little time as possible over London, then faced a return journey fraught with danger. That night the LADA guns fired over 30,000 rounds skywards.

A No. 39 Squadron Bristol Fighter caught a Gotha flying at 10,000ft north of Hainault, at about 12.05am. Following a running fight the Gotha smashed into the ground on open land on the outskirts of East Ham.

The scene of devastation in Sydenham Road after the raid of 19/20 May 1918 where Delahoy's Dairy had stood. Amongst the 18 killed were five members of the Delahoy family, while next door the same bomb killed Rose Westley, aged 47, her son, a niece and her sister-in-law.

Elsewhere Major F. Sowrey, No. 143 Squadron, who had previously shot down a Zeppelin in September 1916, engaged a Gotha V at about 12.25am returning from bombing Peckham and Rotherhithe. Flying an SE5a, Sowrey closed and fired off two drums of Lewis gun ammunition and, despite the Gotha's evasive tactics, closed again to open with his Vickers. But an engine stall caused a spin and

The wreckage of the Gotha brought down in East Ham at 12.20am on 20 May 1918, victim of a No. 39 Squadron Bristol Fighter, the squadron's first 'kill' since their successes against Zeppelin raiders in September/ October 1916.

Another of the Gothas brought down on 19/20 May. In total three were shot down over land, one made a forced landing and two were confirmed as shot down over the sea. The small arrow indicates an unexploded 50kg bomb with its nose buried in the ground. (Colin Ablett)

by the time he recovered control Sowrey had lost sight of the Gotha – but it appears he had wounded the pilot, Vfw Albrecht Sachtler. Doubtful of reaching Belgium the crew began searching for somewhere to land when a Bristol Fighter of No. 141 Squadron, crewed by lieutenants Edward Turner and Henry Barwise, pounced on the struggling Gotha. The first burst, fired by the observer, Barwise, hit the Gotha's port engine as it was attempting to reach the illuminated landing ground at Frinsted, Kent. Attacked again, the Gotha dived, defending itself by firing its rear gun in short bursts at the Brisfit. Then Barwise's gun jammed and, encountering engine problems, Turner pulled away and gave up the attack. However, the Gotha was now in a bad way and despite Sachtler's best efforts it crashed between Frinsted and Harrietsham at about 12.45am. Only the rear gunner, Uffz Hermann Tasche, who suffered a broken arm, survived the landing.

A fourth Gotha met with disaster near Clacton after the pilot came down low to clear cloud cover in an attempt to establish its position. An engine problem meant he was unable to check the descent and, having unloaded the bombs, he made an emergency landing; the commander, Lt Wilhelm Rist was killed. Anti-aircraft guns also shot down two Gothas off the coast but claims for a third went unconfirmed; one more crashed on landing as it returned to Belgium.

Quiet now returned to the skies over London. The city's population, now reassured by the very visible aerial response to this latest attack, steeled themselves for the next alarm and the defenders confidently waited for their next test. A week passed, then a month, two months then three, but the raiders did not return; in fact they never came again.

THE AFTERMATH OF THE FIRST BLITZ

THE END OF THE CAMPAIGN

For Brandenburg, losses on this Whitsun raid were high as the defences demonstrated increasing efficiency, but he and Bentivegni still planned to continue raiding England. However, on 27 May 1918, the German Army launched an attack on the Aisne and both Bogohl 3 and Rfa 501 were committed to supporting the attack. They planned two raids in July 1918 but the OHL cancelled them. However, by August the powerful Elektron incendiary bomb, weighing only 1kg and able to be dropped in vast numbers, was ready. Plans to unleash a fearsome firestorm on Paris and London were in place and in September, with the war going against Germany, the OHL initially took the decision to launch the firebombs. The crews prepared for this desperate attack, bombs were loaded, then, at the very last minute an order arrived cancelling the raid. Since June 1918, following agitation at home, British aircraft had carried out raids on German towns and cities. Now, recognizing the end of the war was near and fearing even greater reprisals against a German civilian population whose morale was already disintegrating, the OHL cancelled the order to unleash the firestorm. For London's civilian population the war was over.

At the beginning of the war, Germany had hoped her bombing raids would break Londoners' morale and force them to demand that the government sue for peace. For the capital's population the raids – first by Zeppelins and then by bomber aircraft – undoubtedly caused sleepless nights, stress, anxiety, fear and anger, but they never induced the people to demand peace; instead, the raids brought forward strident cries for retaliation.

Although the plans to crush London's morale failed, the raids did have other intended effects on Britain's war effort. On two occasions raids caused fighting squadrons to be withdrawn from the Western Front and many new high-performance aircraft, urgently needed elsewhere, were committed to Home Defence. The raids also caused dramatic reductions in munitions production at times, and anti-aircraft guns, ammunition, searchlights and manpower were all required to maintain the defence system to combat these raids, remaining in place until the end of the war despite urgent demands for their redeployment elsewhere.

THE COST OF THE WAR

Yet this came at a price for the German aircrews. As a direct consequence of planned raids on London, Germany lost seven airships (L.12, L.15, SL.11, L.32, L.33, L.31 and L.48) over Britain or her coastal waters, and 60 Gothas: 24 shot down or missing and 36 destroyed or seriously damaged by crash landings in Belgium. In addition two 'Giants' were also lost in bad landings after raids and another three suffered a similar fate after an aborted mission against London.

The airship raids on Britain claimed 557 lives and caused injuries to 1,358 men, women and children, with material damage estimated at £1.5million (1914–18 value), with just under £1million of this inflicted on London. Some 26 raids targeted the capital, but only nine actually reached the central target area, the others deflected by bad weather or hampered by mechanical failure. These raids killed 181 and injured 504, or 36 per cent of the total British casualties in this phase of London's first aerial war. While engaged in defending the capital, 15 aircraft crashed and six pilots were lost in these bad landings.

In comparison, the Gotha and 'Giant' raids caused material damage estimated at £1.4million, of which £1.2 million occurred in the London region. These raids killed 837 people and injured 1,991. Of these casualties, 486 deaths and 1,432 injuries occurred in London (68 per cent of total). Of the remaining losses most were inflicted on coastal towns in Kent and Essex. Of those aircraft committed to defending London, 21 were lost due to enemy action or damaged in crash landings, with the loss of five pilots and one observer.

Good gracious! you haven't been in a raid, have you?

Oh no! they had some beer at the Red Lion, and I tried to get in!

Germany had hoped her air raids would crush the morale of the civilian population but in this aim they failed. Instead, many civilians demanded retaliation against German towns and cities and, in countless numbers, they brought 'comic' postcards to send to friends and family offering a wry view of the air raids.

As a weapon of war, the airship was short-lived. At the beginning of the war they had seemed to many to be the most advanced and terrifying weapons in existence; by the end of the war, airships as long-range bombers were consigned to the pages of history books – a flawed concept, an aviation cul-de-sac. Yet even though far more of London's population suffered at the hands of the Gotha and 'Giant' bombers, the Zeppelins or 'Zepps' as they became known to Londoners, held a terrible fascination for the civilian population. Even when under attack, people were drawn into the streets to watch the skies above as these 'gaseous monsters', as Churchill dubbed them, passed overhead, looking on in both awe and horror in equal measure. Despite the passage of time, this haunting fascination remains to this day – long after the greater impact made on London by these early bombers has largely been forgotten.

LONDON'S LEGACY

Those in authority did not forget the danger presented by the bomber raids. The lessons learnt in dealing with this threat proved extremely beneficial to Britain in the long term. They made the government acutely aware of the necessity to maintain an in-depth aerial defence system. The need to realign the divergent paths taken by the RFC and RNAS led to the creation of the Royal Air Force in April 1918, and a sophisticated central operations room evolved at Spring Gardens in central London during the final year of the war. Here sat the hub of an exclusive military telephone network that relayed information from 25 sub-control centres, each in direct contact with the AA gun batteries, searchlight companies, balloon aprons, aerodromes and observer posts in its own area. In the operations room, information received from the sub-commands was fed via telephone headsets to a team of plotters working on a large map table, who moved symbols representing enemy aircraft across the map, all overseen from a gallery above by Ashmore, commander of the London Air Defence Area, Higgins, commanding VI (Home Defence) Brigade, and a senior police representative. Ashmore was able to speak directly to the sub-commanders and Higgins to the fighter wing HQs, while the police representative had direct lines to the emergency services. According to Ashmore, the system worked very well:

> From the time the observer at one of the stations in the country saw a machine over him, to the time when the counter representing it appeared on my map, was not, as a rule, more than half a minute.

It was the system that, with the addition of Radar, provided the country with its defence against the Luftwaffe when German aircraft returned to British skies in the summer of 1940.

SELECT BIBLIOGRAPHY

Castle, H.G., *Fire Over England*, London (1982)

Castle, I., *London 1914–17: The Zeppelin Menace*, Oxford (2008)

Castle, I., *London 1917–18: The Bomber Blitz*, Oxford (2010)

Castle I., *The Zeppelin Base Raids: Germany 1914*, Oxford (2011)

Cole, C & Cheesman, E.F., *The Air Defence of Britain, 1914–1918*, London (1984)

Fegan, Thomas, *The 'Baby Killers' – German Air Raids on Britain in the First World War*, Barnsley (2002)

Fredette, Major R.H., *The First Battle of Britain 1917–1918*, London (1966)

Griehl, M. & Dressel, J., *Zeppelin! The German Airship Story*, London (1990)

Hanson. N., *First Blitz*, London (2008)

Hyde, A.P., *The First Blitz*, Barnsley (2002)

Jones, H.A., *The War In The Air*, Volume 3 (pub.1931, reprinted Uckfield 2002)

Jones, H.A., *The War In The Air*, Volume 5 (pub 1935, reprinted Uckfield 2002)

Morris, J., *German Air Raids on Britain 1914–1918* (pub. 1925, reprinted Dallington, 1993)

Poolman, K., *Zeppelins Over England*, London (1960)

Rawlinson, A., *The Defence of London, 1915–1918*, London (1923)

Rimmel, R.L., *Zeppelin! A Battle for Air Supremacy in World War I*, London (1984)

Raleigh, W., *The War In The Air*, Volume 1 (pub.1922, reprinted Uckfield 2002)

Robinson, D.H., *The Zeppelin in Combat*, Atglen (USA, 1994)

Stephenson, C., *Zeppelins: German Airships 1900–40*, Oxford (2004)

White, C.M., *The Gotha Summer*, London (1986)

APPENDICES

APPENDIX 1:
IN TOUCH WITH LONDON'S FIRST BLITZ

Inevitably, much of London has changed in the 100 years since this first aerial conflict over the city during the First World War. The destruction caused by the Blitz of 1940–41, the V1 and V2 rockets of 1944–45, as well as the subsequent and ongoing redevelopment of the city, has erased much of early twentieth century London. Even though many roads and buildings have disappeared from great tracts of the capital, there are still a few reminders that link us with this turbulent time if you know where to look.

The first bomb dropped on London, by Zeppelin LZ.38 on 31 May 1915, fell on 16 Alkham Road, Stoke Newington. Despite setting fire to the roof and upstairs rooms, the house still stands. Unfortunately Hackney Council erected a plaque in the 1990s to mark this historic moment, but placed it half a mile away on the wall of 31 Nevill Road, incorrectly identifying it as the first house bombed in the war – and gives the wrong date. A new plaque, however, was erected by Hackney Council in Alkham Road in May 2015, to mark the centenary of London's first air raid, and the old one removed.

Kapitänleutnant Heinrich Mathy's raid of 8/9 September has left the most indicators of its passing. A small plaque encircled by paving in one of the central lawns marks the spot where his explosive bomb landed in Queen's Square, Bloomsbury. Moments later another bomb fell outside the Dolphin public house on the corner of Lamb's Conduit Passage and Red Lion Street. The clock in the pub stopped as the bomb exploded and remains in situ, with its hands frozen in time for many years at 10.49pm. However, in more recent times the hands have slipped to 10.40pm. Interestingly, back in 1990 the group Crosby, Stills & Nash released an album, *Live It Up*, which featured a track called *After The Dolphin*, the lyrics inspired by the raid that night. Further along the route a plaque on the wall of 61 Farringdon Road commemorates the destruction of that building during the raid and its subsequent rebuilding.

Another plaque, on the wall of the chapel in Lincoln's Inn, records the explosion of a bomb dropped by Kptlt Breithaupt from L.15 on 13 October 1915. The bomb shattered the seventeenth-century stained glass window, and the walls below still bear the scars of the blast.

Outside London, in Cuffley, Hertfordshire, a monument erected by donations from readers of a national newspaper commemorates William Leefe Robinson's deed in bringing down SL.11 on the night of 2/3 September 1916, and his subsequent death in 1918. His grave is located in All Saints Church cemetery at Harrow Weald. The bodies of all the Zeppelin crews shot down over Britain – as well as the Gotha crews – now lie in peace in the tranquil setting of the German Military Cemetery at Cannock Chase, Staffordshire.

Perhaps the most poignant reminder of the First World War bomber raids is the memorial in Poplar Recreation Ground, East India Dock Road, recording the deaths of 18 young schoolchildren killed at the Upper North Street School, Poplar, when the first Gotha daylight raid took place on 13 June 1917. Another reminder of that first bomber raid is a ceramic plaque in memory of PC Alfred Smith on the wall at Postman's Park (entrance in Aldersgate Street, EC1), who died while saving the lives of a group of factory girls in Central Street, EC1. The twisted remains of a bomb that fell on the church of St Edmund the King and Martyr in Lombard Street, EC3, now forms a unique memorial to the second daylight raid on 7 July 1917. Although the church is now the London Centre for Spirituality, the bomb remains preserved in a glass case, located where the altar once stood.

In September 1917 the Gothas switched to night-time bombing and, during the first moonlight raid on 4/5 September, a bomb landed on the Victoria Embankment, a few feet from Cleopatra's Needle. Gouges from shell fragments still scar the ancient Egyptian obelisk, plinths and right-hand sphinx. The plaque on one of the plinths incorrectly refers to the raid as the 'first raid' on London by aeroplanes; it was the first *night-time* raid. Later that month, on the night of 24 September, a bomb landed in the roadway in Southampton Row, WC2 outside the Bedford Hotel. The hotel has been completely rebuilt in the intervening years but a framed plaque outside remembers the 13 killed and 22 injured in the blast. Moments later the same Gotha released a 50kg bomb, which smashed through the glass roof of Gallery IX at the Royal Academy, Burlington House, Piccadilly. The blast shattered the room and a small round plaque at the entrance to the gallery now marks the event. The surrounding marble also shows heavy scarring caused by the shell fragments.

In Lincoln's Inn, not far from the plaque commemorating the Zeppelin bomb dropped on 13 October 1915, is another, outside 10 Stone's Buildings. The brass plaque commemorates a bomb that fell on 18 December 1917. A small white disc set in the tarmac marks the point where the bomb exploded and the walls show significant shrapnel damage. Finally, in Chelsea, a plaque on the wall of the north-east wing of the Royal Hospital commemorates its destruction by a 1,000kg bomb (incorrectly recorded on plaque as a 500lb bomb) in February 1918, its rebuilding in 1921, destruction again in 1945 by a V2 rocket and subsequent rebuilding in 1965.

Examples of the aircraft employed by the RFC, RNAS and RAF against the German bombers are on display at the RAF Museum, Hendon (www.rafmuseum.org.uk). There you can see a restored Sopwith Camel, SE5a and Sopwith Triplane, a rebuilt Bristol Fighter and reproduction Sopwith 1½ Strutter. But perhaps the most interesting is a Sopwith Pup. This restored aircraft uses 60–70 per cent of original Pup N5182, which flew from RNAS Walmer and Dover against the Gotha raids of 25 May and 5 June 1917. In addition the Shuttleworth Collection in Bedfordshire (www.shuttleworth.org), regularly include a Sopwith Pup, Sopwith Triplane, SE5a and Bristol Fighter in their air shows. And near Maldon in Essex, the former No. 37 Squadron First World War airfield at Stow Maries (www.stowmaries.org.uk) is undergoing extensive renovation, with many of the original buildings still standing, and has plans for regular flights by First World War aircraft.

APPENDIX 2: CHRONOLOGY

1914

4 Aug   Britain declares war on Germany.

8 Aug   London's first three AA guns positioned in Whitehall.

5 Sep   Winston Churchill, First Lord of the Admiralty, outlines his Home Defence plan as the Admiralty accept responsibility for the aerial defence of London.

1 Oct   Instructions for the implementation of a blackout come into effect.

24 Dec   A German seaplane drops the first bomb from the air on Britain. It lands in Dover.

1915

9 Jan   Kaiser Wilhelm gives official approval for air attacks on Britain – but excludes London as a target.

19/20 Jan   Navy Zeppelins L.3 and L.4 bomb Great Yarmouth, King's Lynn and a number of Norfolk villages during the first Zeppelin raid on Britain.

12 Feb   The Kaiser includes London Docks in legitimate targets.

3 Apr   The Army Airship Service takes delivery of the first of the new 'P-class' Zeppelins – LZ.38

5 May   Kaiser Wilhelm approves London, east of Tower of London, as a legitimate target.

31 May/1 Jun   Army Zeppelin LZ.38 makes the first airship raid on London.

6/7 Jun   Flt Sub-Lt R.A.J. Warneford (RNAS) destroys Army Zeppelin LZ.37 over Belgium. Zeppelin LZ.38 is bombed in its shed at Evère by Flt Lt J.P. Wilson and Flt Sub-Lt J.S. Mills (RNAS).

20 Jul   Unrestricted bombing of London approved by the Kaiser.

17/18 Aug   Navy Zeppelin L.10 bombs Walthamstow, Leyton, Leytonstone and Wanstead.

7/8 Sep   Army airships SL.2 and LZ.74 bomb south-east London.

8/9 Sep   Navy Zeppelin L.13, on a course from Bloomsbury to Liverpool Street Station, causes the most material damage of all the airship raids on London.

12 Sep   Admiral Sir Percy Scott appointed commander of London's gunnery defence.

13/14 Oct   Three Navy Zeppelins (L.13, L.14 and L.15) attack London and outskirts. Bombs fall from Covent Garden to Aldgate as well as on Woolwich and East Croydon. Highest casualties from a single Zeppelin raid.

1916

10 Feb   Responsibility for the aerial defence of London passes from the Admiralty to the War Office.

31 Mar/1 Apr   Navy Zeppelin L.15 brought down by anti-aircraft fire in sea north of Margate, Kent.

April   RFC places order for Buckingham incendiary ammunition.

15 Apr   No. 19 Reserve Aeroplane Squadron reformed as No. 39 (Home Defence) Squadron and concentrated on the north-eastern approaches to London.

May   RFC places orders for Brock explosive/incendiary and Pomeroy explosive ammunition.

30 May	The first of the R-class Super Zeppelins – L.30 – is commissioned into navy service.
24/25 Aug	Navy Zeppelin L.31 attacks Isle of Dogs, Greenwich, Eltham and Plumstead.
2/3 Sep	Army airship SL.11 is the first to be shot down over mainland Britain.
September	Army airships cease raiding Britain.
September	Approval given to commence production of the Gotha G.IV bomber.
23/24 Sept	In a raid by Navy Zeppelins, L.33 is brought down at Little Wigborough, Essex, after bombing East London. L.32 shot down near Billericay, Essex. L.31 bombs Streatham, Brixton and Leyton.
1/2 Oct	L.31 shot down over Potters Bar, Hertfordshire.
28 Nov	A single German LVG C.IV drops bombs on London in daytime between Knightsbridge and Victoria.
December	Lt Col M. St. L. Simon appointed Anti-Aircraft Defence Commander, London.

1917

January	Britain begins to scale down the London air defences in belief of a 'diminished risk from Zeppelin attack'.
28 Feb	L.42, the first of the S-class Zeppelins – the Height Climbers – is commissioned into naval service.
5 Mar	Hptmn Ernst Brandenburg appointed commander of Kagohl 3, the bomber squadron created to attack London.
6/7 May	A single Albatross C.VII drops bombs at night on London between Holloway and Hackney.
25 May	First attempted aircraft squadron raid on London, redirected on Folkestone.
5 Jun	Second attempted squadron raid on London abandoned due to weather conditions. Sheerness and

	Shoeburyness bombed instead. First Gotha shot down by AA fire.
13 Jun	First daylight raid on London by Gotha bombers. Highest casualties on London from a single raid (162 killed, 426 injured).
16/17 Jun	The German navy launches its last – planned – Zeppelin raid on London. L.48 is shot down over Theberton, Suffolk, as the raid fails to reach its target.
19 Jun	Brandenburg, commander of Kagohl 3, injured in air crash resulting in amputation of a leg.
23 Jun	Hptmn Rudolph Kleine appointed commander of Kagohl 3.
7 Jul	Second, and final, daylight raid on London by Kagohl 3.
19 Jul	Release of first part of Gen Jan Smuts' report on Home Defence.
8 Aug	Maj Gen Ashmore appointed commander of LADA.
17 Aug	Release of second part of Smuts' report, recommending creation of a single air service.
28 Aug	Home Defence Group upgraded to Home Defence Brigade.
4/5 Sep	First night-time raid on London by Kagohl 3.
6 Sep	Smuts' report on night raids.
22 Sep	Arrival of Rfa 501 in Belgium, flying R-type 'Giants'.
24 Sep	Kagohl 3 commences 'Harvest Moon Offensive', the first of five raids on London in eight days.
29 Sep	First London raid involving both Gotha and 'Giant' aircraft.
1/2 Oct	Last raid of 'Harvest Moon offensive'.
19/20 Oct	Navy Zeppelin L.45, driven off course by high winds, drops bombs on Hendon, Cricklewood, Piccadilly, Camberwell and Hither Green, the last

Zeppelin bombs to fall on London.

31Oct/1 Nov Seventh night raid on London by aeroplanes.

6 Dec Eighth night aeroplane raid on London.

12 Dec Rudolph Kleine killed in action. Temporary command of Kagohl 3 passes to Oblt Richard Walter.

18 Dec Ninth night aeroplane raid on London. Highest material damage inflicted in an aeroplane raid (£225,000).

18 Dec Kagohl 3 re-designated Bogohl 3.

1918

January Britain establishes the Air Ministry.

28/29 Jan Tenth night aeroplane raid on London. A bomb in Long Acre causes the most casualties in the capital inflicted by a single bomb (38 killed – 85 injured).

29/30 Jan Eleventh London night raid by aeroplanes.

Early Feb Ernst Brandenburg resumes command of Bogohl 3 and suspends further action to allow squadron to regain full strength.

16 Feb Rfa 501 carries out the twelfth night aeroplane raid alone. First 1,000kg bomb dropped on London.

17 Feb A single 'Giant' carries out the thirteenth night aeroplane raid on London.

7/8 Mar Fourteenth night aeroplane raid on London, flown by Rfa 501.

1 Apr RFC and RNAS amalgamate to form Royal Air Force (RAF).

19/20 May Bogohl 3 and Rfa 501 combine for the fifteenth night aeroplane raid on London – 'the Whitsun Raid'. Largest and final raid of the war.

5 Aug Führer der Luftschiffe Peter Strasser killed when Zeppelin L.70 shot down off the Norfolk coast.

APPENDIX 3: THE FORCES ENGAGED IN LONDON'S FIRST BLITZ

THE ZEPPELIN RAIDS
31 MAY/1 JUNE 1915

German force
Two German airships
Army Zeppelin LZ.38 (Hptmn Erich Linnarz) – bombed London
Army Zeppelin LZ.37 – returned early

British defensive sorties
RNAS – 15 aircraft
Chingford: BE2a, BE2c and Deperdussin
Dover: four aircraft (type unknown)
Eastchurch: Avro 504B, Blériot Parasol, BE2c and Sopwith Tabloid
Hendon: Sopwith Gunbus
Rochford: Blériot Parasol
Westgate: Sopwith Tabloid and Avro 504B

17/18 AUGUST 1915

German force

Four German airships

Navy Zeppelin L.10 (Oblt-z-S Friedrich Wenke) – bombed London

Navy Zeppelin L.11 – reached England

Navy Zeppelins L.13, L.14 – returned early

British defensive sorties

RNAS – 6 aircraft

Chelmsford: Two Caudron G.3

Yarmouth: Sopwith two-seater Scout and two BE2c

Holt: one aircraft (type unknown)

7/8 SEPTEMBER 1915

German force

Three German airships

Army Schütte-Lanz SL.2 (Hptmn Richard von Wobeser) – bombed London

Army Zeppelin LZ.74 (Hptmn Friedrich George) – bombed London

Army Zeppelin LZ.77 – reached England

British defensive sorties

RNAS – 3 aircraft

Felixstowe: BE2c

Yarmouth: BE2c and Sopwith two-seater Scout

8/9 SEPTEMBER 1915

German force

Three German airships

Navy Zeppelin L.13 (Kptlt Heinrich Mathy) – bombed London

Navy Zeppelins L.9, L.14 – reached England

British defensive sorties

RNAS – 7 aircraft

Redcar: Caudron G.3 and two BE2c

Yarmouth: three BE2c

Kingfisher (trawler): Sopwith Schneider (seaplane)

13/14 OCTOBER 1915

German force

Five German airships

Navy Zeppelin L.13 (Kptlt Heinrich Mathy) – bombed London

Navy Zeppelin L.14 (Kptlt Alois Böcker) – bombed London

Navy Zeppelin L.15 (Kptlt Joachim Breithaupt) – bombed London

Navy Zeppelins L.11, L.16 – reached England

British defensive sorties

RFC – 5 aircraft

Joyce Green: one BE2c (two sorties)

Hainault Farm: two BE2c

Suttons Farm: two BE2c

24/25 AUGUST 1916

German force

Four German airships

Navy Zeppelin L.31 (Kptlt Heinrich Mathy) – bombed London

Navy Zeppelins L.16, L.21, L.32 – reached England

Navy Zeppelins L.14, L.13, L.23 and three others – returned early

Navy Schütte-Lanz SL.8, SL.9 – returned early

British defensive sorties

RNAS – 9 aircraft

Eastchurch: two BE2c

Felixstowe: two Short 827

Grain: two BE2c

Manston: BE2c and two Sopwith 1½ Strutter

RFC – 7 aircraft

No. 39 Squadron:

North Weald: two BE2c

Suttons Farm: two BE2c

Hainault Farm: one BE2c

No. 50 Squadron

Dover: two BE2c

2/3 SEPTEMBER 1916

German force

16 German airships

Army Schütte-Lanz SL.11 (Hptmn Wilhelm Schramm) – bombed London

Navy Zeppelins L.11, L.13, L.14, L.16, L.21, L.22, L.23, L.24, L.30, L.32 – reached England

Navy Schütte Lanz SL.8 – reached England

Army Zeppelin LZ.90, LZ.98 – reached England

Army Zeppelin LZ.97 – returned early

Navy Zeppelin L.17 – returned early

British defensive sorties

RNAS – 4 aircraft

Grain: Farman F.56

Yarmouth: BE2c

Bacton: BE2c

Covehithe: BE2c

RFC – 10 aircraft

No. 33 Squadron:

  Beverley: BE2c

No. 39 Squadron:

  North Weald: BE12 and BE2c

  Suttons Farm: two BE2c

  Hainault Farm: two BE2c

No. 50 Squadron:

  Dover: three BE2c

23/24 SEPTEMBER 1916

German force

12 German airships

Navy Zeppelin L.31 (Kptlt Heinrich Mathy) – bombed London

Navy Zeppelin L.33 (Kptlt Alois Böcker) – bombed London

Navy Zeppelins L.13, L.14, L.17, L.21, L.22, L.23, L.30, L.32 – reached England

Navy Zeppelins L.16, L.24 – returned early

British defensive sorties

RNAS – 13 aircraft

Cranwell: BE2c

Eastchurch: three BE2c

Manston: two BE2c

Yarmouth: Short 184, two BE2c and two Sopwith Baby

Bacton: BE2c

Covehithe: BE2c

RFC – 12 aircraft

No. 33 Squadron:

  Beverley: BE2c

No. 39 Squadron:

  North Weald: two BE2c

  Suttons Farm: BE2c

  Hainault Farm: two BE2c

No. 50 Squadron:

  Dover: two BE2c

  Bekesbourne: BE2c and one unknown type

No. 51 Squadron:

  Thetford: two aircraft (type unknown)

19/20 OCTOBER 1917

German force

11 German airships

Navy Zeppelin L.45 (Kptlt Waldemar Kölle) – bombed London

Navy Zeppelins L.41, L.44, L.46, L.47, L.49, L.50, L.52, L.53, L.54, L.55 – reached England

British defensive sorties

RNAS –11 aircraft

Cranwell: BE2e

Frieston: BE2c

Manston: three BE2c

Yarmouth: BE2c

Bacton: BE2c

Burgh Castle: three BE2c

Covehithe: BE2c

RFC – 66 aircraft

No. 33 Squadron:

  Scampton: two FE2b and three FE2d

  Kirton-Lindsey: three FE2b and three FE2d

  Elsham: two FE2d

  Gainsborough: FE2d and FE2b

No. 37 Squadron:

  Goldhanger: BE2d, two BE2e and BE12

  Stow Maries: four BE2e

No. 38 Squadron:

Leadenham: two FE2b
Buckminster: two FE2b
Stamford: four FE2b
No. 39 Squadron:
  North Weald: seven BE2e and Martinsyde G.102 (attached)
  Biggin Hill: BE2c, BE12 and BE12a
No. 50 Squadron:
  Bekesbourne: BE2e and three BE12
No. 51 Squadron:

Mattishall: two FE2b
Tydd St Mary: two FE2b
Marham: two FE2b
No. 75 Squadron:
  Hadleigh: three BE2e and BE12
  Harling Road: two BE2e and BE12
  Elmswell: BE2e
No. 76 Squadron:
  Copmanthorpe: three BE2e and BE12
  Helperby: BE2e and BE12

THE BOMBER RAIDS

13 JUNE 1917

Kampfgeschwader 3 der Oberste Heeresleitung (Kagohl 3)
20 Gothas – 2 returned early
Royal Naval Air Service (RNAS) – 33 aircraft
Dover: 3 x Sopwith Pup, 1 x Sopwith Baby
Eastchurch: 2 x Bristol Scout, 1 x Sopwith 1½ Strutter
Felixstowe: 2 x Sopwith Schneider, 5 x Sopwith Baby
Grain: 2 x Sopwith Pup, 2 x Sopwith Baby
Manston: 4 x Bristol Scout, 1 x Sopwith Pup, 2 x Sopwith Triplane
Westgate: 4 x Sopwith Baby
Walmer: 4 x Sopwith Pup
Royal Flying Corps (RFC) – 55 aircraft
No. 37 Squadron: 1 x BE2e, 1 x BE12, 1 x BE12a, 1 x RE7, 5 x Sopwith 1½ Strutter
No. 39 Squadron: 1 x BE2c, 2 x BE2e, 3 x BE12, 3 x BE12a, 1 x FK8
No. 50 Squadron: 1 x BE2c, 1 x BE12, 2 x BE12a, 5 x FK8, 1 x RE8, 1 x Vickers ES1
No. 65 Squadron: 2 x DH5
No. 78 Squadron: 1 x BE12a
No. 98 Depot Squadron (DS): 1 x BE2d, 1 x BE2e, 1 x BE12a
No. 35 Training Squadron (TS): 2 x Bristol Fighter
No. 40 TS: 2 x Sopwith Pup
No. 62 TS: 1 x Sopwith Pup
No. 63 TS: 1 x Sopwith Pup
No. 2 Aircraft Acceptance Park (AAP): 2 x DH4, 1 x DH5
No. 8 AAP: 1 x DH4, 1 x DH5, 1 x FE8, 1 x Sopwith 1½ Strutter, 1 x Bristol Fighter, 1 x RE8
Orfordness Experimental Station: 2 x Sopwith Triplane, 2 x DH4

7 JULY 1917

Kagohl 3
24 Gothas – 2 returned early
RNAS – 22 aircraft
Dover: 1 x Sopwith Pup, 2 x Sopwith Baby
Eastchurch: 2 x Sopwith Camel
Grain: 1 x Sopwith Pup
Manston: 1 x Sopwith Pup, 3 x Sopwith Camel, 4 x Sopwith Triplane, 3 x Bristol Scout
Walmer: 5 x Sopwith Pup
RFC – 81 aircraft
No. 37 Squadron: 2 x BE12, 3 x BE12a, 1 x BE2e, 1 x RE7, 6 x Sopwith Pup, 6 x Sopwith 1½ Strutter
No. 39 Squadron: 3 x BE12, 3 x BE12a, 2 x SE5, 1 x FK8
No. 50 Squadron: 2 x BE12a, 6 x Sopwith Pup, 1 x FK8, 1 x Vickers ES1, 3 x unrecorded aircraft
No. 78 Squadron: 5 x BE12a
No. 35 TS: 2 x Bristol Fighter
No. 40 TS: 1 x Sopwith Pup, 2 x unrecorded aircraft
No. 56 TS: 1 x Spad
No. 62 TS: 1 x Sopwith Pup
No. 63 TS: 2 x Sopwith Pup
No. 198 DS: 1 x Vickers FB12c

No. 2 AAP: 5 x DH4, 1 x DH5
No. 7 AAP: 1 x FE8
No. 8 AAP: 3 x Bristol Fighter, 1 x FE2d, 2 x FE8, 1 x DH5, 1 x FK8
Orfordness Experimental Station: 1 x Bristol Fighter, 1 x Sopwith Triplane, 1 x DH2, 1 x FE2b, 1 x Sopwith 1½ Strutter, 1 x FK8, 1 x RE8
Martlesham Heath Testing Squadron: 2 x Sopwith Camel, 1 x DH4

4/5 SEPTEMBER 1917

Kagohl 3
11 Gothas – 2 returned early
RFC – 18 aircraft
No. 37 Squadron: 1 x BE2d, 3 x BE2e, 1 x BE12a
No. 39 Squadron: 3 x BE2e, 3 x BE12
No. 44 Squadron: 4 x Sopwith Camel
No. 50 Squadron: 2 x BE12, 1 x FK8

24 SEPTEMBER 1917

Kagohl 3
16 Gothas – 3 returned early
RFC – 30 aircraft
No. 37 Squadron: 4 x BE2e, 2 x BE12
No. 39 Squadron: 4 x BE2e (inc. one W/T tracker aircraft), 1 x BE12, 1 x BE12a
No. 44 Squadron: 3 x Sopwith Camel
No. 50 Squadron: 5 x BE12 (three W/T tracker aircraft), 1 x BE2e, 2 x FK8
No. 78 Squadron: 2 x FE2d, 2 x Sopwith 1½ Strutter
Orfordness Experimental Station: 3 x unrecorded aircraft

25 SEPTEMBER 1917

Kagohl 3
15 Gothas – 1 returned early
RNAS – 2 aircraft
Manston: 2 x BE2c
RFC – 18 aircraft
No. 37 Squadron: 1 x BE2d, 2 x BE2e, 1 x BE12
No. 39 Squadron: 4 x BE2e (one W/T tracker aircraft), 1 x BE2c, 1 x BE12a
No. 44 Squadron: 3 x Sopwith Camel
No. 50 Squadron: 1 x BE2e
No. 78 Squadron: 1 x FE2d, 3 x Sopwith 1½ Strutter

29 SEPTEMBER 1917

Kagohl 3
7 Gothas – 3 returned early
Riesenflugzeugabteilung 501 (Rfa 501)
3 Giants – 0 returned early
RNAS – 3 aircraft
Manston: 3 x BE2c
RFC – 28 aircraft
No. 39 Squadron: 2 x BE2c, 6 x BE2e, 2 x BE12 (both W/T tracker aircraft), 1 x BE12a
No. 44 Squadron: 4 x Sopwith Camel
No. 50 Squadron: 4 x BE12, 3 x BE2e, 1 x FK8
No. 78 Squadron: 1 x FE2d, 3 x Sopwith 1½ Strutter
Orfordness Experimental Station: 1 x Martinsyde F1

30 SEPTEMBER 1917

Kagohl 3
11 Gothas – 1 returned early
RNAS – 2 aircraft
Manston: 2 x BE2c
RFC – 31 aircraft
No. 37 Squadron: 4 x BE2e (one W/T tracker)
No. 39 Squadron: 4 x BE2e (two W/T trackers), 2 x BE12, 1 x BE12a
No. 44 Squadron: 8 x Sopwith Camel
No. 50 Squadron: 1 x BE2e, 2 x BE12 (one W/T tracker), 2 x FK8
No. 78 Squadron: 1 x FE2d, 5 x Sopwith 1½ Strutter
Orfordness Experimental Station: 1 x Martinsyde F1

1 OCTOBER 1917

Kagohl 3
18 Gothas – 6 returned early
RFC – 18 aircraft
No. 37 Squadron: 1 x BE2e, 1 x BE12
No. 39 Squadron: 2 x BE2e, 2 x BE12a
No. 44 Squadron: 7 x Sopwith Camel
No. 78 Squadron: 1 x FE2d, 4 x Sopwith 1½ Strutter

31 OCTOBER/1 NOVEMBER 1917

Kagohl 3
22 Gothas – 0 returned early
RNAS – 5 aircraft
Eastchurch: 2 x Sopwith 1½ Strutter

Manston: 2 x Sopwith 1½ Strutter, 1 x DH4
RFC – 45 aircraft
No. 37 Squadron: 6 x BE2e (one W/T tracker)
No. 39 Squadron: 5 x BE2e, 3 x BE12 (one W/T
  tracker)
No. 44 Squadron: 13 x Sopwith Camel
No. 50 Squadron: 3 x BE12 (two W/T trackers),
  1 x BE12a, 4 x FK8, 1 x BE2e
No. 78 Squadron: 6 x Sopwith 1½ Strutter,
  3 x Sopwith 1½ Strutter SS (single-seater
  conversion)

6 DECEMBER 1917

Kagohl 3
19 Gothas – 3 returned early
Rfa 501
2 Giants – 0 returned early
RFC – 32 aircraft
No. 37 Squadron: 1 x BE2d, 6 x BE2e, 1 x BE12
No. 39 Squadron: 2 x BE2e, 2 x Bristol Fighter,
  3 x BE12
No. 44 Squadron: 6 x Sopwith Camel
No. 50 Squadron: 3 x BE12 (all W/T trackers),
  4 x FK8
No. 78 Squadron: 4 x Sopwith 1½ Strutter SS

18 DECEMBER 1917

**Kagohl 3 – now redesignated Bombengeschwader
  3 der OHL (Bogohl 3)**
15 Gothas – 2 returned early
Rfa 501
1 Giant – 0 returned early
RFC – 46 aircraft
No. 37 Squadron: 3 x BE2e, 1 x BE12, 2 x BE12b
No. 39 Squadron: 2 x BE2e, 4 x Bristol Fighter
No. 44 Squadron: 8 x Sopwith Camel
No. 50 Squadron: 3 x BE12, 6 x FK8
No. 61 Squadron: 4 x SE5a
No. 78 Squadron: 9 x Sopwith 1½ Strutter SS,
  1 x Sopwith 1½ Strutter, 1 x BE2e (W/T tracker),
  2 x BE12

28/29 JANUARY 1918

Bogohl 3
13 Gothas – 6 returned early

Rfa 501
2 Giants – 1 returned early
RNAS – 6 aircraft
Dover: 4 x Sopwith Camel, 1 x Sopwith 1½ Strutter
Eastchurch: 1 x Sopwith Camel
RFC – Detailed returns not available
No. 37 Squadron: 15 sorties flown
No. 39 Squadron: 10 sorties flown
No. 44 Squadron: 25 sorties flown
No. 50 Squadron: 11 sorties flown
No. 61 Squadron: 9 sorties flown
No. 75 Squadron: 5 sorties flown
No. 78 Squadron: 22 sorties flown

29/30 JANUARY 1918

Rfa 501
4 Giants – 1 returned early
RNAS – 7 aircraft
Dover: 4 x Sopwith Camel, 1 x Sopwith 1½ Strutter
Walmer: 2 x Sopwith Camel
RFC – 69 aircraft
No. 37 Squadron: 3 x BE2e, 3 x BE12, 3 x BE12b
No. 39 Squadron: 8 x Bristol Fighter (one W/T
  tracker), 1 x BE2e (W/T tracker)
No. 44 Squadron: 15 x Sopwith Camel
No. 50 Squadron: 3 x BE12 (inc. one W/T tracker),
  4 x BE12b (one W/T tracker), 5 x FK8
No. 61 Squadron: 7 x SE5a
No. 75 Squadron: 1 x BE2e, 1 x BE12, 1 x BE12b
No. 78 Squadron: 6 x Sopwith Camel, 3 x Sopwith
  1½ Strutter SS, 3 x BE12, 1 x BE12a, 1 x BE12b

16 FEBRUARY 1918

Rfa 501
5 Giants – 1 returned early
RFC – 56 aircraft
No. 37 Squadron: 1 x BE2d, 5 x BE2e, 3 x BE12,
  1 x BE12a
No. 39 Squadron: 7 x Bristol Fighter
No. 44 Squadron: 12 x Sopwith Camel
No. 50 Squadron: 3 x BE12 (one W/T tracker),
  3 x BE12b (one W/T tracker)
No. 61 Squadron: 7 x SE5a
No. 78 Squadron: 7 x Sopwith Camel, 1 x Sopwith
  1½ Strutter SS

No. 141 Squadron: 4 x BE12 (one W/T tracker)
No. 143 Squadron: 2 x FK8

17 FEBRUARY 1918

Rfa 501

1 Giant – 0 returned early

RFC – 66 aircraft

No. 37 Squadron: 5 x BE2e, 3 x BE12 (one W/T tracker), 4 x BE12b

No. 39 Squadron: 7 x Bristol Fighter

No. 44 Squadron: 12 x Sopwith Camel

No. 50 Squadron: 2 x BE2e, 4 x BE12 (two W/T trackers), 1 x BE12a, 1 x BE12b

No. 61 Squadron: 8 x SE5a

No. 78 Squadron: 9 x Sopwith Camel, 1 x Sopwith 1½ Strutter SS

No. 141 Squadron: 4 x BE12, 1 x BE12b

No. 143 Squadron: 4 x FK8

7/8 MARCH 1918

Rfa 501

6 Giants – 1 returned early

RFC – 41 aircraft

No. 37 Squadron: 2 x BE2e, 2 x BE12, 3 x BE12b

No. 39 Squadron: 8 x Bristol Fighter

No. 44 Squadron: 4 x Sopwith Camel

No. 50 Squadron: 3 x BE12 (two W/T trackers), 3 x BE12b

No. 61 Squadron: 6 x SE5a

No. 78 Squadron: 3 x Sopwith Camel

No. 112 Squadron: 1 x Sopwith Camel

No. 141 Squadron: 3 x BE12

No. 143 Squadron: 3 x FK8

19/20 MAY 1918

Bogohl 3

38 Gothas – 10 returned early

Rfa 501

3 Giants – 0 returned early

RAF – 86 aircraft

No. 37 Squadron: 5 x BE12, 2 x BE12a, 2 x BE12b, 1 x SE5a

No. 39 Squadron: 8 x Bristol Fighter (one W/T tracker)

No. 44 Squadron: 11 x Sopwith Camel

No. 50 Squadron: 1 x BE12 (W/T tracker), 1 x BE12b (W/T tracker), 7 x SE5a

No. 61 Squadron: 9 x SE5a

No. 78 Squadron: 10 x Sopwith Camel

No. 112 Squadron: 12 x Sopwith Camel

No. 141 Squadron: 7 x Bristol Fighter

No. 143 Squadron: 10 x SE5a

INDEX

References to images and maps are in **bold**.

Admiralty, the 7, 10, 11, 12, 34, 47
 and defence plan 18, 56
 and warnings 48–49
Ahlhorn airship base 100
aircraft, British 10–11, 191–92, 195
 BE2c 19, 46, 47, 49, **59**, 64–65, 70, 111; BE12: 64, 70, 94, 111, 136; Bristol F.2B Fighter **126**, 165, 172, **179**; Caudron G.3: 38; F.B.4 'Gunbus' 17; FE2b 111; FK8: 125, 130, 137; Henri Farman 33; Morane-Saulnier Parasol 33; S1 Scout 34; SE5a 125, 165, **179**; Sopwith Camel 125, 137, **138**, 165, 171; Sopwith Pup 125, 127, 165; Sopwith Strutter 125, 148
aircraft, German 11, 94, 95, 102, 104, **108**, 191
 Albatross C VII 117; G.IV 109–11, 117, **118**, **119**, **120**; G.V 137, **145**, 171, **174**; LVG C.IV 91; R.12: **159**, 161, **163**, 164, 171–73, 177; R.13: 180, 183; R.25: 173, 176, 178, 179–80; R.26: 173; R.27: 180–81, 183; R.39: 173, 175, 177, 180; R.VI 144, 149–50
airfields: map 112
airships, German **6**, 7, 9–10, 11, 19, 101, 191, 192
 L.3: 26; L.4: 20, 26; L.6: 76; L.7: 23; L.8: 26; L.9: 26, 33, 35, 76; L.10: 21, 33, 35, 36, 38–39; L.11: 33, 35, 42, 55; L.12: 34–35, **36**; L.13: **35**, 42–43, 45–46, 49, 54–55, 58, 60; L.14: 35, 42; L.15: 48, 49, 52, 58, 60–61; L.16: 48, 55, 66; L.17: 76; L.18: 56; L.19: 58; L.21: 66, 91; L.22: 58; L.24: 92; L.30: 76–77; L.31: 65–66, 68, 76, 80, 82, 87, 90–91; L.32: **57**, 76, 80, 82–86; L.33: 76, 77–79, **80**, 82, **83**; L.34: 91; L.42: 93, 94; L.44: 99; L.45: 95–96, 98–99; L.47: 100; L.48: 94–95; L.49: 99; L.50: 99; L.51: 100; L.55: 99; L.70: 100; LZ.37: 28, 33, 34; LZ.38: 21, 27, 28, 29, 32, 33; LZ.39: 33; LZ.74: 40, 42; LZ.90: 61, 69; LZ.97: 63–64, 69; LZ.98: 69–70; SL.2: 39–40; SL.3: 33; SL.11: **69**, 70, 72–73, **74**, 75, 76; SL.12: 91–92; Z.IX 23
Air Organization and the Direction of Aerial Operations 136
air raid warnings **16**, 118, 125, 126, 133, **134**, 146, 167
Aisne, battle of the (1918) 190
ammunition 155
anti-German sentiment 32, 133
Archway 153
Arkell, Lt Anthony 187
Army Airship Service 26, 28, 32, 33, 69, 75
Ashmore, Maj-Gen Edward 105–6, 133, 134, 136, 143, 165, 192

Balfour, Arthur 34
balloon barrages 143, 155, **156**, 165, 177
Banks, 2nd Lt Charles 171, 174
Barking 121, 153
barrage fire 143–44, 145, 146, 153, 159, 165
Bartikowski, Oblt R. 185
Barwise, Lt Henry 189

Bartholomew Close **24**, 43
Beechey, William 40
BEF *see* British Expeditionary Force
Behncke, KADM Paul 14–15, 23, 26
Belgium 11, 12, 14, 20, 26, 33, 156
Belgravia 164
Bell, Capt D.J. 148
Bentivegni, Hptmn Richard von 105, 144, 148–49
 and 1918 raids 177, 178, 180, 184, 190
Bentley, George 175
Bermondsey **41**, 42, 121, 163–64
Bethnal Green 188
Blackheath **67**, 68, 146
blackouts 18
Blériot, Louis 11
Bloch, Vfw F. 185
Böcker, Kptlt Alois 35, 42, 49, 53–54, 58
 and 1916 raids 76, 77–80
Borchers, Lt Max 178
Boy Scouts **135**
Brand, Capt Quintin 185
Brandenburg, Hptmn Ernst 104–5, 111, 117, 118
 and 1917 raids 119, 121, 125; and 1918 raids 176, 184, 190
Brandon, 2nd Lt A. de Bathe 60–61, 70, 79, 83, 84
Breithaupt, Kptlt Joachim 49, 50, 52–53, 60, 61
Brentford 175
Britain *see* Great Britain
British Army 11
British Expeditionary Force (BEF) 11, 12, 17
Brixton 80, **81**, 82, **84**
Brock, Flt Lt F.A. 62
Bromley-by-Bow 77–78, **81**, 153
Buckingham, J.F. 62
Bülow, Maj Hilmer von 160
Burke, Thomas 122
Bury St Edmunds 27, 58
Buttlar, Kptlt Horst von 35, 55, 66, 76–77

Cadbury, Flt Lt Egbert 91
Calais (France) 8
Camberwell **97**, 98
central London 43, **44**, 49–50, **51**, 52, 138, 140, 146, 195
Charlton 40, **41**, 148, 157
Chatham 137
Chelmsford 38, 79
Chelsea 177, 195
Cheshunt 40, 90
Chingford 128
Churchill, Winston 12–13, 18, 23, 34
City of London **24**, 40, 43, **44**, 45–46, 52–53, 121, 128–29, 195
civilians, British 26, 27, 46, 55, 68, 132, 165, 173, 190–91
Clapham 181, **182**
Cleethorpes 58

Cleopatra's Needle 140, **141**, 195
Clerkenwell 121
Cole-Hamilton, Capt C.W.E. 123
Coombs, Henry 43
Covent Garden 172–73
Cricklewood 96, **97**
Crouch End 140

Daily News (newspaper) **16**
Dalston **31**, 121, 128, 150, 152
Dennis, Capt Arthur 173
Deptford 40, **41**, 66, **67**, 145, 157
Deutsch Luftschiffahrts-Aktien-Gesellschaft (DELAG) 9
Dietrich, Kptlt Max 91
Dover 35
Dulwich 159
Dunkirk (France) 13, 18, 118
Düsseldorf shed 23

East Anglia 28, 69
East Croydon **51**, 53
Eastern Front 102
East Ham 121, 187, 188
Edmonton 128, 140, 154
Edwardes, 2nd Lt H.A. 176
Eichler, Kptlt Franz 94
Eltham **67**, 68
English Channel 11, 26, 125
Epping Forest 127
Essex 26, 27, 28, 39, 58, 63, 155

Farnborough 11
Felixstowe 134
Fire Brigade 32, **73**
Fleischhauer, Hans-Wolf 178
Ford, Lena 183
France 17, 99
Frankenburg, Kptlt Kurt 91
French, John, Lord 57, **114**, 115
Friedrichshafen (Germany) 23
Fuhlsbüttel shed 20, 76

Gayer, Kptlt Hans-Karl 99
George V, King 75, 133
George, Hptmn Friedrich 40
German Army 10, 92
    and bases 20, 21, **22**
        Bogohl 3; 161, 165, 167, 176, 184; Flieger-Bataillon Nr. 4; 8;
            Kagohl 3; 102, 104, **107**, 110–11, 126, 137, 154, 158; Rfa
            501; 144, 149–50, 158, 167, 173, 176–77, 184
        see also Army Airship Service; Oberste Heeresleitung (OHL)
German Navy 10, 15, 32–34, 101
    and bases 20, 21, **22**
    see also Naval Airship Division
Germany:
    and retaliatory bombing 156, 190
    and strategies 20–21
Ghent (Belgium) 33
Ghistelles (Belgium) 8, 110

Golders Green 43, **44**
Goodyear, Lt J.G. 172
Gothaer Waggonfabrik AG 109
Götte, Lt 177
Grace, 2nd Lt F.A.D. 130
Gravesend 33
Great Yarmouth 26
Green Line 136, 143
Green Park 20, 49
Greenwich 40, **41**, 66, **67**, 68, 138, **139**, 157
Grosch, Alfred 45

Hackney 117
Hackwill, Capt George 171, 174
Hage shed 21
Haggerston 150
Haig, FM Sir Douglas 125
Hainault Farm 48, 49, 62
Hall, Lt R.N. 176
Harris, Capt A.T. 63–64
Harvest Moon Offensive (1917) **116**, 144, 145–46, **147**,
    148–49, 150, **151**, 152–55
Harwich 35, 126, 134
Heiden, Walter 171, 174
Heilgers, Vfw H. 185
Henderson, Maj-Gen David 13, 47, 48, 113
Hendon 7, 17, 96
Hertfordshire 69, 195
Higgins, Lt-Col Thomas Charles Reginald 106, 125, 130, 192
Highbury 154
Highgate 140, 153
Hilliard, Flt Sub-Lt G.W. 46
Hirsch, Kptlt Klaus 33–34, 39
Hither Green **97**, 98
Hoeppner, Genlt Ernst Wilhelm von 102, 103–4, 109, 110, 117
Holloway 117, 140, 152
Holt, Lt Col Fenton Vesey 62
Horn, Hptmn Alfred 39
Hornsey **139**, 140
Hounslow 18, 62
Hoxton 28–29, **31**, 32, 128
Hull 33, 58, 66
Humber estuary 26
Hunt, 2nd Lt B.H. 70, 72, 73, 75
hydrogen 19, 39, 62

immigrants 133
Ipswich 27
Isle of Dogs **39**, 40, **41**, 66, **67**, 129, 156–57
Islington 145, 146

James, AM F. 130
Jenkins, 2nd Lt F.H. 49
Joyce Green 18, 49
Jutland, battle of (1916) 64

Keevil, Capt C.H. 123
Kendrew, Lt C. 138
Kennington 150

Kent 27, 28, 35, 66, 69–70, 93–94, 117–18, 156
Kentish Town 140
Ketelsen, Lt Friedrich 164
King's Lynn 26
Kitchener, Herbert, Lord 47
Kleine, Hptmn Rudolph 126, 127, 130, 134–35, 137, 144, 148–49, 152, 154, 156, 157–58, 160–61
Kölle, Kptlt Waldemar 95–96, 99
Kynoch, Capt Alex 183

LADA see London Air Defence Area
Lanz, Karl 10
Leggatt, Samuel 28–29
Lehmann, Oblt Ernst 61, 69–70
Lewis, Capt Cecil 179–80
Leyton 37, 38, 80, 81, 82
Leytonstone 31, 32, 37
Lincolnshire 69
Linnarz, Hptmn Erich 26–27, 28, 29, 30, 32, 33
   and 1916 raids 63–64
Liverpool 57
Liverpool Street Station 45–46, 121, 122, 158
London 7, 11, 14, 15, 20, 100–1, 190–91
   and 1915 attacks 24, 28–29, 30–31, 32, 36, 37, 38–40, 41, 42–43, 45–47, 49–50, 51, 52–55; and 1916 attacks 66, 67, 68, 70, 71, 72–73, 75, 77–79, 80, 81, 82–87, 91; and 1917 attacks 95, 96, 97, 98–99, 121–23, 124, 125, 127–30, 131, 132–33, 138, 139, 140–41, 142, 143, 156–60, 161, 162, 163–65; and 1918 attacks 169, 170, 171–73, 175–81, 182, 183, 184–85, 186, 187, 188–89; and blackouts 18; and defence plan 56–57, 111, 113–15; and false claims 61–62; and memorials 194–95
   see also Harvest Moon Offensive
London Air Defence Area (LADA) 133, 156, 166
London dockyards 26, 145
London Underground 146, 149, 152
Long Acre 172–73
Lorenz, Oblt Fritz 149
Lovell, Albert 28
Ludendorff, Erich 103
Luftschiffbau Schütte-Lanz GmbH 10, 21
Luftschiffbau Zeppelin GmbH (Zeppelin Airship Company) 9, 10, 21, 23

MacKay, 2nd Lt J.I. 68, 70, 72, 73, 83, 84
Maida Vale 181, 183
Margate 61, 119, 126, 134, 135, 137
material damage 27, 32, 38, 46, 68, 123, 155, 158, 164, 191
Mathy, Kptlt Heinrich 26, 33, 35, 42–43, 45–46, 48, 49, 53–54, 60
   and 1916 raids 65–66, 68, 76, 80, 82, 87, 90
   and death 89, 91
Merchant, 1st AM W.T. 172
Millwall Docks 40, 66, 157
Morrison, Flt Sub-Lt C.D. 38
Mulock, Flt Sub-Lt Redford 27
Murlis-Green, Capt G.W. 164, 165, 176
Murray, 2nd Lt G. 130
museums 195

Naval Airship Division 34–35, 57, 58, 86
navigation 25, 144
New Cross 41, 42
Nicholas, Edgar 79–80, 82
Nordholz shed 20, 21, 23
Norfolk 26, 100
North Sea 26, 69
North Weald Bassett 64
Northampton 95
Northolt 49
Nottinghamshire 69, 76
Notting Hill 150

Oberste Heeresleitung (OHL) 8, 144, 190
Odhams Printing Works 172–73
Old Kent Road 148
O'Neill, 2nd Lt T.M. 176
Operation Türkenkreuz (1917) 111, 155
Oxney 27

Palethorpe, Capt J. 130
Paris 26
Peterson, Oblt-z-S Werner 34–35, 48, 55, 58
   and 1916 raids 76, 80, 82–84, 86, 87
Piccadilly Circus 97, 98
Pimlico 154
Plaistow 153, 157
Plumstead 67, 68
police forces 28, 134, 135, 165, 192
Pomeroy, John 62
Poplar 122–23, 125, 153, 195
Powell, 2nd Lt H.S. 60
prisoners of war 61, 80
Pritchard, 2nd Lt Thomas 99
propaganda 6, 7, 39
public opinion 68, 118, 123, 132–33
Pulling, Flt Sub-Lt Edward 91
Putney 150
Pyott, 2nd Lt I.V. 91

radio 25–26, 48–49, 70
Ramsgate 27
RAS see Reserve Aeroplane Squadron
Rawlinson, Lt Col Alfred 52, 53, 152–53
Reserve Aeroplane Squadron (RAS): No. 19; 57, 60, 61; No. 39; 62
RFC see Royal Flying Corps
Ridley, 2nd Lt C.A. 60
riots 133
Rist, Lt Wilhelm 189
RNAS see Royal Naval Air Service
Robinson, 2nd Lt William Leefe 64, 70, 72–73, 74, 75, 195
Ross, Lt C.S. 70
Rotherhithe 41, 42, 145
Royal Aircraft Factory 11, 18
Royal Air Force (RAF) 13, 100, 136, 184, 192
Royal Flying Corps (RFC) 11, 12, 13, 53
   and defence plan 56, 57, 59
   No. 1 Sqdn 17, 18; No. 16 Wing 62; No. 18 Wing 62;

No. 37 Sqdn 111, 121, 127; No. 39 Sqdn 63, 64, 70, 87,
   88, 90, 111, 121; No. 44 Sqdn 176; No. 46 Sqdn 133; No.
   50 Sqdn 111, 121; No. 56 Sqdn 125, 126; No. 66 Sqdn
   125, 126; No. 78 Sqdn 111; No. 141 Sqdn 165; No. 143
   Sqdn 165
Royal Marines 20
Royal Naval Air Service (RNAS) 11, 12, 13, 17, 18, 23, 53, 118
   No. 1 Sqdn 33; Yarmouth 27, 35
Royal Naval Volunteer Service 20
Royal Navy 11, 14

Sachtler, Vfw Albrecht 189
St Pancras Station 178–79
Sassoon, Siegfried 122
Scheer, VADM Reinhard 15
Schoeller, Hptmn Arthur 180, 181
Schramm, Hptmn Wilhelm 70, 72
Schütte, Johann 10
Schütze, Kvtkpt Viktor 94
Schwonder, Kptlt Roderich 99
Scott, Adm Sir Percy 14, 47–48, 53, 57
seaplanes 23
searchlights 27, 32, 36, 45, **87**, 143
Seydlitz-Gerstenberg, Oblt Hans-Joachim von 177
Sharpling, Thomas 29
Sheerness 137
Sheffield 95
shelters 155, 169, 172–73; *see also* London Underground
Shepherd, William 45
Shoreditch 29, **31**, 32, 128, 154, 169
Siegert, Wilhelm 7–8, 102
Simon, Lt Col Maximilian St Leger 57, 113, 114, 115, 119,
   106–7, 125–26, 135
   and barrage fire 143–44
Smith, Charles 80
Smuts, Lt Gen Jan Christian 133, 136, 143
Sommerfeldt, Kptlt E. 75
sound detection 155
Southend 27, 28
Sowrey, 2nd Lt Frederick 70, 83–85, **86**, 188–89
speed 21
Spitalfields 29
Square, Flt Sub-Lt H.H. 38
Stachelsky, Oblt G. von 164
Stagg, AM Albert 187
Stepney **31**, 32, 121
Stoke Newington 28–29, **30**, **31**, 128, 194
Strasser, FKpt Peter 15, 23, 25, 26, 34, 35, 42, 48
   and 1916 raids 68, 75, 76, 86, 91, 92; and 1917 raids 94; and
   1918 raids 100; and false claims 61–62
strategic bombing 17
Stratford 32, 138, **140**
Streatham 80, **81**, 82, 157
Stroud, Capt Clifford 183
Suffolk 26
Surrey Docks 157
Suttons Farm 48, 49, 62, 63
Sydenham 185, **188**

Tannenberg, battle of (1914) 20
Tasche, Uffz Hermann 189
telephone communications 136, 192
Tempest, 2nd Lt Wulstan 90–91
Thames estuary 118–19
Thames River 40
'Theatreland' 50, 52
Thomsen, Lt Friedrich von 171, 174
Tipton, Lt R.S. 49
Tondern shed 21
Tooting 157
Tottenham 128, 140
Tower Bridge 20
Tower of London 28
Trenchard, Maj-Gen Hugh 13, 125
Turner, Lt Edward 189

Underground *see* London Underground
Upper North Street School, Poplar 122–23, **125**, 195

Walter, Oblt Richard 161
Waltham Abbey 36, 40, 61
Walthamstow 36, **37**
Wanstead **37**, 38, **139**, 140, 153
Wapping 129
War Office 34, 48, 56–57, 111, 113, 133
Warneford, Flt Sub-Lt R.A.J. 33, 34
warning maroons 133, **134**, 167, 169
Waterloo Station 150
weaponry, British 64–65
   anti-aircraft guns 18, 20, 36, 40, 43, 45, **47**, 113–15, 118–19,
      121, 125–26, 127–28, 143–44; auto-cannons 48, 52–53;
      bombs 19–20
   'Fiery Grapnel' 20; Hotchkiss guns 20; Lewis guns 58, 60;
      Martini-Henry cavalry carbines 19; 'pom-pom' guns 7, 20;
      Ranken dart 58, 60; RTS bullet 165; Sparklet bullet 62
weaponry, German 43, 110
   Elektron bomb 160, 167, 190; incendiary bombs 28–29, 32,
      158, 160
weather conditions 25, 26, 57–58, 69, 93, 117, 134, 148–49,
   157–58
Weissmann, A. 164
Wells, H.G. 11
Wenke, Oblt-z-S Friedrich 36, 38
Western Front 19, 20, 64, 102, 113, 115, 125, 184
West Ham 138, 153
Whitechapel **31**, 129, 158
Whitsun raid (1918) 184–85, **186**, **187**, 188–89
Wilhelm II, Kaiser 14, 15, 23, 26, 27, 28, 94
Williams, 2nd Lt G.G. 148
wireless-telegraphy 136, 144
Wobeser, Hptmn Richard von 39–40
Woolwich 40, **41**, **51**, 54–55, 138, **139**, 154, 177
Wright brothers 9

Zeppelin Airship Company *see* Luftschiffbau Zeppelin GmbH
Zeppelin, Count Ferdinand von 9–10
Zeppelins *see* airships, German
Ziegler, Uffz Karl 171, 174